Handmaidens of the Lord

Publications of the American Folklore Society
New Series
General Editor, Larry Danielson

A listing of the books in this series appears at the back of this volume

Handmaidens of the Lord

PENTECOSTAL WOMEN PREACHERS AND TRADITIONAL RELIGION

Elaine J. Lawless

UNIVERSITY OF PENNSYLVANIA PRESS

Philadelphia

A shorter version of Chapter 5 appeared as "Piety and Motherhood: Reproductive Images and Maternal Strategies of the Woman Preacher," *Journal of American Folklore* 100 (Oct.-Dec. 1987):469–79. Used by permission.

Maps pp. x–xii used by permission of University of Oklahoma Press.

Library of Congress Cataloging-in-Publication Data

Lawless, Elaine J.
    Handmaidens of the Lord : Pentecostal women preachers and traditional religion / Elaine J. Lawless.
        p.   cm. — (Publications of the American Folklore Society ; new ser.)
    Bibliography: p.
    Includes index
    ISBN 0-8122-8100-4.   ISBN 0-8122-1265-7 (pbk.)
    1. Women clergy—Missouri. 2. Pentecostal churches—Missouri—Clergy. 3. Missouri—Religious life and customs.   I. Title.
II. Series.
BV676.L39 1988
289.9'4'088042—dc19   88-4838
                                                                                  CIP

Second paperback printing 1994

For Buena

And in loving memory of
   Ellen Ryan Dubinski
who greatly enriched the lives
of all who knew her

And it shall come to pass afterward, that I will pour
out my spirit upon all flesh; and your sons and
your daughters shall prophesy, your old men
shall dream dreams, your young men shall see
visions.
And also upon the servants and upon the handmaids
in those days will I pour out my spirit.
[Joel 2:28–29]

Let your women keep silence in the churches: for it is
not permitted unto them to speak; but they are
commanded to be under obedience, as also saith
the law.
And if they will learn any thing, let them ask their
husbands at home: for it is a shame for women
to speak in the church.
[I Corinthians 14:34–35]

Let the woman learn in silence with all subjection.
But I suffer not a woman to teach, nor to usurp
authority over the man, but to be in silence.
For Adam was first formed, then Eve.
And Adam was not deceived, but the woman being
deceived was in the transgression.
[I Timothy 2:11–14]

Contents

Acknowledgments

This book could never have been written without the support, encouragement and cooperation of the women who appear in these pages. I want to thank all of the women preachers who put up with my presence in their churches and who answered my persistent questions. Most especially I want to thank Sister Anna Walters.

My research for this study was made possible largely by generous support from the University of Missouri—in the form of a Summer Fellowship Grant in 1984 and two Research Council Grants in 1984 and 1985. My research was further supported by a Summer Fellowship Grant from the National Endowment for the Humanities in 1985. Writing time was provided by a semester's leave granted by the English Department at the University of Missouri in the spring of 1986.

I want to thank Larry Danielson, for his unfailing encouragement and support over the years since I first discovered the discipline of folklore at the University of Illinois in his classes and those of Archie Green and John Flanagan. I need to thank, too, Dick Bauman, Bert Wilson, and John McCormick (Dean of the Graduate School at Missouri) for their consistent faith in and respect for my work. Finally, I want to thank Sandy and Jesse for taking care of each other so beautifully while I trekked around the countryside going to church day and night, then disappeared to write about it.

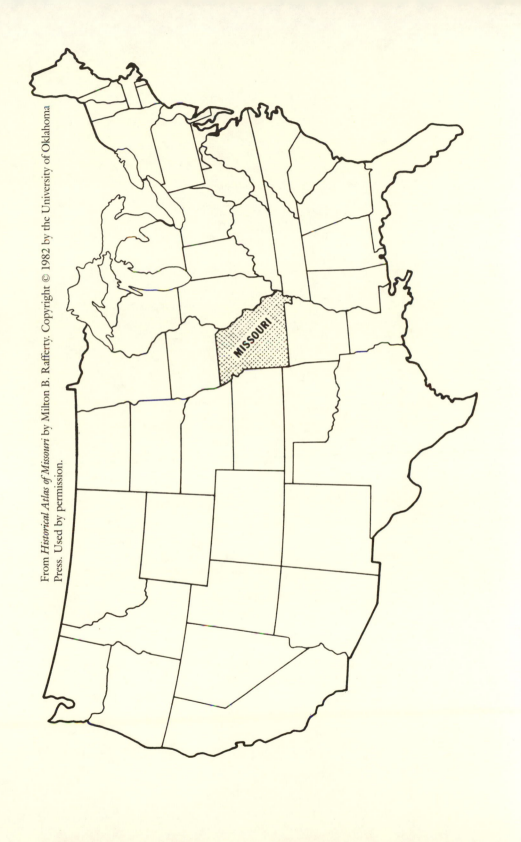

MISSOURI

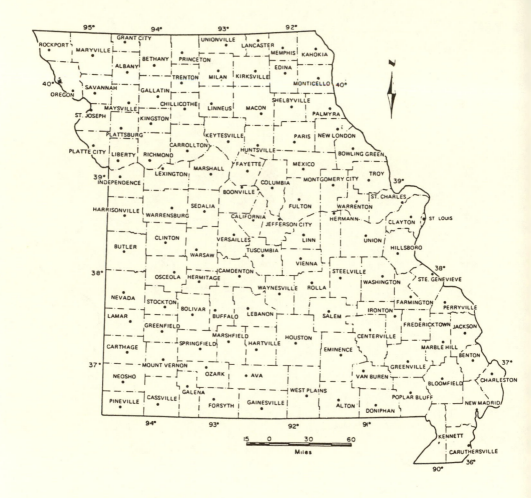

From *Historical Atlas of Missouri* by Milton B. Rafferty. Copyright © 1982 by the University of Oklahoma Press. Used by permission.

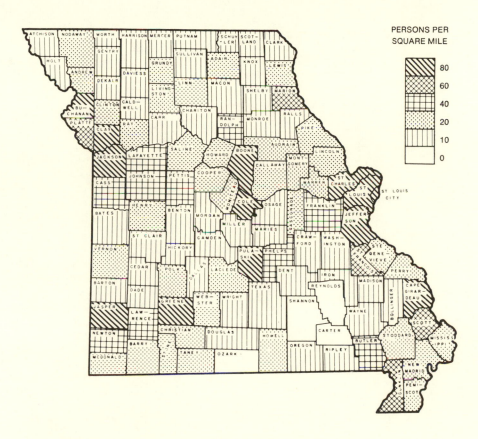

PERSONS PER
SQUARE MILE

	80
	60
	40
	20
	10
	0

From *Historical Atlas of Missouri* by Milton B. Rafferty. Copyright © 1982 by the University of Oklahoma Press. Used by permission.

Prologue

SISTER ANNA

On Wednesdays, Sister Anna Walters rises even earlier than usual because she must prepare to give an entire church service at the Monroe County Nursing Home. She has been giving this service without remuneration for nearly twenty years. Many of the people in this county home are widowed spouses of couples she has known most of her adult life. She has watched these people work, raise their children, lose their mates, grow old, and move into the county home to wait to die. This is a part of her work she takes very seriously. I arrive at her house to accompany her today at eight in the morning; she is dressed and ready to go. The phone rings. I sit for nearly twenty-five minutes as she counsels what appears to my ears to be an hysterical young woman whose husband has been abusing her. Mostly, Sister Anna listens, asserting "yes" and "oh, honey" a thousand times it seems. Finally, she consoles the girl and tells her that she has to leave the house for a while but that as soon as she gets back into town she will come to the girl's mother's house where she has instructed the girl to go, taking the two-year-old baby. She hangs up with promises to come to her later and tells her she loves her very much. Somehow, I get the feeling the girl might be Anna's own daughter, but no, she laughs, this is a very young girl, only 19, who she had married only a short time ago in her own church. And, now, there are big problems at home. She knows she'll be up very late tonight with this girl. But, for now, she says, we have places to go!

Monroe County, Missouri, is a strange mixture of rural beauty and human poverty. The dirt roads that thread their way through wooded lots and over rolling hills suggest a countryside untouched by modern American life—or concerns. Driving from Centerville through central Missouri, one feels the absolute quiet, the only sound the hum of the motor car and an occasional jay or crow. Fences are in various stages of disrepair; farm machinery stands forsaken in a muddy field, slowly rusting and crumbling into the already poor soil. A livestock chute stands with gaping mouth awaiting steers that have long ago gone to market. Weatherbeaten gates stand ajar and swing on their hinges, not needed to keep anything in, or anything out. A surly cur trots alongside the road ditch, left to scavenge or die.

Sister Anna knows these roads by heart; they are so familiar to her she drives them without thinking. She gives directions the way some cooks give recipes—turn a little to the right down by the creek, at the top of the hill go left, curve with the road down where Gilbert Hackman's barn used to be. I've been to the Monroe County Nursing home with her several times, now, but I still don't think I could find it by myself. I'm sure there's a more direct way, on the paved Missouri "B" roads that Sister Anna rarely takes; I am always surprised when we pull up over a ridge and her car wheels hit the gravel of the county home driveway.

First, the eye catches the abandoned brick monstrosity that used to be the Monroe County Nursing Home. But Sister Anna pulls up in front of the low-slung concrete-block building that sits out here on a "B" road and holds within its walls the indigents of Monroe County. She grabs a stack of old hymnals and her large, worn Bible and marches into the home. The staff greet her warmly and tell her how much the residents enjoy her visits—they have so little to look forward to. In the lobby a man sits and stares toward the doorway. Neither our entrance nor the flood of sunlight and cold air we bring with us causes him to blink. His stare is permanent, his lips slack-jawed, his large farm hands limp across the arms of the wheelchair. He is missing two fingers; most of his nails are black from cold weather or hammer blows. He wears bib overalls and work boots and a denim shirt—the same uniform he must have worn all his life. As Sister Anna reaches out and takes one of his large, rough hands in her smaller two, I realize how large a man he really must be, for even as he sits he towers over the tiny preacher woman's head. Smiling, with tears in her eyes already, Sister Anna leans up toward the farmer's face, greeting him by name, asking him too loudly how he feels, telling him she loves him. As far as I can tell he neither sees her nor hears her. She places his arm loosely back onto the chair arm with a gentle, knowing pat.

At the foyer door she is met and embraced by a woman not much taller than she is; mauled would be a better word: petted, coddled, patted, and pulled by a woman of indeterminate age with red hair stretched in all directions framing her wild-eyed face. The guttural sounds coming from her seem to emanate from deep inside her loose, extended belly, which protrudes fleshy and white from the unbuttoned front of her threadbare cotton frock. She slides about on fuzzy socklets and shrugs her shoulders to keep on an oversized ratty sweater of bright orange. Her lips are huge and open and contorted, twisted; her tongue is swollen and flips about. Sister Anna greets her, too, by name, and gently leads her to the large lunchroom where twenty-five or thirty other residents of the home wait patiently for the service to begin. They know which days Sister Anna comes to give them a church service and they make their way down to the lunchroom on their own, or ask the staff to wheel them down with plenty of time to spare. Anna helps the wild lady sit down and then walks slowly around the room, shaking hands and embracing all of the old men and women who wait there for her. In some there is a flicker of recognition, a paralyzed half-smile, the pressure of a handshake, a tear. Others do not seem to respond at all—drugs, senility, boredom have rendered their faces vacant. Many cannot even hold the hymnals that Sister Anna tries to place in their hands.

We are joined in the lunchroom by a man from Sister Anna's church; he carries a guitar. One of the staff members goes to the old upright piano and begins to belt out a favorite chorus. The guitar picks up the tune and Anna begins the song service. For the next hour or so, she leads the singing, prays, heals, teaches, and preaches to the left-over minds and bodies that sit in front of her. The cold winter sunlight floods the tile floor and somehow, for me, accentuates their desperate circumstances. I always cry when I visit this place with her; sometimes the sobs begin very low in my stomach. For days afterward I cannot get the faces of these people out of my mind. I notice that Sister Anna is praying for them, now, with her face lifted to the sky and tears streaming down her face. Her prayer tells God that these people are ready, now, to "come home," that they have lived the life and now they are tired. She pleads with God to make their days comfortable ones, free of pain, and she tells him again they are ready to see Jesus. I cannot but hope that God is listening. From somewhere to my right, amazingly, comes a song. An old woman sits, her hands resting on the cold bars of her walker, and from her mouth comes a song she tells us later was her father's favorite. He taught it to her in the year 1900; she is 98 and has been in the Monroe County Nursing home for 31 years. She has buried her husband and five sons, she tells me, and she "just cannot understand why Jesus just won't come for her."

After prolonged hugs and good-byes, we leave the nursing home and Anna heads back to Centerville. There are several housebound ladies she needs to visit this afternoon, and she's hoping there is time to dash over to the hospital to visit two people who are very sick. She picks up her mail at the post office, and then we begin the house calls. After two calls, she wonders if *I* am hungry (and I wonder what *she* is "running on"), so we go into a local restaurant to get lunch. When we enter the door, greetings hit us from all sides. Everyone in the place, it seems, knows Sister Anna and their greetings are warm and pleasant ones. She has to stop at nearly every table to exchange a little talk and lots of smiles. People, men and women, reach out to shake her hand or touch her arm; some rise to embrace her. Finally, we are allowed to sit down and eat, but not exactly in peace, for as people come in and leave, as the waitresses realize she is here, there are more conversations. I notice she actually eats very little and remember that she weighs a mere 107 pounds.

After lunch, we visit more homes. These visits seem so long for me. The housebound people are sad, some bitter; they cannot move around easily and they feel no one in their family is really willing to cater to their needs, to buy their groceries, to pay their bills. They complain openly to Sister Anna, who volunteers to help out, takes the grocery list, pays some of the bills, adjusts the television that hasn't been working, calls the furnace man who never seems to get there. The conversation is dry, dull. I am bored, but Sister Anna keeps the talk squarely where the woman wants it to be—on her family, her grandchildren, the weather, church activities. The woman complains that no one will take her to church anymore. Anna offers to come get her next Sunday in the church van; the woman noticeably perks up. Then, she seems to collapse as we announce we must go and visit others whom Sister Anna calls by name. The woman acknowledges that those people need Sister's visit, too, but sits in a pout as we have to let ourselves out the door.

At the end of this excruciatingly long day, we arrive back at Sister Anna's house to be greeted by her husband who is obviously bored and very unhappy. He thought for certain that we would be back much earlier and had planned on it. Anna consoles him, telling him in minute detail where we have been and who we have seen. I get the feeling this is a daily ritual for them—he, disappointed that she has been gone so long, she, consoling him, asking him to try to understand her lifestyle. The phone rings and he remembers, then, that the young woman from the morning has been desperate to talk with Sister Anna. She answers the phone and begins to listen. After some time, she suggests that the girl come to her house while Anna gets some dinner and changes clothes for the evening service. I head home, knowing that Sister Anna will, perhaps, get to bed by midnight if she's lucky, and that before the night is over she will have a difficult time, again, with her new husband about being away from the house so much. She probably will not be able to sleep because of the stress, because of the pain in her back, because of her pinched nerves. But Thursday morning she will rise and have another day very similar to this one.

Sister Anna Walters is the quintessential church pastor. Twenty-four hours a day she is available to her congregation—"my children" or "my people" she calls them with such affection after eighteen years of serving as their pastor. Sister Anna's notion of the role and duties of a pastor is all-encompassing: she is comforter to those who are grieving; she is counselor to those in trouble; she is chauffeur to those who have no car; she is organizer for all adult and children's activities of the church; she is God's ambassador to the unfortunate who cannot attend church; she is spiritual guide and leader to the congregation as a whole. Although our conception of what "pastor" means, for a Protestant Reverend, a Catholic priest, or a Jewish rabbi, may inherently include any or perhaps all of the above, rarely does the twentieth-century pastor take on all of these responsibilities all of the time. Yet, Sister Anna does. Her days are filled with her "work"— yet, oddly, neither she nor the community would perceive of her as a "working woman," regardless of the fact that she is gone from her home nearly all the daylight hours and most evenings until late into the night, and regardless of the fact that she does, in fact, make her "living" by being the pastor.

Sister Anna takes her "commission" seriously: she is there to serve the needs of her congregation. In order to get the strength to do this, she says she must maintain a close relationship with God and Jesus. She rises in the morning and "hits her knees," saying "Good Morning" to God and imploring him to give her physical and mental strength to get through her hard, long days. Since she has always been physically frail and often wracked with pain, she needs this source of strength. She believes that God helps her through the day; her perception of God and Jesus is a personal one and they are available simultaneously to her as companions. She has affectionately dubbed her car "God's Car," and she moves everything out of the front seat so Jesus can sit next to her. She talks out loud to him as she drives, telling him all of her concerns and asking for his advice. She believes the personal care of God and Jesus has kept her from any harm or serious car trouble all the years of her ministry.

Sister Anna staunchly denies any "feminist" leanings. To acknowledge any desire to be considered a "liberated" woman would be to castigate herself in her own community. She does not have to fight for liberation; she is in many ways liberated. But, what does this statement mean in terms of her everyday life? Anna is not the usual housewife; she is rarely at home to perform "housewifely" duties, though somehow she manages to get this work done as well. She alone determines whom she will visit on a given day, what activities need attention, what meetings she must attend. She answers to no one except God, she says. In essence, she is self-employed; of course, she says she is doing "God's work." This is a crucial point that must be comprehended in order to understand her role and her own manipulation of that role. To say "God laid it upon my heart to go visit Sister Stewart this morning" grounds her visit solidly in God's prerogative. Sister Anna carefully disavows her own thoughts about visiting Sister Stewart. To say she woke up thinking about Sister Stewart and that probably Sister Stewart needed a visit would be presumptuous. Interpreting all her own thoughts to 'read' "God told me . . . " or "God dealt with my heart . . . " justifies her actions and legitimizes her work. Another woman in the community, for example, who daily arose from her bed and traveled all over town and county visiting people in their homes, and visiting the sick in the hospital and the elderly in the nursing homes, would be considered a wonderful, giving person, but the line between wonderful woman and "busy-body" is a fine one, and if the woman is neglecting her household in order to do her "good deeds," then her activities might be looked at askance. Importantly, Sister Anna couches all of her travels and visits as "God's plan," which, while appearing to be a constriction and a denial of her own creative capabilities, actually provides for her freedom. The "call to preach" is an available strategy, perhaps the only strategy available to women in this milieu, to become independent—independent enough to leave their husbands and babies and travel far distances and stay away from home for weeks at a time. Anna did that when she was younger. In the early days of her ministry she would leave her husband and take her young children with her to travel all over the state preaching children's crusades, then later preaching adult revivals that lasted sometimes one week, sometimes three or four. Finally, initiating her life as *pastor*, she took her three children and left her husband working in Kansas City and took the pastorship in Millerville, a tiny town in central Missouri. Widowed several years ago, Sister Anna recently remarried. Now, this husband must sit at home long hours while his wife travels all over the county continuing her work as pastor of the church.

The photographs following illustrate the Sunday life of Sister Anna and her congregation, beginning as she and her husband arrive at the church and ending as she closes the building. All photographs are by Miguel Fairbanks.

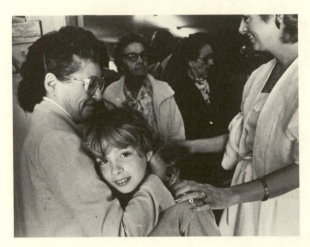

Handmaidens of the Lord

Introduction

Most people, when they think of Missouri (if they ever think of it at all), think of St. Louis, or Kansas City. Certainly, the Interstate-70 Baseball Series in 1985 put Missouri on the map for a lot of folks who didn't quite know where it was before. Ironically, most of Missouri has nothing to do with the cities of St. Louis and Kansas City. These metropolitan centers hang precariously on the edges of the state, St. Louis leaning toward the east and all that it always wished it could be, and Kansas City stretching toward the frontier, boasting of its dust and the flavor of the west. It is telling that there is an East St. Louis on Illinois soil and a Kansas City, Kansas that, in name anyway, can make a greater claim to the city. There are no other large cities in Missouri. Other towns of any size are, importantly, linked to the religious intensity that has long been a significant part of Missouri history. Independence knows too well the violent history of the Mormon Church in this midwestern state, and Springfield stands as the hallmark of the Bible Belt, the center for the ever-growing Assemblies of God and a profundity of Bible Colleges.

The largest college in the state is the University of Missouri, which is located in Columbia, a town located almost exactly halfway between St. Louis and Kansas City and not much larger than the population of the university itself. A few miles south of Columbia, halfway to the tiny capitol of the state, Jefferson City, is the airport that serves the entire interior of the state, an airport that is quite literally located in a cow field. If you drive from Jefferson City south toward the largest tourist trap in the state, the Lake of the Ozarks, your sensibilities are slapped with gaudy advertisements for plush resorts, marinas, rich eateries, water slides, surf, and sand—an odd assortment of imported delights not at all native to the farming soil of this midwestern state. In fact, if you pull off the highway anywhere from Columbia south, you leave the lure of the Lake and enter the real world of Missouri in very small, rural towns like Millersville, Holts Summit, Brazito, Russellville, Centerville, Versailles, Tuscumbia, and Iberia. Most, if not all, of the folks in these towns have never spent the night at Tan-tar-a Resort Estates, and never will. Some drive down to Osage Beach and clean the rooms of the rich visitors, or work in the machine shops that service the foreign cars that find their way to the lake, but most say they don't care anything about the lake, admitting it has very little to do with their lives.

For the very religious in the area, and many are, "the Lake" has come to epitomize the very seat of evil and temptation; they are certain that drugs, alcohol, and prostitution lurk in those posh resorts and they try hard to keep their kids close to home. Perhaps this juxtaposition of native and imported is not unique, but here in the very heart of Missouri the brassy incongruences seem to strike very deeply. The poverty and wreckage that have resulted from a rapidly declining agricultural way of life are evident in the abandoned farm houses and barns, the boarded-up feed stores, and the grain elevators that have rusted from disuse. These are contemporary changes; historical changes are also evident in the delapidated cotton gins that dot the land and the migrant worker shanties that now house unemployed families. In many ways, Missouri has not kept up with the rest of the country, at least not with the rest of the industrial northern part of the country. For many people, Missouri still owes its allegiance to the deep South; "Little Dixie" may only cover a small portion of the state in name, but in reality, much of the land south of Columbia and Jefferson City, much of the area we know as the Ozarks, and much of the bootheel, is southern in mentality and inclination.

This is largely "cracker" country. The better-known enclaves of Missouri French and Germans are further east; those immigrants to the state planted roots near the rivers—in Montgomery, Ste. Genevieve, and Perry Counties. The people of Cole, Morgan, and Miller Counties are Anglo; their grandparents came to Missouri from Virginia, North Carolina, Tennessee, and Arkansas. By and large, they are farming stock with little or no formal education. Missouri schools are some of the poorest state supported schools in the nation. In fact, most of the folks I know from this area are distrustful of educational institutions and educated people. Like "the Lake", the colleges are thought to harbor wanton morals, dangerous innovators, and free-thinkers that are a bane to the staunchly religious life most of these people favor. The religious denominations that thrive in this region strive for the straight and narrow way, dictating for their followers a life free of all worldly temptations, which include smoking, drinking, movies, and dancing.

Represented in this area is a religious spectrum ranging from the strictest Pentecostal and Holiness groups which denounce television and baseball games to some of the more liberated Methodists and even more contemporary charismatic groups who enjoy Christian rock music. But the core of religious sensibility in the heart of Missouri is fundamentalist Baptist and Pentecostal—both adhering closely to a Bible-inspired religion that places a great deal of importance on living the Godly life, regular attendance at church, child-rearing in the way, and strong family ties. In general, people in this area believe that everyone ought to get married and stay married to that same person for the rest of their lives. Divorce is a dirty word. This is not to suggest, of course, that people do not divorce. They do. Just as many of them smoke and drink. But that still does not mean they think it is right. What is right is for men and women to marry, to have kids, to build a home and a strong home-life. Most of the kids in the area marry life-long friends, kids they have known from school and church. People tell me that most of the "broken homes" are a result of a marriage with an outsider, someone who came in to visit, or someone from the city, which means, usually, from "Jeff" (Jefferson City). The family is sacred; the family structure is Bible inspired. The man is the head of the household, just as God is Lord over all. Jesus is second in command, after God, and after Jesus, comes man. Woman was made from man and for man; therefore, she is subservient to her husband, who is lord of his house. The children are subservient to their parents in all things. And the home is a very private place.

Most of these people think it is preferable for the woman to remain secluded in the home, taking care of the household, rearing the children, creating a haven for the man who must go out into the world to face the hardships of that outside world and make a living. In times past, this was always the case; it was unheard of for a woman to take a job outside the home. But hard times have hit this region and many of the women in these households work. The work they can find is almost exclusively limited to domestic work in the lake region, clerk positions in the chain stores that have moved in, such as Walmart and K-Mart, and babysitting for other women who have found work outside their homes. In most cases, women leave their youngest children with their mothers and grandmothers—the strong sense of family remains traditionally linked to the extended kin of both the husband and the wife. Socializing is limited largely to the extended family, but may include some special friends from church. In fact, the church is referred to as a "family"; favors and obligations among members often take on the same familial distinctions as those with blood kin.

This book focuses on white Pentecostals in the mid-Missouri region, specifically on women preachers in the Pentecostal religion in the area. Although the study in its larger capacity ranges from Assembly of God believers to Church of God-Holiness believers, in many respects the more general survey aspects of my work have been honed down to center directly on one particular woman who has pastored an Assembly of God church in Centerville, Missouri for eighteen years. Relying on her "story" to stand as representative will later enable me to indulge in the more refined facets of analyses. But first it is important to supply some background for my research and explain why I have chosen to study women preachers.

This work actually began nearly ten years ago at Indiana University, where I began my work with Pentecostal groups. My first narrative collections were from my neighbors, women who lived south of Bloomington in what is lovingly referred to by the natives as the "limestone capital of the world." These women had lived with limestone workers all their lives: their fathers, husbands, and brothers all worked the lime. The stories they told me were personal experience stories closely akin to stories I had read about coal mining families in states to the east, Tennessee and Kentucky, the region known as Appalachia. The narratives revealed a hard life, full of deprivation and heartache. Because the limestone can only be worked when it is warm, most families were forced onto welfare rolls for many of the long cold months of Indiana's winters, or their "men-folk" had to find temporary, poorly paying jobs for approximately six months of every year. I was surprised to learn how dangerous, too, the limestone work was; many of the women had been widowed at an early age with a house full of children, or they were tending a crippled husband who had been injured in the quarries. Only three or four miles from Bloomington and Indiana University, these folks lived lives that rarely, if ever, intersected with those of the folks "in town."

Socializing and entertainment for these people were tied closely with religion. On many of the one-lane dirt roads that spidered across the fields, tiny clapboard one-room churches stood unpainted and stark in the bright daylight, but glowed and pulsated with raucous religious fervour at night. Most of the women I interviewed in 1977 belonged to one of these small Pentecostal churches, and they continually invited me to come to church with them. Finally, I did. And I went back again and again, convinced that I had located a "laboratory" for researching oral, traditional religion.[1] Eventually, that work led to a Ph.D. dissertation on the expressive religious language of Pentecostal women, primarily their spontaneous testimonies.[2] And I am still attending Pentecostal churches, convinced that there is so much more we need to learn and understand about this important constituency of folk religious life in America.

Pentecostalism is a twentieth-century, American-born religion. Religious histories pinpoint its birth as a denomination around the turn of this century. Actually, however, the enthusiastic worshipping style which characterizes Pentecostal church services today dates back to Methodist revivals and camp meetings of the early 1800s. And the strict fundamentalist taboos and regulations imposed upon Pentecostal believers stem from the strong "Holiness" tradition that was itself an outgrowth of John Wesley's Methodist notions of sanctification. The complex story of the development of the Movement and the various Assemblies of God that emerged from the roots of Methodism and the Holiness Movement has been documented from several different perspectives.[3]

The Pentecostal Movement in the United States began when a small group of believers equated the experience of tongue-speaking with salvation. Certainly, tongue-speaking, or glossolalia, had occurred among fervent religious folk long before 1900, but it was not until a small group of religious students at Bethel College in Topeka, Kansas, under the direction of Charles F. Parham, sought to replicate the Biblical "upper room experience" that tongue-speaking came to be recognized as a *requirement*. Parham's group sought the "fire" of the Holy Ghost and declared that all in the room received "the baptism of the Spirit" *en masse*.[4] Because the original New Testament upper-room experience occurred on Pentecost, these believers took for themselves the name "Pentecosts." Parham and his believers spread their message to the countryside admonishing all to be baptized in the spirit as well as in water. Tongues was the evidence of the possession of the Holy Ghost, and Pentecostal preachers began to preach what they called the "full gospel," a term still used today to identify a legitimate Pentecostal group. The "full gospel" is a combination of old doctrines and new emphases: Biblical emphasis on salvation and justification by faith; a stress on divine healing; the doctrine of the premillennial return of Christ; and a belief in a Holy Spirit whose baptism empowers a Christian to live victoriously and to witness effectively, and who enables the believer to perform the supernatural.[5]

In my work in the American midwest, I have collected much of the "folk history" of the Pentecostal Movement. Older people clearly recall when the Pentecostal preachers arrived in their area. Believers recount with happiness the day when they first heard the "Pentecostal Message," usually in a revival or camp meeting. The experience, they always say, changed their life. When the traveling Pentecostal evangelist left their area, often the newly converted left their home church and started new congregations, giving them such a diversity of names that the confusion about Pentecostal assemblies continues today. They called their new churches Apostolic Temple, Apostolic Assembly, Assembly of God, Apostolic Church of Jesus Christ, Inc., Pentecostal House of Worship, Pentecostal Assembly, Pentecostal Holiness Assembly, Pentecostal Church of God, Pentecostal Church of Christ, and a host of other confusing combinations.[6]

As was typical with many of the smaller, more fundamentalist Methodist and Baptist congregations, these new Pentecostal churches took for their pastors any person who declared that he or she had had a "call from God" to preach. To this day, most Pentecostal churches in the rural areas, and even many in the urban centers, require no more than this spiritual call to preach or pastor a church. Only the more organized Pentecostals, for example the United Pentecostal Church, have established Bible colleges for the religious education of those called to the ministry. Some lay preachers and pastors who have never attended such a Bible college, however, do take a mail-order test that enables them to procure a license to officiate at weddings and sign death certificates.

My early work with Pentecostals sought to understand this group as a religious "folk group" and to delineate the various verbal genres that were operating within the religious service; thus, my work has focused on the maintenance of religious boundaries and self-imposed segregation through semiotics and religious language;[7] on testimonies within the religious service;[8] on the structure of the religious service and the gender-linked roles of service participants;[9] and on a variety of other aspects of the Pentecostal religious experience. From the beginning, it has been apparent that female attendance and participation in this religious group far surpassed male participation in the services: women sang and led the singing; women testified and led the testimony service; women prayed simultaneously with and just as loudly as did the men; women played as many musical instruments as the men did, and usually more; and sometimes, in southern Indiana, a woman preached the sermon.

I moved away from the midwest for a while, but when I found myself back in Missouri, the state where I had been born and raised and where I received my undergraduate schooling, I knew that I wanted to continue my work with Pentecostalism; specifically, I wanted to find out about women preachers.[10] Knowing the state, and knowing these fundamentalist people so well, I found it incongruous that a woman might be allowed to stand at the altar, behind the pulpit, and preach a sermon. The male dominance, female subservience hierarchy that persists so strongly within the privacy of Pentecostal homes also remains firm within the walls of the church. At least in Indiana, none of the women whom I had heard preach were actually *pastors* of churches. In one case, one of the women preachers was in name only the "assistant pastor" to her husband, who was clearly the authority figure in the church. In fact, her opportunities for preaching were dependent upon his allowing her the opportunity to do so and were severely limited since she shared the "assistant pastor" slot with another, older, well-respected male minister. In 1983, I began to conduct fieldwork in central Missouri to determine how many women were actually preaching in Pentecostal churches, and to find out if any women held positions of power and authority within those churches; that is, I wanted to ascertain if any women held the sole position of authority as *pastor* of a church. My work in Missouri has been fruitful and exciting, frustrating and, at times, intimidating.

Sharing a letter I received during my work on this project will illustrate the general attitude in this area toward my work and toward the general topic of women preachers. An article about women preachers appeared in the Poplar Bluff *Daily American Republic* on Friday, August 30, 1985. The journalist, Jim Vogel, had been working on this feature all that summer and had contacted me on several occasions, knowing of my own work with women preachers. In the article he quoted me several times and prompted a local citizen to send the following letter to me (reproduced with original spelling):

> 11/5/85
> Rt. 1 Box 13
> Poplar Bluff, MO 63901

> Elaine Lawless
> University of Missouri
> Columbia, Mo. 65201

> Hi Elaine;

> Finally getting around to writing in response to your article that the Weekly American ran sometime back.

> I might would like to be like Paul Harvey and say, "You know what the news is, now here's the rest of the story."

> Women preachers are big news I guess maybe, but lets look at the rest of the story, Biblically.

> In the beginning, they were created for a help-mate, not to take the lead, nor to be walked on either as for as that goes. (Gen.2:20).

> Its hard to be the head when you weren't made for it. I know the Lib hates statements thus, but the Lib didn't make theirselves, God did.

> We might look at a scary picture for right now. But, by the way, lets clear up something so you can have confidence in the "OLD Fogy Book" as its reputation is, the Holy Bible. The description of Noah's Ark in Genesis the sixth chapter has been found, and right where the Bible said it was--on Mt Ararat close/around the Turkish border--although its in half with one half being

slid down the mountain side. The movie and book, "In Search of Noah's Ark", brings this to light. Plus all the prophecies it has brought to pass!

Anyhow, back to the scary picture now; our government offices (a few key offices I think) are beginning to be invaded by women, which by our great constitution they have that right. I'm regretfully saying that rights here in this particular case can destroy us--America, a great nation!

The Apostle Paul, one of the greatest men ever to exist has this to say; "I will that the younger women marry, bear children, guide the house,—" I Tim.5:15.

He wasn't talking about the House of Representatives either! The house he was talking about is the greatest one in the world we might say, the home!!

But, here's the line that's gonna catch up with us sooner or later unless there is some voluntary action on the part of women to preserve, or, help to preserve our America; "--giving honor unto the wife, as unto the weaker vessel,--." 1 Peter 3:7.

One might say that that is referring to their physical condition, but, it doesn't just stop there as we might compare. The lovely ladies' thinking is also weaker I believe we can say, as to solving world problems, war, building and I don't know what all. Paul just flatly stated the term 'weakness' which can apply to many categories.

In a poll taken, 60% of the women were against the invasion of the island of Granada I think it is, by President Regean. Of the which invasions can prevent the spread of communism in certain cases. It takes a strong constitution and stamina to go forward, and, especially to be a leader in the forward march. And according to Paul, the helpmates don't have that, as well as according to late examples maybe. Also, as says God.

So, I would like to say about your heading in our newspaper, "Women Preachers Fight Barriers to Serve God"; Maybe someday, or, we had better someday, see a heading, "Women Fight Barriers to Stay in Their Place"--namely the households, as they have been ordained to do so.

Elaine, many thanks for your time and may you educate many through your writing of the truth.

Sincerely,

Howard R. Edwards
[name changed]

Because they are not generally accepted and because they can rarely pastor the larger town churches, locating women preachers or women pastors is no easy matter. Itinerant women preachers, first of all, are not listed anywhere. No perusal of telephone directories or newspaper church listings will yield names of preachers who do not hold the pastorship of a church. On the other hand, women who do hold the pastorship of a church are most often pastors of churches that are very small, are so far from the typical "main-line" denominations that they are never listed, or are simply too rural to be included in directories that cater to town populations. Often, too, women pastors will be listed only by their initials, making sex differentiation nearly impossible. Fieldwork, therefore, is often a slow and tedious process.

In the central counties of Missouri, working with Columbia as my home base, I first relied heavily on very small town newspaper offices to get me started. Often one of the editors on these newspapers knew at least one women who preached or pastored; from there it was generally a matter of making contacts with contacts. Women preachers tend to know about other women preachers and welcomed the chance to share their information with me. On the other hand, I found many male preachers and pastors reluctant to share names and information with me because they were, by and large, against the very notion of a woman preaching. Like the man who wrote the letter to me, I would most often get a "sermon" from them which extolled the virtues of women but pointed out the dangerous implications of females behind the pulpit.

The survey portion of my work has taken three years and, in some ways, continues to date. People who know what I am doing call me now when they hear a women preach, or hear about a woman preacher. In spirit, however, the survey phase is over because I am no longer following up new leads that are sent to me. Adding more names to my roster of women preachers is important, but at this point I feel the research has yielded enough information to enable me to make statements and analyze data based on that information that will only be substantiated by further work with additional subjects.

Once my work began, I had no trouble getting more names of women than my work-day would allow me to visit. But fieldwork in religion has its own unique problems. Simply getting a woman's name did not suffice to insure her as a candidate for an interview. Most often, I would learn that a certain woman was to preach a revival in a particular church or would be preaching a Sunday night service. In order to assess the characteristics of the religious group as well as listen to the woman preach, the easiest first step was to visit the church and hear her. If possible, I tried to hear one woman several times. My presence in these churches would without fail arouse curiosity at the least, and sometimes raise concern, but certainly I was never asked to leave. After having visited a church

11

several times, I usually approached the woman preacher, identified myself as a teacher at the University, and asked permission to tape record her sermons. Since inexpensive tape recorders are readily available now, and because recorders are often used at these religious services, mine was generally accepted without any problem. As the woman and her congregation began to get more used to seeing me in the services, I usually began to linger after the service was over and talk with people, waiting to talk with the preacher. Finally, I would approach her about a possible interview. In addition to the interviews, I have recorded hundreds of hours of church services led by women and sermons delivered by women preachers. In two cases, the women themselves have been recording their own sermons for many years and have shared their private collections with me, increasing my total number of recorded sermons.

Surprisingly, a large number of women in central Missouri feel that God has called them to preach the gospel. The range of actual, consistent preaching activity on their part is variable, however. This variability results from several factors. In many cases, the women are wives of preachers or pastors and their opportunities for preaching are likely to be times their husbands are ill or out of town, or times that the husbands have designated as "wife preaching" nights. Often, the wives will be allowed to preach the Sunday evening service or to conduct the Wednesday night service. Generally, however, the Wednesday night service is not a slot for an actual sermon but is more often perceived as a "teaching" night. Other women preachers in the area who are not married to a preacher have even fewer opportunities to stand behind the pulpit. These women are traveling, itinerant preachers who must rely exclusively upon invitations to preach. They are often called to preach revivals, to act as a stand-in when a pastor is ill or gone; they are sometimes asked to preach simply because they "show up" at a service. This traditional courtesy of asking a visiting preacher to preach is extended to both men and women preachers. A substantial number of women preachers in this region are frustrated by the fact that they feel God has clearly given them a directive to preach his Word, but they often do not have the opportunity to carry out that directive. Some feel especial apprehension because they feel they will be held accountable for all the lost souls that they did *not* save during their tenure on this earth.

On the other hand, the most surprising outcome of my research has been the discovery that a number of women preachers in central Missouri actually do hold the position of *pastor* of a church—that is, they solely occupy the single most authoritative position in the church and assume all of the power and responsibilities that that position implies. In fact, while their numbers are by no means great, nearly every small town in central Missouri is likely to have one congregation that will be pastored by a woman, often several. In almost every case, these churches will be Pentecostal. Rarely, if ever, will the Baptist or Methodist churches have a woman pastor.[11]

My intention in this work is multi-dimensional, both a "humanistic" study of women preachers and pastors and an examination of the "artistic" aspects of women's sermons. I am concerned with the life stories of Pentecostal women preachers and their perceptions of themselves within a cultural milieu which does not condone their occupational decision, and I am concerned with the way in which they manage to become pastors of congregations and how they conduct themselves as leaders of the church and as community figures. In the first chapter, I have selected representative spiritual life stories of four women preachers. In Chapter 2, I focus on the similar backgrounds and influences that enabled these women to dare to assume in the first place that they had had a personal calling from God to preach, and on their strength to pursue that determination against all odds. Then I offer an argument for looking at their personal narratives as traditional narratives that serve as alternative "fictions" for their lives. I am also concerned with the stylistics and poetics of the female sermon as an artistic form created in performance. Chapter 3 begins an examination of the preaching styles of women preachers. Here I offer a contrast between the sermon of an evangelist preacher and the pastor of a church. The study of women's sermons continues in Chapter 4 with an examination of the two most dominant themes in women's sermons: sacrifice and salvation. And, finally, Chapter 5 focuses on the important reproductive images and maternal strategies that appear to aid the woman in acquiring and maintaining the position of pastor of a congregation; these images and strategies are expressed both in the woman's role within the congregation and the community and in her sermons. The Epilogue brings the reader up to date on the life of the central figure in this book, Sister Anna Walters. The Appendix, provides several verbatim sermons, parts of which have been analyzed in this study.

The women I have interviewed and taped for this work have been at once surprised, honored, and often dismayed by my attentions. For most of their lives they have had to deal with the criticism of their families and friends; most of them have met with overt resentment for their "calling." Their husbands, fathers, and children have openly displayed their own discomfort in having a preacher for a wife, daughter, or mother. To be a woman preacher is *not* to be popular; respect is tenuous and hard-earned and tolerance is most often served up with heavy doses of suspicion. Such women *may* be looked upon by the community as terribly brazen, even as troublemakers. Husbands and children have suffered the pain of

13

hearing their wife or mother publicly condemned or ridiculed; certainly, the masculinity of a man married to a woman preacher is perceived to be in jeopardy. For the folklorist, then, to enter this world and bestow attention on these women *as* preachers is to invite more pain. While the women have claimed their right to preach or pastor, they have elected to proceed quietly, in proper deference to the world as it exists. My attentions thus served at times to exacerbate an already festering problem; especially if their husbands were around, many women preachers preferred *not* to have my obvious interest. In fact, in one case, the husband, who was also a minister, kept insisting that it really ought to be he that I interview, not his wife. In some cases, the women have specifically requested that their real names not be used, just in case someone might think they were trying to boast or call attention to themselves. Therefore, given the tension that serves as the very foundation of their lives and their "calling," I have determined to use pseudonyms throughout the book; names of counties, towns, churches, and individuals are fictitious. No real purpose could be served by an adamant stance on real names; what we can learn about fundamentalist religion in general and women preachers in particular can be accomplished without causing further apprehension to the participants in this study.[12]

NOTES

1. Folklorists remain undecided about a satisfactory definition of "folk religion." Nevertheless, most contemporary folklorists studying religion are primarily working with a common understanding of "folk" and/or traditional religious aspects as dynamic, performed, and believed constructs that direct and give meaning to people's lives, in both their sacred and secular spheres. Folk religion has often been described as the "unofficial" and orally transmitted characteristics of religion that remain in tension with or serve in contradistinction to the more codified "official" and doctrinal aspects of religion. This approach, however, must be modified when one is studying autonomous, smaller American fundamentalist congregations whose orally transmitted belief systems are, in fact, quite "official" in their own church context and may or may not be in tension with another hierarchically "higher" religious governing body. Appropriately, the genres folklorists focus on include spontaneously performed, but traditionally rule-governed, genres such as sermons, testimonies, rituals, specialized language, legend, and even dress and behavior. Important contributions to the study of folk religion include the work of Don Yoder, Bruce Rosenberg, William Clements, Jeff Todd Titon, Gerald Davis, and William Wilson. Full bibliographic references can be found at the end of this book.

2. Elaine J. Lawless, "Women's Speech in the Pentecostal Service: An Ethnography;" and *God's Peculiar People: Women's Voices and Folk Tradition in a Pentecostal Church*.

3. Histories of Pentecostalism include: Vinson Synan, *The Holiness-Pentecostal Movement in the United States*; John Nichol, *Pentecostalism*; Melvin Dieter, *The Holiness Revival of the Nineteenth Century*; Nils Block-Hoell, *The Pentecostal Movement*; W. J. Hollenweger, *The Pentecostals*; Robert Mapes Anderson, *Vision of the Disinherited*; Stanley H. Frodsham, *"With Signs Following"*; Elmer T. Clark, *The Small Sects in America*; and Bernard A. Weisberger, *They Gathered at the River*. See also Dickson Bruce, *And They All Sang Hallelujah: Plain-Folk Camp-Meeting Religion, 1800–1845*, for an excellent survey of the early camp meeting tradition.

4. See Synan, p. 101; Nichol, p. 27; and Block-Hoell, p. 19. See also Steve Durasoff, *Bright Wind of the Spirit*.

5. Nichol, p. 8.

6. Cf. Block-Hoell, pp. 58–69.

7. Lawless, " 'What Did She Say?' An Application of Peirce's General Theory of Signs to Glossolalia in the Pentecostal Religion"; and "Brothers and Sisters: Pentecostals as a Folk Group."

8. Lawless, "Shouting for the Lord: The Power of Women's Speech in the Pentecostal Service."

9. Lawless, "Make a Joyful Noise: An Ethnography of Communication in the Pentecostal Service."

10. Most work with spontaneous sermons has been confined to the study of male preachers. Both Bruce Rosenberg's *The Art of the American Folk Preacher* and Gerald Davis's *I Got the Word in Me and I Can Sing It, You Know* focus on the African-American tradition of male preachers. Jeff Todd Titon's "Powerhouse for God" record and forthcoming book on Rev. John Sherfey deal with a white male Baptist preacher. Catherine Peck's 1983 Master's thesis is the only work I know that deals exclusively with the Afro-American preaching styles of female preachers. I have published several articles on the tradition of white Pentecostal women preachers.

11. For several years the University of Missouri College of Agriculture published research bulletins on "The Church in Rural Missouri." These bulletins offered statistics on the number of sectarian and nonsectarian churches in the state, education of clergy, size of congregation, etc. It is telling that as late as 1975, no statistics were available on the number of women preachers in the state. The only bulletin that I could locate that even mentioned women preachers (#633C) dismissed the issue in the following manner: "Women Preachers. It is unfortunate . . . that the number of women in the sample was not large enough to warrant separate analysis. The nine women included in this investigation constitute only 2.6 percent of the total sample" (p. 163). Thus far, I have not been able to locate more contemporary figures on the number of women preachers in the state. I suspect that the information is not much better for 1987, primarily because these kinds of statistics are based on questionnaires and published information and not on fieldwork; such a study would, in fact, miss the numbers of women preachers and pastors in the state.

12. Tapes of interviews, services, and transcripts are housed in my personal archives at the University of Missouri.

This Is My Story:
This Is Where I Came From

Beginnings are difficult. "Where do you want me to start?" Sister Anna asks me. "How do I tell you about my life? I was saved when I was nine years old; I was seventeen when God called me to preach. But those are *my* markers. What are the markers you are looking for?" Such a good question. We are so tuned to biographical data as a linear progression: she was born in 1892 to E. Jacobs and S. Jacobs, née Bishop; there were twelve children, four boys and eight girls; she went to school in Sparta; she married William Richards at age seventeen and bore four children of her own . . .

But when I ask a woman preacher, "Tell me about yourself, about your life," the markers are all different. I've had to learn to listen; I need to learn their markers rather than teach them mine. Their accounts are more like the patchwork quilts that grace their beds. Certain moments come to mind first, remind them of another similar day, a different moment. Their lives are a mosaic, some events more textured than others. Some occupy a whole block on the quilt, others only share a space with related times and memories appliqued one on top of the other. Remembering lifts the layers. Digression is a religious pattern itself, woven like the coverlet's shuttle, forward and back, to reveal perfection on both sides. Yet, a look at their various individual stories reveals a traditional pattern, a common story with uncommon embellishments. Not only in the story style and performance, but in the content as well, these stories prove to be examples of folk narrative.

The "life stories" of four women preachers included in this chapter are representative of the kinds of stories I have gotten from women preachers throughout the central counties of Missouri. Most of the material that comprises their personal stories is taken from interviews; however, because parts of these stories remain in the active repertoire of these women *as* preachers, some sections are quoted as performed within sermon texts. I have chosen to include these four women's stories because in many ways they *are* representative and because they offer the range of spiritual life stories of Pentecostal women preachers in this area; that is, their actual life experiences range from those of an itinerant preacher who has never pastored a church, to a woman who preaches on occasion only at her husband's church, to a woman who has pastored one congregation for eighteen years. Their individual lives, then, represent the range of possibilities for a woman preacher. Their accounts of their experiences allow us to see the broader similarities as well as provide for the particular integrity of each woman's story.

Finding a palatable way to present these orally delivered life stories to the reader has been a difficult task. One is tempted, of course, to offer verbatim, untampered transcripts of interviews, complete with interview questions and without concern for chronological sequence—since we are not pretending that these represent life "histories". Although I will agree that these stories *are* fictions and can be viewed as *texts* in their own right, many of them were not actually delivered in an uninterrupted flow. Therefore, I have "framed" the transcripts—in terms of introducing the stories, putting them into context, describing the women, and creating transitions. There are two "voices" in the stories—theirs and mine. Although my voice may be interjected at any point in the narrative (and will always be evident), the quoted portions of their stories are fully intact and are verbatim.

Favorite stories and accounts of the women may appear in several different interviews. Differences in recounting should be understood as different accounts of the same stories. In the case of Sister Anna, many stories have been recounted to me on numerous occasions. Some of the material about Sister Anna was actually written down by her as she would remember accounts she wanted to share with me.

SISTER RUTH

Murray, Missouri, is a very small typical farming town in north central Missouri. Here, on a side street, on the corner, stands a tiny gray building, long, with a center front double door. No steeple adorns the top of this dwelling, no stained glass refracts the light, and no billboard announces services or the pastor's name and Sunday's message. Hand lettering on the front, above the door, spells out "APOSTOLIC CHURCH OF JESUS CHRIST, INC." Half the double door is broken and sticks; the other half sports an oversized, rusty doorknob and leads into the sanctuary. The windows are all open, with no screens. Outside, within hand's reach, I can see the goldenrod that has taken over the abandoned lot next door; huge bumble bees cruise in and out of the open squares; a large fan stands in the corner and hums noisily, oscillating precariously on its rickety frame. The pews are old theater seats, their crushed red velvet worn smooth and shiny. I push one down and sit quickly. There is an ancient upright piano to my left up front and a large wooden pulpit in the center, flanked by a rough wooden bench which serves as an altar. A banner, hung high above the pulpit near the ceiling, reads "Be Not Afraid, Only Believe" and two large vertical posters, hand-lettered in red crayon on mill paper, read:

I am blessed. I am blessed. Everyday of my life I am blessed. When I wake up in The morning till I Lay my head to rest. I am blessed. I am blessed.	Lord you are more precious than silver. Lord you are more costly than gold. Lord, you are more beautiful than diamonds. And nothing I desire compares with YOU!

I wonder about the very large mayonnaise jar bulging with scraps of paper, the only object honored on the wooden altar. Actually, it will be many months before this group will trust me enough to allow me to see them push yet another piece of paper into the "prayer jar," form a circle with the jar, with each person closest to the jar on either side touching the glass sides as they pray aloud, all together, for the person whose name has just been written on a slip of paper and added to the other names in the jar. Since its beginning many years ago, that jar has never been disturbed except to swallow another prayer name. They weren't sure, they told me later, what I might think about this particular custom of theirs. I suspect my name is in that jar.

In time, I learn that the fortyish woman at the piano is the pastor's daughter. She was once a rising country-western singer but suffered an acute case of agoraphobia years ago, before she moved to Murray and joined her mother's church. She smiles broadly as her mother goes around the tiny room shaking hands with every person, hugging some, exclaiming "Praise the Lord," and "We're *so* glad to have you here."

Sister Ruth is a slight, energetic older woman—the epitome of every-one's favorite grandmother. She has gray hair which she pulls back severely at the nape of her neck in an old-fashioned bun. She is spry and spicy. "Mostly," she tells me, "the problem with being a woman preacher is that some folks will just sit there. You can't move them. You talk about some-thing being hard. They'll sit there and never say 'Amen!', never boost them. And you saying 'Amen!' to a preacher is like saying 'Sic 'em' to a dog that's running a rabbit. He'll go that much faster. It helps." And she laughs heartily.

"I've got a determination that I am not going to give up. Those that endurest to the end are the ones that are going to be saved. When God has something for us to do, he means for us to do it."

Born into a church-going family in Alabama, Sister Ruth has fond memories of attending the Baptist church during her childhood, although now that she's a Pentecostal, she recalls just how inhibited all the Baptists were, how quiet and reserved the services—so quiet you could hear a pin drop. And, she could remember the "protracted meetings" that the Baptists used to hold down there. "They'd have it day and night. They'd have it of a morning, 11:00 in the morning, and they'd have it seven nights a week and it'd go on for two weeks."

Ruth married a Pentecostal boy in 1933. She'd heard about "Holy Rollers" from her step-grandfather when she was growing up, but she never associated that reference with Pentecostals. She could never remem-ber *exactly* what her granddad would say, only she knew he didn't much care for them, that he didn't believe in what they were doing. He lived nearly 100 miles away from Ruth's family, so it's possible that he was describing a religious group not found in their immediate region. "And when he'd come down to visit Dad, he would always be talking about it in a slang way, you know, talking about the Holy Rollers." When she first began to visit her new husband's church, she was appalled. She told the following account during one of her sermons; in fact, she recalls it often. (I have typed it as she performed it on October 10, 1984.)

> I met my husband,
> 60 Naturally he was raised Pentecostal
> And I wasn't.
> So, ah,
>   . . .
> 75 We went to church that night
> And my, my, my they had such a time, praise God.
>   . . .

100 And I tell you I heard messages preached in there that I'd never
      heard.
    And, ah,
    The first night
    I went in there and I sit 'cause
    Oh, they were shouting all over the place,
105 Just having a marvelous time,
    Talking in tongues and
    My, my the people were falling out
    Under the power of God.
    But I was taught
110 Not to do that,
    See?
    You go in—it's very quiet
    You can hear a pin
    Drop anywhere in the whole church
115 Very quiet
    You couldn't hardly hear the minister,
    Even the singing
    That much.
    But these people put everything they had into it.
120 And, my, my you could just see it
    Just bubbling, bubbling up here
    And they were just shouting!
    And I sat there with my head down,
    Said, "Lord, what have I got into this time?" [laughs]
    . . .
148 And going home that night, ah,
    Somebody said something about the church—
150 About the service,
    And I said,
    "You told me we were going to church."
    "And we did."
    And I said, "Well,
155 If I'd a known that, I'd a stayed home!"

But actually, Ruth continued to attend the Pentecostal services with
her husband's family, and, she said, "The Lord began to deal with me."
She remembers specific Bible texts that were used for the sermons; Acts
2:38 sticks in her mind as the text for several services. Her internal dilemma
became a dialogue between God and the devil.

164 The Lord began to deal with me and
165 The devil did, too, he was right there.
    He said, "Now, you know if you go up
    That you're gonna have to be baptized,
    You haven't been baptized according to Acts 2:38,"
    He said, "you go up you're going to have to be baptized."
170 Devil talking to me now,
    And he said, "it's too *cold*!"
    It was in February
    And ice was all over everywhere.
    They didn't have baptizing tanks
175 To baptize you then.
    They took you to the creek.
    Didn't have a car,
    We had to go in a wagon
    And it was cold, my, my, my.
180 But I was gonna defeat that devil
    Because I was obeying the word,
    What I'd heard.
    Went on
    And broke the ice.
185 Went down in,
    I could take you to the very spot today,
    Broke the ice
    Laid me down into the water
    Baptized me.
190 You know, when you first hit the water
    It's a little cold,
    But the longer you stayed there
    The warmer it got!
    . . .
100 Yep, they got me out,
    Up in the wagon and drove home.
    I don't know how many—about five miles, I believe it was—
    before I could get home to change clothes.
    By that time I was really warmed up!

    Eventually, Ruth had three children, two boys and then a girl. She and her husband moved to St. Louis, Missouri, in 1942. She worked there in a factory for thirty-five years and attended church almost every night, taking her three small children with her. And she kept two boarders, sometimes three, to make ends meet, and did the washing and ironing by hand. She speaks of her children as her primary joy; becoming a mother had a particular significance for her: "I had Betty, you know, I had—you know a lot of times people get ahold of a baby, want to hold a baby, just want one that's all yours? Well, I used to be guilty of that. I had her. She was only a few months old and I was, with my children, I was picky about them. I didn't want nobody else holding them, cause I was afraid they'd hurt them. And when it cried for me, it just, it just thrilled me to the bottom. Because they'd cry and want to come back to me, see. And, of course, I look back and remember that when I was a kid, I used to try and get ahold of a baby to play with it and hold it and carry it around, more than anything in the world. Let the boys go. Let everything go. I wanted to play with that baby, hold that baby, take care of it. But finally that baby would start crying and I couldn't do anything for it. I wasn't the mother, see, and I couldn't nurse it. And when it started crying, it just wanted its mother. And when I had my own, and somebody'd come and take them out of my arms, they'd cry and want right back to me, and then I could look back and remember what had happened when I was a kid. There's nothing like being a mother."

Early on, Ruth felt that her pull toward God and religion was stronger than most people's. Her dedication was so strong; her convictions kept her going where the convictions of others seemed to wane. But, she says, she put off "getting the Holy Ghost," having that personal spiritual experience that would be marked by the speaking in tongues. Perhaps she realized that this move was not going to be an easy one to coordinate with her life and her family. In fact, when she tells the story of the night she "got the Holy Ghost," the narrative pivots on the fact that in order to go forward to "get it," she had to leave her child behind without thinking about it crying for her: "See, I had her in church, my husband was there and my two boys. And the Lord began to deal with me that night. And I don't know who took her. And she didn't cry, as far as I know of. Somebody got her cause I made a start for the altar and then I received the Holy Ghost. I shouted all over the place. The sweetest—I don't think I ever felt, I don't think I ever felt that good—I know I didn't, before I received it."

Ruth began, then, to become more and more involved in church activities. For years, as her children grew up and got married themselves, she would participate in the church services, leading the singing, leading the testimony services, taking care of the various details that needed attending to. In a way, folks began to think of her as a preacher, even then. When her daughter wanted to marry, the young man said he didn't want "no preacher for a mother-in-law." Her daughter tells me that her mother, "always did all the work, you know, but he did all the preaching." Her daughter will laugh and say, "Mom was a real one-woman show." And Sister Ruth will recall how she could lead the singing and "be" the band at the same time she'd care for her little granddaughter: "Let me tell you we had some time in that church. That's when I played the piano, held one of my granddaughters in my lap, beat the foot drum, and led the singing. Well, now, when I get to thinking about that sometimes I look back and I wonder, 'how in the world did I do it?' " She claims she only learned how to play three songs on the piano, but that folks just loved to hear her play and would always plead with her to play the piano: "And I tell them, I say, 'Now, I don't know music.' I say—this is what I always tell them, 'I play by ear and sing by letter. Play by ear and open up and let 'er fly!' "

Sister Ruth cannot quite pinpoint *exactly* how she got the call to preach, how she knew that she was supposed to take a church herself. Her daughter, musing, trying to recall the year of her mother's decision, said: "I was married and had Debby, so it must have been about '58, when you got blessed." I insisted, "How did you get the 'call'?" And Sister Ruth recalled, "Something just said 'Go'! When I'd begin to play that piano and begin to sing, the words would just roll out of my mouth and the thoughts out of my mind, and just, something just, it just said, 'Do it!' "

Apparently, she became disgruntled that she was doing so much work in the church and not receiving any credit for it. She told me, "you know that pastor, my pastor, at that time I didn't have a church then. But he *never did* call on me to preach. I taught every one of the classes, done everything there was to be done in the church, but never the preaching. He never did call on me to preach." This statement is a bit difficult to understand, because the "I didn't have a church then" implies that, at least in her own mind, she was already *supposed* to be preaching; her comments further imply that the pastor of her church ought to have known this as well. Once, in a sermon, she suggested that she left this man's church because he failed to close his services with an altar call: "They just kind of were in and out, you know, they just stood and was dismissed, see, and there were people there who wanted to pray. So, we kind of, there was another lady, Helen, and I, and the Lord moved upon us to move out." On another occasion, she told me she thought this pastor and his church just were not very friendly, either: "They'd never go and shake hands with them, invite them back. They'd never do that." Sister Ruth knew these personal touches were important, so, in 1957, she and her friend Helen left the church to try and found their own. My prodding to get Sister Ruth to tell me how she *knew* this was what she was supposed to do resulted in her relating to me the following narrative.

"Like, uh, I can tell you this little story that happened when I got that first church. Had a wedding coming up. Of course, at that time I wasn't ordained. And, a lot of people said you had to be ordained to preach, but you don't. You do have to be ordained if you give marriage ceremonies, you know, or something like that. But, I had this wedding and I had gotten another man to come up and marry them. And, that evening, that afternoon and evening, it done a little bit of everything. It thundered. It lightninged. It hailed. The wind blowed. The sun shined. It . . . oh, it was an awful evening. And still at it when it was time for me to go up to unlock my church. And my husband came in that night and he said, 'Well, I wouldn't go. I wouldn't get out in this kind of weather. They won't be there.' I said, 'Well, I gotta be there whether anybody else is or not.' And that's always the way I felt about it. So I went on. Got up there and there's three carloads sitting in front of the church waiting to get in. Well, I got a message that night. We got in there and they didn't have no flowers on their coats, on their clothes, and they left the church to go to the florist to get flowers, and it was raining. And they were gone, gone, gone. Already past time they were supposed to have gotten married, and me holding that preacher there. Finally, they come back and the minister went ahead and married them. But I got a message out of it. It sticks to today. Like the ten virgins? Five were wise and five were foolish. Five of them *thought* they were ready to go in when they wasn't. When they got back it was too late. So, we think a lot of times we're ready to do this or do that, but are we really?"

It is typical of Sister Ruth to answer a question with a narrative. It was clear to her, at least, that it was just "time" for her to find a church of her own, but it would have seemed presumptuous of her to say that directly. She recalls noticing a small rock building that she'd been passing every day on her way to work; this particular day it had a big sign on the front—"For Rent." She and her friend got the landlords to come in and ascertain how difficult it would be to turn the place into a church sanctuary. They explained that she would need exit signs, and the door was hinged wrong for a "public" building—things that seemed pretty alien to her. The building had been a paint store, so there was lots of old paint around, but there was even more paint on the floors, great ugly blobs of it. There were layers and layers of cardboard piled high in the corners and pieces of old linoleum piled one on another. And under these, more spilled paint. The women went down there and scraped paint every Sunday afternoon until they got it cleaned up, down to the bare concrete floor, which they painted, all except for a small section that would have to serve as the "altar" area. They just couldn't face the terrible stains on that part so they brought in a small piece of carpet and carefully laid it down across the front, covering the worst spots with yellow pile.

"We got it all cleaned up and painted and we didn't have a chair one. My husband said to me, he said, 'What're you gonna do for benches?' And I said, 'Well, if nothing else we'll take our own, let everybody bring their own chair.' Well, he thought that was pretty stupid, that wouldn't look like a church. And a few nights after that I had a dream that I was going to church and I didn't know where I was going, but I was going to church and I had my chair with me. And when I got down to the church—at first I didn't know I was going to *my* church, I just thought I was going to church but I was taking this chair—but when I got there the building was full of seats and the seats were full of people. And the next day we saw this ad in the paper for theater seats. We had ten dollars and they were a dollar apiece. And we bought a hundred of them. Two ladies, now, are going to do all this. Well, he brang the men down to make sure to get a hundred good seats, but they wasn't no way in the world that you could get a hundred real perfect seats out of that bunch. But I said, 'But I don't have but ten dollars.' And he said, 'Well, that's all right, you can send the rest of it.' Well, we got the rest of the money and paid for the seats."

This first church was near the baseball stadium in St. Louis, in a run-down neighborhood that eventually became part of the black ghetto, a fact that seemed to make Sister Ruth terribly nervous. Even then, she recalls, the neighborhood was almost entirely black, and with the ballpark so close she had incessant parking problems. Eventually she bought a lot adjacent to her church for parking, and, it appears, learned to love the role of church pastor. She often relates the story of how she got a platform for her church, the same platform she preaches from today in Murray, Missouri: "Some very dear friends of mine, their children were small and they went out and picked blackberries and sold them and bought the material and went down to the church the night before we had service and put the platform in. When I went down for service they were all standing outside, you know, this was summertime. And I thought, 'What are they all standing outside for? They've got a key. Why don't they go on in?' But, see, they were waiting for me. Well, I got there and opened the door. I walked in. That platform had been put in there and I was just rejoicing. Praise the Lord." Eventually, though, Sister Ruth felt more and more uncomfortable in this small building wedged between the growing black neighborhood and the rowdy ballpark crowds, and she sold it to a black church group. Then, she said, "I just went here and there, you know, with no home church, just searching out." Ironically, the pastor from her original church called her during this time to preach a revival at his church, and she recalls that in 1962 a stranger gave her a message of hope. She had taken some girls down to sing on a radio broadcast. Here, the piano

---

player, whom she had never seen before, said to her, "You know, God shows me that you're gonna be a great leader." She said, "You're gonna be a great leader, have a lot of followers. God is really gonna bless you." Sister Ruth said she didn't stop to ask her what it would take to get there, and she says that didn't "puff me up or anything like that." For a time, between 1965 and 1970, she actually had her own fledgling radio broadcast, but soon the financial burden became too great. Only years later, in 1977, was she able to broadcast her Sunday morning sermons again on a St. Louis religious station, where to this day she still sends her sermons.

Sister Ruth's first large church fell into her lap. She was, as she stated, "searching around," occasionally visiting one church in particular, whose pastor had been transferred to Arizona and then Louisiana by his company. The pastor's wife sent the key to the church to Sister Ruth and asked her to keep the church open until they returned. Finally, it became clear that the couple were never going to return, and they asked Sister Ruth to just take over the church. Sister Ruth felt uncomfortable about just taking the church and its fixtures, so she insisted on working out a plan to pay the couple for the fixtures, and she took over the building lease.

Sister Ruth kept that church open and active in St. Louis for nearly fifteen years and nurtured a congregation of nearly 150 people. In 1971 her daughter, the one who had suffered a severe case of agoraphobia, followed her brother Richard and moved her family to Murray, Missouri. As their mother neared retirement age, they encouraged her to move to Murray as well. Finally she agreed. And no sooner than she had gotten herself and her husband, who was not well, established in Murray, she began to look around for a church building. It didn't take her long to discover an abandoned storefront church within walking distance from her home. Covered with tattered gray siding, the one-room structure had served other small religious groups well, no doubt, over the years. She discovered that the owners were in no mood to rent the building to her, but they did want to sell it and get it off their hands. She beat the sidewalks in Murray until she found a bank that would give her the loan to buy the building. Then she moved her own platform, altar bench, and some church pews from storage in St. Louis to her new little church. Here she started her "work" in Murray. For nearly ten years now, she has faithfully kept the doors of this tiny Apostolic Pentecostal Assembly open for Wednesday night, Sunday morning, and Sunday night services. She is the Sunday School teacher, the testimony leader, the song leader, the preacher, and the pastor. The strongest core of her congregation is her own family, a not-unusual occurrence in small fundamentalist churches. Her daughter, who loves to testify about her short-lived stint as a recording country-western singer, plays the piano for her, thankful to have her mother in town and to have a piano to play for God. Other townspeople drop in regularly, whether they are actually "members" or not. They just appear glad to have found a place like this, a religious context for "shouting" and "getting happy," when the mood hits them. Several older people are consistent in attendence; a few young mothers sit quietly with their broods of children in tow. Some tell me this is just like their home church back in Virginia, or that it reminds them of a church they used to go to in Detroit. Actually, the town isn't all that pleased with the revival of this "eyesore"; some of the more prominent residents of Murray would rather not hear the sounds of tamborines and religious shouting pulsating across the early evening air. But, if Sister Ruth has her way, she'll be there to open the church, early, as long as she has the strength to walk down the street and pull open the doors.

More likely than not, should you visit Sister Ruth's church, you will eventually hear her narrate her favorite poem—her favorite because God caused her to hear it twice on the same day a long time ago in Alabama. It is called "Heaven's Grocery Store."

I was walking down life's highway a long, long time ago
When I saw a sign that read, 'Heaven's Grocery Store.'
As I got a little closer, the door came open wide,
And when I came to myself I was standing inside.
I saw a host of people, they were standing everywhere.
One gave me a basket and said, 'My Child, shop with care.'
And everything a person needs was in the grocery store.
And all you couldn't carry you could come back again for more.
Well, first I got some patience and love was on the same row.
Further down was understanding you need that everywhere you go.
I got a box or two of wisdom, a bag or two of faith.
I just couldn't miss the Holy Ghost; it was in every place.
I stopped to get some strength and courage to help me run life's race.
By then my basket was getting full, but I remembered I needed grace.
I didn't forget salvation, for salvation was free
So I tried to get enough of that to save both you and me.
Then I started up to a counter to pay my grocery bill
For I thought I had everything to do our master's will
As I went up the aisle I saw prayer; I just had to put it in
For I knew when I stepped outside I would run right into sin.
Peace and joy was plentiful; they were on the last shelf.
Song and praise were hanging near, so I just helped myself.
Then I asked the angel, 'Now, how much do I owe?'
He just smiled and said, 'Take your purchase everywhere you go.'

28

Again I smiled at him and asked, 'How much do I really owe?'
He smiled again and said,
'My child, Jesus paid your bill a long, long time ago.'

SISTER MARY

Mary Harris is a woman preacher. She lives on a quiet, unassuming street in Wheaton, Missouri. She is not the pastor of any church, nor has she ever held the position of church pastor. She is typical of many women preachers in the area who preach special services in local churches and revivals only where she is invited. During my interviews with her, Sister Mary stressed that when she got busy with the duties of being a wife and raising her children, she had gotten away from preaching. When she did that it always made her feel really bad about herself, because she feels her call to preach is her first obligation, even before her husband and family. Sister Mary's right hand is severely crippled—she accurately describes it as more like a claw, now, rather than a hand. The fingers are stiff and she cannot bend any of the fingers back. She can barely pick up the telephone and has trained herself to write in a somewhat legible style by holding her pen upright between the first two fingers of her hand. Mary Harris is a very slight, quiet woman in her fifties, whose rhythmic, punctuated style of preaching comes as a surprise.

Several years ago [January 8, 1974], she fell on the ice and injured her right arm. Her interpretation of that incident was that God was giving her a warning. "When my arm got hurt, I told my husband, I said, 'The Lord really dealt with me.' Cause I was a bookkeeper, you know, and I had just laid my preaching down for a while, just preached once in a while and that's all. And then I told my husband, I said, 'the Lord really dealt with me,' that I had laid aside what God had told me to do, and that I had become too interested in bookkeeping, and I'd come to like my job too much. And that's why, my arm had just got [healed] just so far, you know, just to a certain place and stopped. And it was my right arm, and my right hand. And I was very right-handed, and I couldn't do hardly anything. And I told him, I said, 'When I get able,' I said, 'if I can get some revivals lined up, would you not stand in my way.' And he said, 'If you can get some lined up, if it will make you feel better and you feel like that's what you've got to do, then you go.' So I did and that summer, I kept busy.

"I went to Farmington, and let's see, I think it started on Thursday night. I think I had Thursday, Friday, Saturday, Sunday lined up. And then, we were having such a real good revival. We were having soul saving. So, the minister said, 'Don't you think we'd better go on into next week.' And I said, 'Well, I have to face the Lord and find out. Yes, we are having

29

a good revival, but I want to be sure it's in God's will or otherwise there's no need to go on.' So I prayed and I asked the Lord, I said, 'Lord, I want ... I haven't seen anyone receive the Holy Ghost. And I want someone to receive the Holy Ghost, somebody to receive the Holy Ghost Sunday night. By that, I'll know that I should go on.' And you know that night there was a lady in front of me, and I don't know if she'd ever gotten the Holy Ghost before, but she got the Holy Ghost in about fifteen minutes. And so I stayed. And we had, oh, I don't know how many we had, but we went on a few more days.

"And I went to Mountain View and I held a service down there and I had a terrible time trying to get down there. I had to take the bus from here. I took a bus from here to Rolla and I took a mail hack from Rolla all the way into Mountain View. And, see, Mountain View is about a hundred and fifty miles. And I stayed with the pastor. I don't remember how many days I was actually there. But I held a revival, I held it about eleven days, I guess, a revival in Rolla. I went down there and I was hoping for Thursday through Sunday night. Then we started having a lot of people saved, and young people, and some getting filled with the Holy Ghost. So the pastor, he just sort of prayed about it and asked God that he would show us and so we went on and ran the revival, then, the following week. All week.

"Now, last summer I kept busy. I was trying to think of all the places I went. I think I preached at California, Missouri, and I preached at Farmington and Mountain View and Rolla and Warrensbury. Lots of times I would go to a revival some place and I'd come back just for one or two nights. Like I went to Farmington and it was the fourth of July, over the fourth of July, it was in a Church of God-Prophecy. And I don't just hold revivals only in one denomination—I didn't ever get my license, only see, I just got my license. Through the years I never got my license, because I felt that my ministry [would be damaged]—I just preach the word of God. I don't preach any doctrine because I don't believe in that. I held a revival in St. Louis at a "oneless" [Oneness][1] Church, and they're very strange. And they let me hold a revival. But I just told them. I said, 'Now, I won't preach anything that will go against what you believe, but I will preach the whole word of God and what God gives me, that's what I'll preach.' And they said, 'Well, if you preach the word of God,' they wanted me to preach that. But they did try to convince me that I needed to be baptized again in the name of Jesus only, but we have a good revival. They don't believe in jewels. They don't believe in even wearing a ring. So, I went down there to this minister and I told him, I said, 'I have'— well, I had on my wedding ring—but anyway, I told him, I said, 'Do you think I'll have more influence over the people if I don't wear my rings? If

30

you do, I'll take them off. Cause,' I said, 'The Bible says for us not to offend anyone in any way. And I believe that if our brothers are offended, we need to try and not do that thing in front of him. Even though I don't believe that way.' And he said, 'Well, you can do whatever you feel like you want to do. I won't tell you.' But he said, 'I will say this, that probably you would have more influence over the people since we teach that.' So I just took my rings off and put them away while I was there. And I feel like, you know, the Bible says we have to use wisdom in what we do and I think sometimes we don't use our wisdom. And then what we do—we don't win anybody, because we haven't used wisdom that God gave us to use.

"My mother got saved when I was four years old. My mother was born at Milford, Missouri, but she was raised around Lincoln. And my dad was raised here and 'round. He was born in Monroe County, around Bloomsdale, down in there. He was raised by his grandparents a lot. I know that Grandpa Rowar—my maiden name is Rowar—and my mother's name, maiden name, was Hines. And her dad was German. And she took us to church from that time on, well, as long as I can remember. I remember she'd had such a habit of going to the theatre, it was hard for her not to go. And she'd take me. Just me. I was just four when she had three children. And she would take me with her, we would start, even after she got saved, we'd start to church and she'd say, 'well, let's go to the show,' and I wanted to go there. But we would go to the show and before long she'd sit there and cry the whole time. And she'd say, 'No, I don't want to leave, well, but we've got to leave. I just can't stand it any longer.' What she was, she was under conviction, and it was just like she had such a habit of going to the show that it was, you know, it was just like smoking or drinking or anything like that. She said she was just a fiend for it. Now, the first time she got saved, she was going to a little Methodist church in Lincoln, and the Methodists shouted then. And, she said that she really got saved, and she was just a small child, but then when she got older she got away from God. Her mother was always a Christian. She used to tell us she'd never seen her mother ever get mad. And she'd say that her mother, I heard her the other night testify, and she as talking about Grandma and how that Grandma—and I can remember this too—that if she heard someone singing "I'll Fly Away", why Grandma would just start shouting. She'd just start dancing and I can remember that. It always seemed like that song just made Grandma feel happy. But when I was four years old, my mother got, that's when she really got saved and she got filled with the Holy Ghost. Later, my aunt and uncle went to this, the Pentecostal Church of God—it was the only Pentecostal church here in Wheaton at that time and it was down, it was in an old, Yellow Cab building and it was a big building. I can remember that big building and it was in an alley. It was just like you would pass the Central Motor Bank as you come in. It would be just right there at Wheaton Street, but there was an alley that went through—that was before the Expressway, and they called it Bradford Street and it was back in there. It went all the way through to Washington. And I can remember that church being so full of people and people didn't understand about Pentecost and they'd throw rocks on the building. We didn't have a car and we walked from one side of town to the other, but she was very strict and she taught us that we had to have a standard that we lived by. She made—we had a family altar in our home and every morning before we went to school we had prayer and she read the Bible to us. We started our day out that way.

"I can remember back when I was in the sixth, fifth or sixth grade, I went to the principal, see, because I had some friends and they didn't understand the way that I believed, you know, because I did belong to a real strict church and my hair was never cut from the time that I was four years old. And Mother braided my hair and put it around my head and pulled it straight back and they made fun of me at school, but I always tried to explain to them why. And I remember this time I went to the principal and there was two girls that was good friends of mine and I told them, I said, 'Why don't we try to have prayer meeting during recess?' And, so, I said, 'I'll got to the principal and ask him if we can.' And, you know, they allowed it. And we had prayer meeting during our recess. And I led that service.

"But I got saved when I was eight years old, and I'll soon be fifty-seven. And, when I got saved, I remember there was a revival and this minister that was preaching, when he gave the altar call, I had always been taught that you had to ask God for forgiveness for your sins when you reached the age that you felt things were wrong. And that night I felt real confession and I can remember, I can see the place, I can't remember the exact date, but I know I was eight years old and I can remember going down to the altar, and I was right on the end of the altar. There were some others there praying. But I got down on the end and I remember that I really cried and I was sorry of my sins. I really felt like I was really a bad sinner. And I really prayed through.

"And, then, when I was nine years old, I received the Holy Ghost. At a children's prayer meeting. We had a children's prayer meeting on Sunday afternoon and I received the Holy Ghost through speaking other tongues, and there was several children that received it the same time I did.

"See, when I was fifteen, my mother got real sick and she miscarried, had a stillborn baby. And I had to quit school. And you know how teenagers are, I felt real bad, I'd never failed. I'd always been right with my class that I started with—the group of young people that I'd went from kindergarten and all the way through school—and I felt real embarrassed. But I had to tell them, 'well, I have to quit school,' after my first semester and take care of my mother, cause I was the oldest. So, I never did go back to school. But, later I took the G.E.D. test and I just prayed and asked God to help me and I got my diploma. And I was just thrilled to death.

"And, then, when I was sixteen [this would be 1943], I was asked to go along to sing, just to help out and sing. There was another lady, she was just a young girl, she was in her teens, and she had been called to preach quite a while and they'd asked her to go help out with the preaching. There were two ministers and this young woman, and this one minister took his daughter along so everything would look right, took her along to help sing. And it was at Blue Springs, Missouri. And this one afternoon, they said that the minister that was supposed to preach, he said, 'I just don't have any message. I've prayed and prayed and I've sought God and I just do not have a message for tonight.' And he asked some of the others if they did, and he said, 'I think we really need to pray, because I just can't get a message.'

"So the girls went—the men prayed in the house—and the girls, we decided that we'd go down in the woods. It was wooded around that little town. And we went down, way down in the woods, and we knelt down to pray and God started dealing with my heart. And I never will forget that place because there was a big old grape vine, it was just about this big around [she makes the shape of a circle with her hands that is 8–12 inches in diameter], and it was just hanging right down. And when I—it seemed like God just slew me cause I was down on my back, flat on that ground and I couldn't get up. And I started praying and God started dealing with my heart and the Lord started saying, it just seemed like—not in an audible voice—but I could just, just hear the Lord speaking in a small, still voice, saying, 'Will you go where I want you to go? And will you do what I want you to do?' And, you know, it was hard for me because I thought, 'Now, is this me?' Because I had admired this other girl that preaches *so much*. I'd always all my life, you know, I had always thought, 'Oh, I would like to be an evangelist.' When I was growing up I used to think, and Mama always taught me that so many things was wrong, you know, that I just was almost afraid to do anything. So, the Lord dealt with me, but the thoughts came to me, 'How can I preach?' How can I do anything? But the Lord just kept dealing with me and I couldn't get up and finally I said—I just felt I had come to a place that I could say, 'Lord, whatever you want me to do, even though I within myself, I'm

33

not, I know I'm not worthy of this calling. But I'll do anything you want me to do because I know that it's in your power to speak through me. And I'll go anyplace you want me to.' And you know, when I did that, the Lord just started blessing me and I really got a blessing, from God. And, then, God gave me the first scripture he ever gave me, it was John 3:16. And the words just rolled over and over in my mind and I felt real happy. I felt real free and real happy. I just felt like that I was released from—from what I had felt bound to before that. And we got up and I can remember leaping, almost, through that woods back to that house. I just felt like my feet was like, just like I was walking on clouds, they just felt so high.

"And when we got to the house, I said, 'I know who's going to preach tonight,' I said, 'I am.' And I said, 'because the Lord really spoke to me.' And so this one minister said—he was just kind of like a second Dad to me—he said, 'Well, if you have the message, somebody had to have it, cause I didn't.' And he told this other girl, 'Now, you get a message ready in case that girl don't make it too long.' And, you know, the Lord—there was several people come and it was too many to be in this little small church—so they strung the lights out under the trees, out through the trees and they put all the seats—they took the seats out—and they put them down, out under the trees, and they put the pulpit out there and that's where I preached my first message. And the Lord really anointed me, because within myself, I didn't know that much. I read the Bible, but I didn't know that much about the word of God and how to go ahead and I really didn't hardly know how to yield to the spirit of God, but the Lord just took over. I just prayed and asked God that he would give me a special anointing, and if it was for me to preach that message that God would speak through me. I couldn't do it, so the Lord did.

"But, then, when I came home and after I came home, I felt like well, maybe that wasn't—maybe it was me [rather than God]. You know, the devil will do that to you. And there was this other minister, he come to me several times and he said—he pastored a little church up at Boonville, Missouri—and he said to me, 'Mary, when you going to come hold us a revival?' And I said, 'Oh, I can't preach.' And he said, 'Oh, yes you can, because I know God called you to preach.' And I said, 'but I don't know, maybe it was just that one time.' And so I just kind of pushed it aside.

"But, then, one night I was in California, Missouri, probably two or three months, maybe four months later, and they had this little church that had a old wood stove and it had a concrete floor in this little church. And that night it just seemed like the Lord started dealing with me. And I felt real [bad]—like I couldn't get any place with God. I felt like I was vacillating too much. I just felt like I had such a burden on me that I just felt like I almost had to repent. And I started praying and, again, it just got me down flat on my back on the floor. And I couldn't get up. And I laid there and I cried and I cried and I cried and the Lord started healing my heart again, in the same way. And not until I told the Lord that positively I'd do anything he wanted me to do did I get up. And then the Lord just really blessed my soul. And this minister came to me and he said, 'Well, are you going to hold me a revival? I feel like that you really need to hold this revival.' And I said, 'Yes.' and he gave me a two-week revival. I was just about—well, I don't guess I was seventeen yet. Let's see, it was in the winter, and it was in the summertime when I was at Moniteau Springs. It was in the winter, cause I remember it was real cold, and I went to this little church about a mile out of Lewisborough. It was just a little, tiny church, little country church, and it was Church of God-Prophecy."

Mary says her mother and her father were very supportive about her call to preach. "My mother," she said, "was real thrilled. And my dad was, too, even though he wasn't saved until after I got married. But he always tried to push me, you know. He wanted me to do that. Once I went with some ministers to Statlin, Missouri, to help set a church in order, and I was gone six weeks from home. First, I'd gone to Bloomsborough and up around there, and then I went from there down to this little church, and we were down there about a month, I guess, or more.

"And, we had to walk. This minister, his car had broken down, so we always had to walk. We didn't have any way to church and we stayed with a lady that lived two miles out of town. And we had to walk two miles to church and two miles back, unless someone would volunteer to bring us home. And this lady, when we got down there, she was sick. So I had to—she lived out in the country and she washed on a board and boiled her clothes in a boiler and, so there was two of us girls, and so the two of us, we had to do all the housework and cooking and washing. With men, there was two men, we had to wash their white shirts and boil them out of that boiler and we walked to church. And, you know, it was kind of hard on me, I preached, and I had to do those other things."

It was in this same poor woman's house, too, that Mary got lice in her hair. It had been rumored that some of the people in that town had lice and this particularly upset her. Her hair was her pride, it was long and fell down the middle of her back. One day, as she stood ironing her fellow preacher's shirts with difficult flat irons, she felt something itching on her neck. The woman of the house, who was still quite ill, began to use a fine comb on her hair and discovered that Mary had a head full of nits and lice. Mary was appalled—"I just cried and cried, cause I thought it was such a disgrace. And I thought, 'Oh, here I am way off from home, all alone.' And I didn't want to hurt their feelings, but it really went against what I thought was proper. But sometimes, I learned, you've got to put your pride behind you. So, when this man came in, whose shirt I'd been ironing, came in, I was crying. I told him what she had found and he walked all the way into town, those two miles, to the local drugstore. But they didn't have a thing but powder for fleas and lice on dogs and he brought that back to me. And I told that woman to just rub my scalp yellow with it and she did. Then I washed my hair in Oxydol water and rinsed it in pure vinegar. It's a wonder it hadn't all come out."

Mary tried to recall for me the women who had had the greatest influence on her early years and who might have influenced her to believe she could be a woman preacher. She recalled a woman, Sister Meyers, who was taller than her husband and "sort of heavyweight". She was a traveling preacher when Mary first knew her, but later on she remembers that Sister Meyers took over the pastorship of a local church. For a time after her mother took ill, Mary recalls that her mother insisted that her father drive the family to California, Missouri, to a small "old-time Pentecostal" church down there. That's where she met Brad Harris, the young man she would eventually marry. That's also where she met Lucy Williamson—"She was a lady minister. She evangelized. I don't think she ever—I don't remember her ever pastoring. But she was a person that, a lady minister, and I always thought, 'Oh, I wish I could be like her.' And then, also, there was Sister Donna, her daughter was a real close friend of mine. She was something. Her husband was Catholic, but he didn't hinder her in any way. He didn't believe like she did, but it didn't hinder *her*. She'd start a new work—I remember she started a new work down in Mokane, and I can remember going with her and her daughter and singing when I was a child and she was starting a new work down there. And then, she started the Concord Pentecostal Church of God, down on 179. She started it. She either bought or rented a little schoolhouse down there, a little old schoolhouse, and she and her daughter and her daughter's husband, they started that. Ah, Sister Lucy, she was just—I don't know, it seemed like she stood out from anyone else. And there was another Sister, Sister McDaniel. She was an older lady, and I can remember her preaching—her children was older than myself. But she was a little, short woman. She didn't have very much waist and she was real bow-legged. But I can remember that so much—I can just see her, but, oh, she *was* a fiery preacher. She really did preach the word of God."

After Mary married Brad Harris and moved away from the California area, she felt compelled to go back to that little church. She wasn't preaching and she knew she had been called to do that. She seemed to be compensating by pushing herself to trudge back to the little "home church," traveling more than fifty miles each way. "For a long time I drove by myself, and I drove, I would drive on Sunday morning to church and back home, fix our Sunday dinner, and then I'd go back to evening service and back. And Wednesday night, I'd go on Wednesday night and back. And I felt like I needed to help do things in the church, so I would go then another day and clean the church, so I was just, really doing a lot of traveling and it cost a lot of money." Finally, her husband became frustrated with her and suggested she find a new church closer to home. She did, but the move caused her a lot of pain. When she left her home church, The Church of God of Prophecy, to attend another church, The Pentecostal Church of God [a different denomination altogether], the first church struck her name from their rolls and insisted she was committing "spiritual fornication" because she was going to a church that was not the "bride of Christ." This phase in her religious career left a deep impression on Mary, causing her to hold fast to her determination that denominational differences are dangerous and not of God. Even today, years later, as an established evangelist, she is not accepted in that small "home" church, not allowed to "participate."

Sister Mary prides herself on the fact that all denominations in the local area call on her to preach, now. Even the Baptist church invited her to preach. She relies on an "anointing" from God to make certain that she does not say anything contrary to one denomination's beliefs or say anything that would offend anyone. Actually, knowing the Baptists' recent public denial of women as preachers, she was surprised to be invited to a Baptist church. Like so many women preachers, she turns to the Bible for proof that she should be allowed to preach from the pulpit. "But God said in his word that in the last days, he would pour out his spirit on his handmaidens and they would prophesy and he said, you know, he said that because it's true that you can almost always find more women in the congregation than you will men. And so God had to have somebody to carry on if there's not enough men to carry on, then God has to choose somebody. And if a woman is faithful and she is a vessel of honor then God can use her. But I think that you have to get to a place that you have to dedicate your life . . . you first have to put God first. You have to. That's one thing I've always told my husband. I've said, 'I love you. But God told me to love Him first and then you.' And I've always said, I've said, 'First, God comes first in my life. Above all things. And then you come second.' And you know, it's—sometimes there's things that happen and you have to make a decision. Just like, now, my husband has never objected to me preaching. He's never stood in my way, but, now, he always said, though, 'I want you to go and, just go any time to get there for your services, but come home just as soon as it's over.' Well, that's not asking too much . . . I do feel that you owe something to your husband and to your family. A certain amount of your time. So, I don't feel that he asks too much from me to do that, but now, like the revival I held in Farmington . . . well, I had told him I would be home on Monday. He was expecting me home on Monday. But when that night I pleased God and I felt the service should go on, I called him on Monday, and he really thought I was on the way home and he was kind of angry cause he was expecting me home. He said, 'But you told me,' which I did, but I said, 'Brad, I feel like I need to stay a few more days, and I have to put God first.' Well, when I got home he was—that was all over, but at that moment he was angry. And so, there's a time that you have to choose. And you have to say, 'now, listen, God has to be first.' And it is hard for you to do that. But God will bless you for it."

When I ask her if most people would think she should be home rather than out preaching, she said, "most of my family, yes, but not, not my mother."

One day while I sat in bright sunlight in Mary's kitchen, my tape recorder between us on the worn oilcloth, she described in great detail the excruciating physical therapy she endured trying to get her paralyzed fingers to work again. The hospital staff would take turns pulling on the frozen fingers, breaking them loose while she screamed in pain. Finally, seeing that this wasn't solving the problem at all, a specialist was called in. He wanted to put a catheter "right through at the collar bone into the seventh vertebra." By injecting fluids into that vertebra, they could get the entire right side of her body to droop, to collapse, so that they could work on her stiff fingers. Finally, they asked her if they could make that permanent, but they warned, the right side of her face would be deformed. She declined. She stayed in the hospital, then, for almost two months, and the whole time, she said, God was talking to her. "God dealt with me and let me know that I had let him down in what he told me to do. That I had taken a job and that I liked the job so well, that I laid my preaching up on the shelf and forgot about it. And that it was time for me to put God first in my life and to forget about working."

While her arm was still in the cast, a routine check revealed that Mary had some "foreign cells" growing in her cervix, and she was scheduled for a total hysterectomy. She remembers that she had to be careful for a long time not to hit her stomach with her cast and how painful it was to try to sleep. She would surround herself with pillows and try not to move all night. She recalls being so terribly tired all the time. Her troubles did not end there. Later on that morning, she told me she had cancer.

"God said he wouldn't allow more to happen to us than we can bear," she declared, a bit cautiously it seemed to me.

38

SISTER ALMA

On a quiet side street in Smithville, Missouri, was a very small Assembly of God church, unobtrusively set back from the street, brown without steeple or cross. The glass-encased sign in the front lawn announced that the pastor of the church was Rev. Joseph Cotton. Now, nearly two years after I visited this church, I cannot recall what made me think I would find a woman preaching within those walls. But, somehow, I discovered that sometimes, when her husband would let her, the woman married to Rev. Cotton would preach—often on a Sunday night or on Wednesdays. So, I began to haunt this sacred place hoping to hear the lady of the house speak.

And when she did, I was thoroughly engaged, glued to her face, her manner, the incredible force of her voice and her language. She had the strength of a lion behind that pulpit; she punctuated each line with a powerful gasp; she drew her audience to her in a way to put shame to the man who owned the pulpit. But she didn't preach very often, and I never knew if I would visit there and have to listen to him—or have the privilege of listening to her. Even if I called during the week to check, they were never sure just who would be leading the service. And once he knew of my interest in *her*, he preached more and more, filling up the space, hoping I would next want to interview him. And then, one day, I drove by the church, just checking, and a new name appeared on the billboard. Rev. Jimmy Smith had come to take over this tiny parish, and I lost Alma Cotton forever.

Alma and her husband lived in what served as the parsonage for this Pentecostal assembly, a true hovel. I knew she was embarrassed by our surroundings, for Alma had not always lived this way.

As a young child, Alma sat in the pews in a large Holiness tabernacle in Zion City, Illinois, and watched her daddy carry sick people down the aisle to be healed: "that was my heritage, a heritage of divine healing and the old-fashioned songs and Holiness. My folks were real strict in the old-fashioned way of Holiness." That heritage had stuck with Alma, as she still wore the long, braided bun of traditional Pentecostals; her long skirts and dress sleeves; her face void of any make-up; her fingers without adornment; her legs solidly encased in dark, heavy stockings marked her strict heritage, unusual in this central Missouri region.

But her family didn't start in Chicago. She loves to tell about her mother, an orphan, who was born in Cincinnati but eventually made it to the big city as a very young girl, destitute, looking for work. Her grandparents on her father's side, the Lamberts, were "out northwest of Buford, Missouri, eight miles northwest of Butler. Grandma and Grandpa

Lambert were headed for Kansas and as they crossed the little creek there
the wheel of the covered wagon broke, so they just settled there and
homesteaded. Now, my parents never did receive the baptism of speaking
in tongues. They were Holiness as far as appearances, you know, places
you go, things you do, such as this, but as far as the speaking in tongues,
my parents never did accept that. My daddy had been a preacher in the
Methodist church at one time, in his early years. Then, in Chicago, he
worked under Dr. Dowie. If you know your religious history, Dr. Dowie
was a great man of God as far as divine healing is concerned, at the turn
of the century. I think he was more inter-denominational, if I'm not
mistaken.

"My folks always went to the camp meetings and the country brush
harbor [arbor] meetings[2] and the schoolhouse meetings. A lot of those
meetings were by Pentecostal preachers coming through, in the early days
of Pentecost. And they always went because there were a lot of good
services. But my parents never accepted the baptism. But I had some older
sisters that did receive the baptism of the Holy Ghost at the Assembly of
God church in Butler, was where they started. That's when the church
formed and moved to Butler, that's when they began receiving it. I must
have been about fourteen."

Alma, too, "got the Holy Ghost" there in that Assembly of God
church in Butler. "It was during a revival. A number of the young people
were receiving the baptism, but I was not. I guess I was a little jealous
because I was always the first one to the altar. But they received it and
they saw visions and danced in the spirit, but I did not. But it was the
next day in typing class. See, we were real poor—real poor, and the next
day in typing class, I began to think that the third person of the Godhead
would dwell in me, so poorly clad, no friends, ugly, but he would dwell
in me and the joy of the Lord came in. And from then on, of course, I've
appreciated the moving of the Holy Spirit, so much."

Not long after this experience, Alma began to feel that God had
called her to be a preacher, but she met with heavy resistance. "That was
when I was sixteen, I guess, fifteen, or sixteen. I always read my Bible,
you know, took my Bible to school and kept library and during library
and study hall, it just seemed like every scripture I read, there was something there, a sermon, a thing to say, points that you could get out of
that. And I used to make these up in my head. Then, finally, one day I
talked to my pastor about it. And he, of course, he didn't believe me, you
know, a little ignorant country girl. What did I have that God could use,
he said? But, he did tell me that if God has really called you, then he will
make a way for you."

Alma believes God did make that way. She continued to believe fervently that she had been called to preach. So, when she graduated from high school she had earned a scholarship. She called her pastor and asked him to talk to the people at the Bible college and see if the scholarship would transfer. "He contacted the people at the Bible school and they offered me a scholarship for my tuition. That was the *only* time in Central Bible Institute's history they'd ever given *anyone* a scholarship, even to this day."

From the beginning, once she announced that she wanted to be a preacher, she was given opportunities to preach, here and there. She remembers preaching a sermon at the age of sixteen. She distinctly remembers preaching a revival where she used as her text "Man shall not live by bread alone, but by every word that proceeded out of the mouth of God. I remember that was the first revival I preached at, that was the first." After Bible college, she tried desperately to get her own church. The church superintendent took her out to several "possibilities," but, he said, he was always afraid to leave her alone at any of them. He cautioned her against taking the churches saying they were in "real rough areas." She remembers him saying, "I'm not gonna leave you, a single girl, up there by yourself." And he always took her back home.

For a while Alma attended nurses' training because she "did not receive encouragement from the folks to go into the ministry." But she recalls that she felt "out of the will of God" and was miserable for one whole year. She became an ordained preacher, and she preached off and on, when she could, until she was twenty-one, when she married. She considers herself the co-pastor of the congregation in Smithville, but admits that she does not get to preach that often. "He takes the lead, he preaches, I only have the Wednesday night services and once in a while the Sunday night service. But I think it's best for the man to take the lead. I really do. I think it's—God meant for it to be that way. I really think he did.

"When we first started out, he hadn't preached hardly at all. So I took the biggest part of the load. Until finally God began to deal with him and told him either you get in or get out. And so, then, for a while, we would preach each turn, like if I preached Sunday morning, he'd preach Sunday night and like that. But since we've been here, he has taken most of the responsibility and he's done the ministering.

"But when we were at Houston, Missouri, there was a church out by Ft. Leonard Wood that was going to close. So I drove out there and pastored that church by myself. But we were actually pastoring both places, see. While I would do the preaching, he would always take care of the administrative end, the business part, which I think is God's plan.

"And then we were at Bell City, Missouri and we learned that a little church at Jackson was closed. We couldn't get anyone to go there because there was no one, I guess, no one close by. So I drove to Jackson and we did that for six months, I pastored that little church at Jackson. Then, we moved to Jackson and my husband took that church. Joe and the kids lived there, then and we found out there was a little church at Crump, out north of Poplar Bluff. There was a little community there, used to be just a little store. But the church out there burned and so Joe built the church back. And I stayed with them to pastor until we got it built up enough to where they could support a man, you know. And so, for four and a half years while we were at Jackson, I pastored."

Alma and Joe had five children. Their children's lives revolved around the religious endeavors of their parents; both their mother and their father were preachers. Often, when Alma was pastoring a church by herself, she would have to take the children with her. She recalls that when they were little, "I'd hold two kids in my arms and preach, you know. They'd cry on without me, so I'd hold them and preach. I always said I've got more sermons over the ironing board and the dishpan than I ever did on my knees."

I asked Alma if she'd ever heard folks criticize women preachers. She had, of course. She talked about how no one would support her in her endeavors, how they thought it was dangerous for her. "It's been a real barrier, of criticism, because they've used the scripture that the women keep silent in the church, and so on. But I usually tell them—and it's usually a man, I've never found a women being critical—they've never spoken to me. Now, they might have, in their hearts, but never said anything—but it's usually a man, and I tell them, 'If you men will do what God wants you to do, we women won't have to!' and that usually hushes them." She laughed. Of women being pastors she said, "I think a woman has more a tendency to mother the people than lead them, you know, like a shepherd does. And it's hard [for a man] to follow a woman [be the next pastor]. Because they don't take a firm stand on things, it's more or less 'yes, honey, I understand,' you know, like that."

Alma sees her life as a life of submission—submission to her God's will and submission to her husband's will. She concluded our conversation by singing a song for me. In a loud, clear voice I shall never forget, she sang:

Not what I wish to be,
Nor where I wish to go,
For who am I that I should choose my way?
The Lord will choose for me.
Tis better far, I know,

That he should bid me go
Or stay.

SISTER ANNA

The reader has already met Sister Anna Brock Walters. In my lengthy description of one woman preacher's day, I traced the steps of Sister Anna on a typical Wednesday. Sister Anna is the pastor of a fairly large Assembly of God church in Centerville, Missouri. She has been the sole pastor of this church for eighteen years. Without a doubt, I know Sister Anna's story better than I know any of the stories of the other women featured in this book. For so many reasons she seemed to epitomize the essence of what it means to be a woman preacher and, miraculously, the pastor of a church as well. Throughout this book, I will rely heavily on Sister Anna's story and her art to make this account less fragmentary and more real.

My information about Sister Anna and my understanding of her life come from a combination of sources. I have interviewed her several times in her own living room; I have "interviewed" her in her car as we traveled together going about her work; I have gleaned information about her and about her ministry in interviews I have conducted with other women in her presence; she has written an autobiography that I have been privy to and have typed for her—a work of incomparable importance; and her sermons are a constant source of information about her life and her work. [Note: Brock was the surname of Anna's first husband; Walters is the name of her second and current husband.]

"My grandmother was a minister for many, many years. She was Church of God-Holiness—now that is not Pentecost. And so she, Grandma, wasn't pastoring but she was an evangelist for many years and she had five children. And my grandmother was holding a revival down at a little old schoolhouse and they called it Anton then, and there was a store there. Course my mother was about middle-ways in the family and I've heard my mother say, course she had long hair, and that grandpa's hands were so rough. . . . So, when Grandma was out in the hills down in southern Missouri, holding revivals, why Grandpa then would get the kids up early every morning to go to school. And my mother said, 'Oh, he'd braid my hair so tight, I would always shut my eyes.' So, she always hated it when Grandma was gone to revivals because Grandpa had to braid her hair. But, then, Grandma'd come home and instead of money—about all they could give her were squirrels and rabbits or deer meat, because that's all they could give her, but she'd be so thrilled to bring that home—course that wasn't what she was in it for."

Anna Brock Walters recalls the stories her mother related to her as a child about her grandmother, a Church of God-Holiness preacher. It never seemed strange to her young ears to hear that Grandma often left the family of five children in the hands of her husband and traveled alone, often with other women evangelists, to country churches far from their home to preach revivals. She recalls that both her grandmother and her grandfather were influential in her young life; both participated at the little schoolhouse that on Sundays became the church. Grandpa was a great Bible teacher and Grandma's reputation as a preacher stretched far beyond Christian County.

Anna lived with her own mother and daddy in a 'holler' near Minton several miles from that small schoolhouse. No one lived close by for miles in all directions. Recently, she returned there, she says, and her late model auto had trouble with the road that was hardly a road, twisting and curving, up good sized hills and down, bottoming out in the huge potholes that tried to eat her car. But she was determined to see the house. Halfway there she saw "in my mind's eye, that two-wheeled cart my father built . . . Dad and Momma would walk these very same miles. And they would push my brother who's nineteen months younger than me. At that time, he was a tiny baby and of course, then, I wasn't quite two years old, so they put quilts in a—Daddy made a two-wheel cart—and they would walk those miles and push we two—to church. And then they'd go back home. And Daddy showed me a big old tree out there where he and my mother used to go then and sit under that tree to rest.

"He showed me the rock—a big rock slanted up by the tree. And [he told how] he happened to see that coiled up behind that rock was a copperhead and, he said, 'it frightened your mother so. She reeled in terror, struck her back, fell against that rock.' Some say you can mark a child, other say you can't. But when I was born I was so deformed in my spine it makes you kind of wonder.

"Daddy looked for the schoolhouse that was the church, too, but it was gone. But we could still see where the grass was different, we could place our feet in the grooves that marked the boundaries of the school. And over there, near that bare spot was the stove, and near it a small school bench, a little desk, where I remember sitting, swinging my feet because even then I was always so little, short-legged, my feet wouldn't reach the floor and I'd get so tired. But we didn't dare peep a word out loud in church.

"I remember once they were singing 'Standing Outside the Door.' I knew the words; I'd heard them singing that song many times before, it was a favorite. But I'll never forget . . . *this* time they sang that song, and here I was, just small—but I have used this as an illustration many times in my own messages, that they sang this old song 'Standing Outside the

Door.' 'Oh, what an awful picture. Left standing outside.' That made such an imprint upon my mind that I think that's why I can preach with such vividness heaven as a real place. But this is really where I came from, this is my story.

"Later we had an old Essex car and we'd start out and my grandmother would be so terrified. She was a real prayer warrior, so as we'd start up the hill Grandma Fink would start up, too, with 'Oh, Jesus, help us get over this hill.' Then, when we'd start going down the other side, she'd close her eyes up real tight and start pushing her feet against the floorboards, you know, and pray we'd be saved from the speed. I fear that a lot of our ministers coming up now—I've listened to them—and so many of them coming right out of Bible schools today—I fear that they lack that heartfelt, you know, that *touch*, that says 'this is real, this is real.' But we weren't Pentecost then. Church of God-Holiness—now that is not Pentecost—they believe in sanctification as a separate work of grace. But they don't believe in the baptism of the Holy Spirit. They just stop one step too soon. But they do believe definitely in a born again experience.

"When I first heard of Pentecost it was when an Assembly of God pastor in central Missouri got stuck in a snowdrift in front of our house. My mother was in bed sick. She was a good Christian woman, but there was this huge snowstorm. And the snow had drifted across the road, and he had come to the town where I lived. He was so determined, bless his heart, to have a work [a church] going in that area. There was none for miles and miles and miles. None of us knew anything about Pentecost. Well, I'd heard that he'd built a brush arbor. There was a tale going about that there had been some 'One-ness' come in, held church in a little schoolhouse just down below us. And they said they did some things that were really 'in the flesh,' you know, what we call 'in the flesh.' Like, I heard they'd been getting up and walking on the piano keys and knocked down the stovepipe. But such as that left such a bad flavor with the folks around, you know. That's when this minister came in with the Assemblies of God. Everybody thought he was the same thing. But he wasn't. He had a real tough time. He just had to prove himself, what it amounted to.

"Just like I've had to prove all of these years that a woman can be called into the ministry. And I've kept loving the people even when they criticized me and I just keep telling them, 'Look, this wasn't my choice.' I've stood in front of the mirror lots of times and said, 'God, are you sure you know what you're doing? I'm a wife. I'm a mother. I didn't ask for this.' I was contented even in holding children's crusades, which wasn't nearly as difficult. It wasn't having to be the burden bearer for everybody, you know, like you have to be when you're a pastor.

"But I believe in prophecy. It was at a real tiny church, not where

45

the schoolhouse was where we went to church, but at another schoolhouse my grandmother was holding a revival. There was a store there and CBC [Christian Bible College] students would come down there and play the accordion. I didn't get to see them, but I would hear people talking about it, that they talked in a different language. Well, when I was just a wee little girl, my dad's brother—I'd sit down in a little rocking chair and I was about two or three years old then—but he didn't know how much of a prophecy he was saying, but he'd say, 'listen to Anna. There she goes off in those unknown tongues again.' You know, I was just a chatterbox. And was talking. And I've thought of that a lot since. He never heard, you know. He never knew anything about Pentecost, but he just made that statement. But I look back and I think, 'Lord, that must have been a prophecy.' One day I would.

This was all before I was married. So, I was married in '49, my mother died in '49, so this, when this happened, it must have been in '47 or '48 . . . but, anyway, when he [Brother Daniels] came I was dressed in my brother's overalls and shirt and jumper and cap and he thought I was a boy. Later, when he came back and he saw me, he said, 'Do you have a twin.' I said no. Then it dawned on me and he said, 'Well, I thought sure you had a brother the same size as you' and I burst out laughing and said, 'That was me in my brother's clothes.'

"I loved it when they came. She would come and fix jello salads when they found out that my mother was bedfast there and a whole bunch of us kids with just me to take care of them. I guess in a way he just really loved us into the Assemblies of God. Really, my heritage is really rich. But we were very poor people. And Daddy was only off and on for the Lord.

"My mother remained bedfast until she died. Later, Daddy wouldn't go to church and my mother wasn't able to. But that didn't damper my spirit. I would go and I'd walk. One place we lived I'd walk two or three miles one way just to go to church. Now I think that was a long way for me to walk. That was to go to the Methodist Sunday School. Then when we moved to a different farm on the other side of town I'd walk and go to the Missionary Baptist Church. And I was always in pain. It never seemed to go away, just sometimes it got better. You see I was born that way so I just never knew anything but just pain in my body.

"In fact, my aunts were talking about that just this last weekend when I was down home on Thursday and Friday. When I was about three years old, I think, three or four, one day my grandmother was making me a little dress when my two aunts—one was eight years older and one was ten years older than myself—when they got through something it was handed down and Grandma would make me coats and dresses out of it.

Well, she had made me a dress and she discovered that one of my shoulders was a lot higher than the other one. And she said to my folks, 'You must have taken this baby by the arm and set her over a fence by one arm.' She said that because we'd crossed a lot of fences between our place and Grandma's. And they said no, not that they knew of. So she made an appointment at a clinic in Springfield and took me there herself. The doctors told Grandma that I would have to be taken to the Barnes Hospital in St. Louis and be put in a steel jacket and leave me there, at least a year. They explained that really it was like a cast where they'd stretch one leg one way and the arm the other to see if those bones would straighten out.

"Well, my folks had never heard of scoliosis of the spine. And to tell them that they had to take me to St. Louis, well, that was almost as much as if today you'd tell them to take me clear across the country, you know. They didn't have the money to do it, anyway.

"They never dreamed this would ever cause me any trouble. Mostly, I depended on God, like one day when my mother was sick, just to show you, and I hadn't even been taught in this line, but to show you how God was even working with me even as a little girl while I was taking care of my mother... Daddy drove a milk truck, and that day, the big old oil heater we had in the living room didn't have enough oil in it and it was going out. And it was getting late in the evening and I knew Daddy was going to bring some coal oil in for it, so I walked over and laid my hand on that stove. And I prayed. I prayed that the Lord would keep that stove going because it was too cold and I knew my mother shouldn't be chilled. And that thing just went 'Choo!' like that and it began to burn and burn till my daddy pulled into the drive with the kerosene.

"A year after my marriage, we lived in Kansas City. Then one day the Lord spoke to me and said he wanted me to begin a children's church there in our church. It was a large Assembly of God. And they didn't have a children's church. And I said, 'Lord, I sure would sure hate to give up my Sunday morning service.' He said, 'But the children need to be taught.' So I called my pastor and he said, 'Oh! You're an answered prayer. I'd been praying that somebody would come along and take our kids.' So I started being with fifteen children. And by the time I left there I had— was running eighty-five boys and girls.

"One day, I had begun to hear of children's crusades, children's revivals, you know. So I said to my husband, 'Oh, I wish that the pastor would get an evangelist to come hold us a children's revival, a children's crusade.' My husband was a man of very few words. He said very little. He did a lot of thinking. But when he did say something, he meant it. And he just looked up at me and he said, 'I think you can do it yourself.' Oh! I just about melted and ran down my shoes. And I said, 'Me?' And

47

he said, 'I think you can do it yourself.' So, I thought, 'Well, Lord, I guess I better listen to you. Is this you speaking to me again through him just like you spoke through my mother?'

"I was saved when I was twelve years old. But the summer before, I remember we were studying about missions in our girls' auxiliary. We were studying about missions in China. The woman who was our director told us, I remember so clearly, told us to bring a little pillow to sit on, just like the ladies in China did. They sat on little cushions. I didn't have any little pillows. But I remember I had a little purple satin cushion. So, we sat down on the ground, out in the grass under a large tree next to the church, sitting on our cushions. And the Lord really began to deal with my heart. He told me what he expected of my life.

"Later a woman came to our church. She had *been* to China. She was a missionary. I was so intrigued by her. I don't remember her name, now, but I can remember everything about her. I remember her coming and speaking. I knew God was speaking to my heart, but I had a problem. Here God had called me, a woman, to the mission field. But more than that. I knew he was calling me to be a minister. I was not—it wasn't just to go along as a partner to somebody—*I* was going to do the preaching.

"I told them at church next meeting. The director became upset, red in the face. 'Oh,' the minister said, 'you can give meditations, you know, and you can give devotionals, but that's all you can do.' He didn't know it then and neither did I, but my mother's illness would show me God's plan for my life.

"After Ward Daniels was stopped, see, in that snowdrift, I was still Baptist, see, up to that point. He was an Assembly of God pastor, and he started coming to our house to talk to my mother. One day my mother said to me, 'I wish that you would see if your pastor wouldn't bring me communion.' She'd been bedfast so long she hadn't been able to have communion in years. But I made a dreadful mistake. I was so innocent. This particular Baptist church would not do that because she wasn't an official member of their church. She was actually Church of God-Holiness, but my mother was a beautiful Christian. And here she was, just a while before she knew *she* was going to die. That hurt me so bad. And I thought, 'Brother Daniels' church wouldn't be like that.'

"When I thought I was going into the mission field, well, my mother said to me one day 'sometimes it's harder to stay than to go.' But you know how that she was sick while I was planning to go to Rio de Janeiro in South America. And I took speech class in school, everything was to prepare me, see, better for God's service. But then I decided I had to stay home and take care of my sick mother until she died. But that's because God didn't intend for me to be a missionary...

"And, now, here I was in the city directing the children's church. And I had started the Women's Missionary Council and the church began to sponsor missionaries then. And we'd keep them in our home when they'd come through. I loved that. They came from Spain and from all over. And my kids would say, 'You know, there's a lot of drawbacks, you go through a lot being a preacher's kid.' It was hard, I know, on them.

"After that first children's crusade, ministers began to call and pastors began to have me come in. Wasn't long until one pastor told me I needed to get my 'worker's permit.' And that was the beginning. Oh, I had prayed for that day. I'd agonized before God. I got my Christian worker's papers, like all the other ministers. It used to be called your Exhorter's papers. And that's the first step of being recognized as a minister. So, I began to conduct children's crusades all over.

"One day, after about four years, there was a pastor and he pastored the Postoak Assembly of God Church. That church had just gone down and gone down until they didn't even have enough to support the church. And God spoke to that Brother and told him to call me for a revival. And the deacon of that church says, 'What? A woman preacher? Nothing doing.' They had a young man in mind for the revival. They were going to call him. The pastor says, 'I don't have anything against this young man, but God just told me "Call Sister Brock." ' And those deacons would not budge an inch because they had had a pastor who had preached against women preachers. But, this brother, says, 'Brothers, this is one time that I'm going to have to go over your heads. I know what God told me.' So he called me. And that first week, I'd first go down and work with the children. Early on, you know. Work with the children. And then, I'd go up and preach.

"That week I saw that one brother just turn his face toward the wall and put—he'd reach his hands up high as he could toward the ceiling— because the church just begin to fill up and fill up until the pews were packed out. And the Holy Spirit just moved, Elaine, and fell like I see him move in our services over here. And I just could hardly stay on that platform. At the end of that week, they just scheduled me for another one. And those deacons one by one came to me and apologized and said, 'We had no idea. We stepped in where we shouldn't have.' This old pastor, who had preached *against* women preachers, he and his wife came one night to see what was going on. They're both dead now. But they came and were amazed at the services and he became a good friend of mine. Because he saw that God could use me, after all. We're a vessel. And God's going to use a vessel, for he said, 'In the last days I will pour out my spirit.' And he said, 'Old men are going to dream dreams,' and 'young men are going to see visions. And upon my handmaidens'—he's going to pour out his spirit and 'they will prophesy.' It's neither Jew nor Gentile, Greek nor barbarian, male nor female. It's whoever."

Life in Kansas City was pretty good for Anna and her husband. There Anna began her life as a married woman. She had already been pregnant once, but her severe scoliosis caused her to lose this first baby. The doctors had warned her father that she would never be able to have any children. But Anna did not ever see things that way and in her typical fashion, she began to pray to God for children.

"But I prayed and prayed to get pregnant. I just pleaded with the Lord. And I lost my first one, but, I don't know, maybe it's stubbornness—God has given me a lot of something—God has given me a lot of determination and will-power. I have three [children] now. They fixed a support and I would go and they would adjust that support every month, then, for me to be able to carry my children. And the last one I had to have Caesarian. But the first two, I carried through. My first one weighed eight pounds, six ounces, and for my size [Anna probably weighed less than one hundred pounds then] . . . well, I had a hard time having it. I know to some people it would just seem far-out, but I prayed to have them—I was suffering so bad during the time that I was carrying my children and each time, of course, it spread the spine more and crippled me a little bit more, so God was so good to me.

"I told the minister and his wife, who were with us one evening, and I was suffering so bad, and I said, 'I wish that you would come and—I wish you would pray for me.' Well, they just crawled out of that car. They got out and came in the house and they kneeled down and prayed for me. And from then on—now, the Lord didn't see fit, I don't understand why, but he didn't see fit to close the spine and to straighten it—but I felt a hand, *I felt a hand*, just an invisible hand on my *spine* at that moment. This was with my youngest one. I still had a lot of complications with him.

"But as far as that agonizing pain . . . I went right through. I was in labor ten hours and they finally ended up taking a C-section. But the Lord helped me through that and it didn't do any more to my spine through all of that. That's why I say God has been so good to me. I feel like maybe it's like the three Hebrew children. God didn't see fit to deliver them and keep them out of the fiery furnace but he went right in with them. Some say, 'Oh, Sister Walters, that's just a governor.' Maybe. Maybe that's my governor. Put on so I won't work myself to death."

In the city, Anna started her own cake decorating business. She had a thriving catering service and her family moved into an eight room house, "all on one level," with two full baths. She was very active in the church during these years, working with the children's crusades and women's mission work. As her reputation grew, more and more churches began to invite her to their churches to carry children's crusades and revivals.

"I'll tell you, the faith begin to build. God was moving in spite of the obstacles. And the church begin to fill up and, do you know, we had a choir full of young people then that would come and sing. And they begged me to stay. I believe there was thirty-some that was filled with the Holy Spirit and saved—all different denominations. One woman—just to show how that God was breaking down those barriers, to show me that he could use me because I was constantly asking, Lord, I've been put down so much, can you use even me?—but a little lady that was to enter the TB sanitarium the next week, she had TB so bad. And I told her, 'Sit down on the altar' and I prayed for her and God instantly healed her lungs. Miraculously. This was the first I knew that I had the gift of healing. This was the first."

From then on, the telephone began to ring. Pastors from all over began to ask Sister Brock to come do her work in their congregations. And then one Sunday in 1963 there was a phone call that was to change Anna's life forever.

"One Sunday afternoon the telephone rang and this Brother from Sedalia called and he said, 'Would you come to Millerville and fill in for them? And then, if you feel that it's right and they do, would you try out as their pastor.' And I said, 'Where is Millerville?' I'd never even been to Jefferson City. I was doing good to be in Kansas City. So, he said, 'I'll tell you what, they already don't want you.' Said, 'when I told them that I was going to call you, the deacons said, "What?—a woman?"' "

With trepidation, Anna packed up her husband and children and traveled the 150 miles from their home in the city to Millerville. She recalls that even counting her family there were only 16 or 17 people in the church that morning. Their walk around the church grounds revealed a church in need of repairs and a parsonage that was in "bad, bad shape." It leaked, and it was a lot smaller than the eight room house they had in the city.

"But, anyway, I went there that morning. I knew nothing about pastoring. I'd never tried out for a church, and, in fact, I was just filling in for them. But the Sunday School Superintendent, what does he do but after his part was over with he just turns it over to me. I didn't know what to do—it didn't even dawn on me I had to take up an offering. Forgot to have a song service. The kids and I got up and sang some specials, and I went right into preaching. Later they really teased me and I told them, 'Well, at least you knew I didn't come for the money.' But at the end of the service, one of the deacons came up front and stood right in front of the platform and said, 'It's been a long time since we had

51

a service like this.' And then that night, I preached again and the Holy Spirit just fell in a miraculous way again. And at the end of the service, this other deacon walked up and says, 'Would you like for us to vote on you, now?' And I said, 'No. I wouldn't. I've got to do some praying about this.'

"And so, when we moved into that old parsonage, of course I had to store my dining room set and all that because our bedroom had to be in the dining room. So, it was grand central station. There were no doors to close it off. We had one bath.

"Oh, I guess I'd better back up a little bit to tell you how I knew to go to this church. . . . First of all, my children thought God wanted us to move there. I was really surprised, because my three kids had always lived in the city—to want to come to this little bitty town like this? And move into that old parsonage like it was—when each one had their own separate bedroom? But here they are saying, 'I think we're supposed to move.' And my husband said, 'Now, you know, if you do this, you'll have to be down there all by yourself with the kids.' My husband would have to work in the city all week and then drive home weekends, until we could get all of our bills paid, you know, and see what to do with our place and everything. Then I thought, 'Well, Lord, now it's up to nobody but you and me.' Well, this was a frightening thing because I knew nobody down there. I had no relatives down there; I knew no one. And the responsibility of three children in a new school, and a *church*—and I'd never pastored before! So, I said, 'God, I've got to know.'

"But I knew beyond a shadow of doubt that God had called me because I agonized over a basket of clothes one day, and I just—the Lord just kept speaking to me hard, and I just slumped over that basket and I said, 'I've got to know. I've got to have some answers.' And I'll tell you how I knew to go to Millerville. So, I said, I made it just as hard as I could. 'Lord,' I said, 'If this is to be, a certain pastor, and I named him, James Simmons from Millerville,' I said, 'He will be the one to call me the morning after the vote. And he will say these words: "Will you do us the honor of coming to be our pastor?" And, Elaine, he was the one that called the next morning and he said the very words that I had put before the Lord. I tell you, I almost just—it just about did me in because I thought I had made it hard enough that, you know—"

"The church grew until sixty-eight was our congregation at one time. And the town was just a little over 200 in population. And there were churches all up and down the street. But the Lord gave us four wonderful years there. But it was also there that I got the anonymous letters and the anonymous gift of a book called *Bobbed Hair, Bossy Wives and Women Preachers*. Oh, that became such a stigma to me that I finally just destroyed it. This was sent to me and underlined in red ink that I was going to hell for preaching and going to take millions with me. I put that book on the bed and I dropped to my knees and I cried and cried and cried till I was nearly sick. And I told the Lord, I said, 'Lord, I'm sorry if I made a mistake. I'm not in this for my health, and I'm not in it for the fun of the thing.' I remember slumping over a basket of clothes one day and begging God, 'I've got to know. I've got to have some answers' and always God would just keep speaking to me real hard.

"But I knew beyond a shadow of a doubt that God had called me, and that's how I knew he had called me to Centerville. One day I was coming through town and I thought, 'Well, now, I like this town and I don't know why.' And my husband didn't like it at all. But every time I would come through here for any reason, it would come to me—'You like this place.' Well, one day the Lord spoke to me and he said, 'You may as well start packing. I'm going to send you to Centerville.' I found out that the pastor was leaving; he had resigned. I asked him at a fellowship meeting who I could talk to about it and he told me. I went to the church, then, didn't even tell them I was coming to "try out" cause I didn't know what you were supposed to do. I'd never changed churches like that. I just came and preached for them that morning. I told them, 'I know this is where God wants me. I know that beyond a shadow of a doubt because,' I said, 'he's already told me that I may as well start packing, for this is where I'm coming to.' And some of them were not for it at all. But God works in mysterious ways his wonders to perform and here I am. I've been here fifteen years last February [this was in 1984].

"Some of them were not for this—a woman preacher. When my husband was driving for Skelly Oil, there was a man—my husband hauled him fuel oil and gas. So one day I had to go in, up at the pumps, to talk to my husband about something while this man was still in there. So, my husband introduced me to this man and he tore into me, because I pastored a church. My husband said later, 'I had no idea that man would do like that or I would never even have told him who you were.' Because it just made my husband sick. That man stood there and he belittled me and he told me I was on my way to hell and that there was no place for women preachers and that all the reward I was going to have was what I had right here in this life.' And I said to him, 'well, you send missionaries, so what is the difference?' He told me, 'You ought to come to my church . . . you'd see who runs it!' Funny part is, I know this man's pastor, and he stood up not long ago and said, 'There is one woman minister here,' he and I usually bump into each other making hospital calls a lot because we made more hospital calls than any other pastors here in town, and he said, 'that's Sister Brock. I have the highest regard for her ministering.' But there are some in his church, of course, who are that way and this one man, he just put me down in just such a harsh, cruel way, well, his spirit was enough to turn you off, you know. I thought, 'well, say, Brother, I didn't ask for this. All my husband did was introduce me. And for you to tell me that I was on my way to hell . . .' So I said, 'well, you know, I'm sorry you feel that way about it because God is the one that called me to preach.' Then he tore into me on that, too, like I just didn't hear right. Well, I just started walking off, and I said, 'Well, if I don't see you any more here, I'll see you in the rapture.' And he yelled out across that parking lot, 'I *know* I'm going to be there, but I don't know so much about you.' You know, it wasn't very long before that man died. He didn't live very long after that. I don't know if that's the reason or not, I have no idea. But what I do know is God said, 'Touch not my anointed and do my prophets no harm.'

"I am very fortunate that all three of my children are living for the Lord. One of them went on to be a minister of the gospel, a pastor. I heard him say one time, which was a great compliment, he said, when he was introducing me to preach in his church here a while back, he said, 'I'm going to introduce you to a lady that I have the highest admiration for.' And he said, 'I was raised in a parsonage,' and says, 'my mother made the ministry so beautiful and so appealing in spite of all the hardships . . . that I wanted, I desired to follow in her footsteps and answer the call of God.'

"There's been a lot of people that have tried to take advantage of me because I am a woman. But God has helped me with wisdom a lot of times—wisdom to be able to come back and it really startles people. But God says in his word whom he calls he qualifies. So, it doesn't made any difference one bit whether it's a man or a woman."

NOTES

1. Pentecostals make a distinction between "trinitarians" and "Oneness." This distinction became necessary when one group of Pentecostals sought to abandon the standard trinitarian concept of the "Three-in-One" Godhead—Father, Son and Holy Ghost—as both the same and yet separate entities. "Oneness" or "Jesus Only" Pentecostals strive toward an understanding that Jesus was the embodiment of God on earth. Although they do speak of the Holy Spirit or Holy Ghost as a separate entity, they baptize only in the name of Jesus and deny that they can conceive of God as a Three-in-One idea. For them Jesus *is* God. While theologically the point of view is complex and difficult to understand, it has, nevertheless, served to distinguish among groups of Pentecostals. The large United Pentecostal Church, for example, is a "Oneness" Pentecostal group, while the Assemblies of God are "trinitarian."

54

2. People in this region often speak of early "brush arbor" meetings, which were essentially outdoor revival meetings held in makeshift quarters, generally consisting of a brush roof constructed to form a large open-air "tabernacle." Straw would be brought in to provide flooring, and benches were often rough-hewn logs.

2

Spiritual Life Stories: Traditional Narratives as Alternative "Fictions"

The preceding four examples of what I have chosen to label "spiritual life stories" are representative of the kinds of stories women preachers tell me about their lives. The narratives clearly embody both unique life experiences and folk narrative elements that are surprisingly similar from narrator to narrator. Similarities in actual content are evident, as are storytelling styles and story frames.

Various narratives within the women's "life stories" illustrate how the creations can be viewed both as personal experience stories and as traditional religious narratives. The test of God to validate an action or a stance is a standard motif and the style of narrating such an incident remains identifiable from one corpus of stories to another. Importantly, the style illustrates the dialogic style of storytelling preferred by these women: "I didn't know if this was of God or of the devil (or of myself), so I said, 'God, if this is of you then tomorrow morning at exactly 8:00, Brother Simmons is going to call me and he's going to say, "Anna, would you consider coming to be our pastor?"' And, Elaine, the very next morning at exactly 8:00, Brother Simmons called me and he said the very words that I told God. He said, 'Anna, would you consider coming to be our pastor?' And it nearly knocked the breath out of me."

Sister Anna loves to tell this story, and she has recounted it to me on several occasions. It has the flavor of a story told often and with conviction. Her account has analogues in nearly every interview I have conducted. Sister Mabel Adams, from Hooperton, Missouri, recounted how she had resisted God's call for her to preach: "I felt like, no, I can't do that. So I began to pray, 'Now, Lord, if you really have called me to preach and you want me to preach, you have her call on me tomorrow in church to preach.' That was my point of contact, you know, for certainty. And every time the Lord would give me a dream the night before, and in the dream he would give me the message, the scriptures and everything, and then the very next morning, on Sunday, she would call on me to preach, see, and then I knew."

This motif—the profession of a testing of God for validation—is typical in these women's narratives and illustrates how so much of what they are doing is, of necessity, couched in terms of what *God* has called them to do. The particular importance of this point will be examined in greater detail later in this work.

That many of the stories imbedded within these women's "life stories" are identifiable "traditional" ones, either in structure or in content, can be further illustrated with examples taken from two different states. The explanation for clear analogues collected in places over 500 miles apart must rely on an understanding of the "core" Pentecostal experience. Although the Pentecostal women in Missouri have probably never sat in the same church as the women from Indiana, their experiences have been similar. Large camp meetings and revivals, where women testify and tell their stories provide a forum for exchange of not only performance structure and style, but content as well. Two similar stories illustrate this point.

> My husband thought they were all crazy, and I knew he wasn't going to want to go to the Pentecostal church. Really I had never had the Holy Ghost, but I had been exposed to it and I knew the Holy Ghost was real. But he would come in and say, 'Well, where do you want to go. Let's go to church.' And I would say, 'Well, where do you want to go to church' because I wanted him to make the decision. I didn't want to. But the Lord just sort of worked things out for us. He sent my sister and her husband to visit us and told us they were having a revival and really invited us out. But Tom would look at me and he'd say, 'Now, I tell you, I'll go anywhere you want to go, but don't expect me to go up on that hill,' which is where their church was, 'don't expect me to go up there. These people are crazy and you do not have to live like that to be a Christian.' O.K., well, we did go to church that night to the Pentecostal church and we both were really hungry for a change and I really feel the Lord was talking to us all this time and really directing us and leading us.
>
> (*Helen Davis, Bloomington, Indiana*)

> After they had gotten saved, I don't know, they enticed me to go one night and, you know, it was a Pentecostal church, you know how they shout and everything. It really upset me because I'd never been

to anything like that and it scared me to death. But it was something that really worked on me. It was something there that, how do you explain it, something that tugged, you know, it was something that I wanted.

(Mabel Adams, Hooperton, Missouri)

Pentecostals are clearly aware of the stereotypes that non-Pentecostals people hold about them. They are aware that people view them as "freaks" and refer to them in a derogatory way as "Holy Rollers." While they, as members of the Pentecostal religion, wish both to maintain the important boundaries between themselves and "the outside world" *and* to illustrate that they actually are not *all* that different from other people, they often develop an important "conversion narrative" which outlines their entrance into this strange and "dangerous" religion. These narratives begin at the point of disgust and suspicion—exactly the point where the narrator's audience might currently stand. Compare the following:

My girlfriend and I, when we first entered into this Pentecostal church—this is kind of going back. And, I remember seeing the people raising their hands and speaking in tongues, and some of them just really overjoyed. And one little lady shouting. And we sat back there, and and I would just laugh. Because I thought their—this is really unreal. Because in the—when I was raised in the Baptist church, if I coughed, you know, my dad was pulling my hair, and saying, 'Be quiet. You're in church. You're supposed to reverence the house of God.' And when I seen these people clapping their hands, and raising their hands to worship the Lord, I thought, this is really out of place for them to do this in Church. . . . But, then the Lord really started convicting my heart, because I realized it was more than just watching people—that they did have something that they were expressing, and it was real.

(Pam Davis, Rogers Ridge, Indiana)

Well, my baby sister had gotten saved in one of those churches, you know, and they're the ones that invited us to church. And, of course when they first invited us we said, 'no, we don't have time for that kind of religion.' But finally I just kept feeling the spirit just, just felt something tugging on me, you know, that I needed to go. So, we just kept refusing, but finally I said, 'God,' said, 'if this is of you, then she'll ask me just one more time and next time I'll say yes and go.' And I just started wishing that she'd just ask me one more time and sure enough, you know, she did, and I knew I had to go. And so I told my husband that night, I said, 'I'm gonna go to church with them tonight.' I said, 'I've just got to. I'm gonna just go to visit tonight. Won't you go?' And he said, 'No, I'm not going.' And so I said, 'Well, I'm sorry, but I know I gotta go anyway. I'm gonna go without you.' And that made me feel kind of funny.... And so we set down at the supper table and he said, 'Well, you go get my dress pants ready cause I'm going too!' [laughs]

(*Pat Roberts, Centerville, Missouri*)

These stories are recognizable analogues of some of the stories embedded in the four women's stories included in Chapter 1 above, especially the story Sister Ruth loves to recount about marrying a "Holy Roller" boy and shaking her head in dismay asking, "Lord, what have I gotten into this time?" But, she, like her counterparts, "comes around" to an understanding that the Pentecostal style of religion is, actually, a better one.

Sister Ruth's account of her water baptism also has numerous analogues in my own data and exists, I am convinced, as a kind of traditional recounting of the baptism ritual. One account in particular stands out. This story was told by a woman near to Sister Ruth's age, but who lived in southern Indiana.

I was nine years old and we lived over in Sanders, and I got baptized there at Sanders church, got the Holy Ghost and spoke in tongues one night. And we went to church the next night it was cold, below zero, walked down the railroad and went there and I was baptized, the night after I got the Holy Ghost. And we came home, walked all the way home and I had long hair and had ribbons on the ends of it at that time. On the way home, my hair froze real hard, but it never even give me a cold. I went right on and we went back there to church.

(*Rebecca Carter, Rogers Ridge, Indiana*)

There has been a fairly longstanding concern among anthropologists and folklorists about the differentiations that ought to be made among "life story," "personal history," "[oral] autobiography," and "life history."[1] I prefer to label the accounts given to me from women preachers as "spiritual life stories," for I have become aware, especially in my extended work with Sister Anna, that the recollections are to a very large degree "fictions," in the sense Jeff Titon suggests: "In its root sense, *facio*, fiction is not a lie but a 'making'..."[2] The stories are creations; they cannot be viewed as "pure history" (although that term itself is suspect). Furthermore, I use the term "life stories" because I am skeptical of the living existence of an oral "life story" or "life history" that is carefully constructed, formulated, and delivered in chronological order and somehow fits our etic notions of "oral autobiography." "Spiritual life stories" enables us to assume that one's "life story" is, in fact, not a perfected entity, but rather is a collection of stories, many of them based on both personal experience and tradition at the same time.

In the course of this study, I have been fortunate to read a written autobiography written by Sister Anna. This written account provides rich possibilities for comparison with the oral accounts, an approach which will not be pursued in these pages, but it is important to note that on the written pages Sister Anna is obviously attempting to place her life story into chronological sequence. It is instructive to find all the little yellow sheets of paper tucked between pages, sheets that include stories she has remembered to include late in her account, but which she returns to their "proper" place in the historical sequence. In many ways, the individual stories that clearly emerge as Sister Anna's oral favorites appear in the written pages without substantive changes. Even the dialogic storytelling style survives the transformation from verbal narrative to written. In fact, in many ways her "written" autobiography is but a transcription of her oral stories, with the exception of the conscious attempt to put things into chronological order and an obvious intrusion of religious clichés that "frame" the discrete vignettes and act as transitions between stories. Paragraphs often begin "It is important to learn to listen to the voice of God . . ." or "When God has a special work for his children to do, Satan fights them very hard . . .," but the stories remain very close to their oral renditions.

This particular case of a woman preacher actually writing out her life story is unusual. By and large, very few people in this region have an opportunity to recount their autobiography, spiritual or otherwise, in any context. Even the opportunity to give one's testimony in a testimony service affords only a short forum for "life stories." It is certainly within this church service slot and from behind the pulpit in the sermon slot that church members and/or preachers are allowed the time to tell their own stories, but this time is limited and it is fairly unlikely that at any one time a speaker would attempt to tell his or her entire life experience. Just such an example does appear on Titon's recording of the "life history" of Rev. John Sherfey, but I suspect that that recounting was much like the only one that I have ever encountered in my own fieldwork—the performer delivered what he/she thought the fieldworker had come to record. Once I had telephoned a woman preacher to ask if I might interview her after the Sunday morning service to tape record her "life story," telling her I was interested in how she got the call to preach, how long she had been preaching, etc. She assured me that she would be happy to comply, but I was somewhat alarmed when I realized that her morning sermon was, in fact, her "life story," which she was delivering from the pulpit, to me, either because she had misunderstood my request or because she felt more comfortable in that context. Whatever the reason, it remains the longest and most cohesive "life story" I have collected, but its unusual circumstances mark it, I believe, as an anomaly. I wonder whether Rev. Sherfey's life story might be an example of a similar case. My point is that I feel it particularly fruitless to set out to collect oral autobiographies, as they appear to be a genre that is not likely to exist as a living oral tradition in the lives of the people we study. Far better for us to recognize that, perhaps like the epic songs, the "life story" of these individuals is, in fact, a series of smaller components, vignettes, each developed into a concrete story that follows the rules of traditional religious folk narrative. Importantly, Titon has made the following suggestions in relation to the life story of Son House:

> His life story is not a historical description, and it does not obey historical laws. It is a fiction, a making, and, like all powerful fictions, it drives toward enactment.[3]

> The life story's singular achievement is that it affirms identity of the storyteller in the act of telling. The life story tells who one thinks one is and how one thinks one came to be that way.... So life storytelling is a fiction, a making, an ordered past imposed by a present personality upon a disordered life.[4]

Most important to this study is the recognition that the identity to be "affirmed" in the personal narrative is the pivot around which the storyteller will spin her or his tale. It is unrealistic to assume that one can innocently ask the narrator, "So, tell me your life story" and the storyteller will lean back and tell her life story uninterrupted to the folklorist who sits quietly nodding, waiting patiently for the narrator to continue when there is a pause, resisting the temptation to distort the flow with a question. Almost invariably, *at least* one all-important directive concerning the interviewee's identity has already been relayed, perhaps long before the taped interview session. The first visit the folklorist makes to a potential interviewee irrevocably sets the stage for all further interaction. Titon first visited Son House, for example, because House was a blues singer; Roger Abrahams went to see Almeda Riddle because she was a ballad singer[5]; Theodore Rosengarten went to visit Nate Cobb [Shaw] because of his union affiliation[6]; I visited the women featured in these pages because they are women preachers. While our perception of the identities of these people and their perceptions of themselves with that identity may certainly coincide, we must be prepared to recognize that they have many *other* identities *as well*. In fact, as the case of Granny Riddle illustrates, Abrahams had a difficult time convincing her that her rank among ballad singers was as *he* perceived it to be; her own perception was that she just wasn't all that important. This was not false modesty on her part, and as her story unfolds we do have a sense that Granny sees herself as more complex than singularly being "a ballad singer." However, she tries to give Abrahams the "story" she knows he came to hear. Similarly, Rosengarten describes the very first time he went to visit Nate Cobb:

> He knew why we had come by our appearance: young, white, polite, frightened, northern. . . . Nate took off his hat and sat down with us by the fireplace. We asked him right off why he joined the union.[7]

This first visit eventually led to many tape recorded sessions that resulted in the book *All God's Dangers: The Life of Nate Shaw*. But that first question—in fact, Rosengarten's very appearance at Nate's home— set the stage for their entire interaction. They came to hear about the union—and, by and large, that is what Cobb told them. Even as long as the volume is—and with all its digression—we know Nate was selective. He did not tell all of his "life stories"; he only told, basically, one of them. By listening carefully, we can see that if Rosengarten had been writing a book on prison reform, for example, Nate might have told him a different "life story".

> Our sessions dealing with the prison years were more even-tempered, just as Shaw had had to keep cool to live out his sentence. I asked him about conditions at each of the three prison camps in which he served.[8]

Implied in this passage is that Nate's tendency to narrate in a natural "flow" when talking about his union experiences bogs down at this point, requiring Rosengarten to ask specific questions about, say, prison conditions. In fact, this long and important period of Nate's life is covered quickly in comparison to the story that Rosengarten has come to hear.

The case of women preachers can better illustrate this point. Early in my interviews with many different preachers, I became aware that their life stories certainly followed a pattern. Pivotal points of their narratives seemed to be the experiences of: 1) being saved; 2) being baptized in water; 3) being baptized in the spirit; 4) getting the call to preach. The following represents the first few minutes of an interview with a woman preacher from Hooperton, Missouri.

> Well, I was born of very poor people, they both had to work, there were four of us kids, and my mom is Hettie Monroe and my daddy was Johnny Monroe and my dad's dead and my mom's still living in

North Carolina, Burlington. I was born down there in North Carolina and then I graduated from high school in 1945 and in '46 they were having a camp revival there in my home town and it had been going on all summer long so I got in on the tail end of it and the Lord saved me and I spoke in tongues, was baptized, and from that he called me to preach.

(*Mabel Adams, Hooperton, Missouri*)

Actually, as Mabel Adams tells her story, we learn that her call to preach was not nearly so matter-of-fact. We learn that she was, in fact, quite reluctant even to attend a Pentecostal church, proclaiming it "scared me to death." She, as do the others, continues to attend the meetings, however, and feels something "that tugged." As for the call to preach, she likewise resists in full force, only agreeing to become a preacher by making a deal with God that if he will heal her mother of cancer, she will preach the gospel.

At first, it seemed fairly remarkable that the women I interviewed so often structured the story of their personal life with a reference to when they were "saved," then moved to their baptisms in water and in the spirit, and then to their call to preach, leaving out virtually any references to their home life, their family, or any female adolescent concerns they might have had. Two factors account for this, I think. First, this is the patterning that has come to shape their identities—these events, these experiences do make sense of chaos and confirm their identity, first as a good Christian woman, and second as a woman preacher. But, the other factor must be acknowledged as well: I came to visit them in the first place *because* they are women preachers. I identified them in that way; my initial contact with them was based on that single identifying characteristic. They knew I came to see them *because* they are women preachers. Coincidentally, they are many other things as well: they are their mothers' daughters; they are midwestern Anglo women who grew up in the farm lands of Missouri; and they are wives and mothers. But I did not seek them out because of any of those components of their very complex characters (although those aspects certainly came into play as we talked more). In my interviews, in their daily lives, and in their sermons certain stories are told and retold, remaining fairly consistent and standardized in each telling. The history has become concretized into a developed "fiction." We must recognize, of course, that literally thousands of other life events have not been fictionalized, are not part of "the story", perhaps because they do not contribute to the narrator's development of her identity (or the identity presently in focus) or because these events have not yet been honed to represent an aspect of that identity.

Based on my interviews with women preachers, I would like to suggest that we view "life stories" as consciously constructed "fictions." I use "consciously" with hesitation; for the narrators, if asked, would say they are telling history as it happened, that they are telling the truth. If pushed, they might admit that maybe it did not happen just quite that way or so-and-so did not say exactly those words, but it happened nearly that way—and this is how they like to tell the story. These fictions follow the same inclinations most personal experience stories share—that is, the narrator's sense of a good story often overrides pure truth, while specifics, especially dialogue, often become formularized or crystallized so that the story comes to "say" what the narrator wants it to "say." It is, after all, a story delivered to make some point or to entertain a certain audience. It will, therefore, have a focus. "You won't believe what happened to me on the way to work" begins a narrative that promises to deliver the extraordinary or the unusual. "Hey, I'm a good guy, I went out of my way to . . ." promises to provide an account meant to convince the listener(s) of the narrator's good nature. History will be modified, melded, pushed, and molded to create a "fiction" that is based on truth, but is, in fact, a created story. The narrator's perception (or admittance) of this process is greatly deterred by the understanding by both parties that history modified may become a lie; therefore, there is shared between the narrator and the listener a pact that disallows scrutiny and allows for a measure of fantasy, as long as it is within mutually agreed bounds. These boundaries will be variable depending upon the nature of the fiction(s)—a story told solely to entertain, to make the audience laugh, may be allowed more liberty than one told under oath. The context determines the flexibility of the boundaries. Religion happens to be one area in which the range for creativity in personal experience fictions is quite broad, largely because the narrator takes refuge in the fantastic world of the supernatural. Here we find a strong pact that allows for stories of visions, possessions, and healings that, delivered in any other context, might be met with scoffing, scorn, disbelief, or hilarity.

In the religious person's construction of a "life story", selection is critical. Which events, what themes will emerge as most important? What will be developed, what excluded? The key appears to be just how concisely the narrative(s) affirms the identity of the storyteller in the act of the storytelling. I would argue that the degree to which a life story has been formulated, honed down, and developed will be in direct proportion to just how secure the narrator's sense of identity actually is. With the women preachers interviewed, there is a clear relationship between the elaborated life story, complete with its crystallized most important components (specific vignettes that are utilized in various contexts), and the degree of positive self-identification. Women who have "made it" as preachers—as pastors, especially—have much better developed fictions than those who have not. Some of the accounts are considerably longer than others; some of the narrators need more prodding than others, need the interviewer's questions to keep them going; others include many more developed, self-contained stories within the story—events crystallized into narrative form, often complete with dialogue. Women who remain their husband's helpers, on the other hand, and have not fully developed their identity *as* preachers or pastors have not formulated their stories into fictions to the same degree as women who have. Their accounts are, in fact, closer to "life histories" than to "life stories", although the pivot points remain the same. The women who have the greatest sense of self, whose identification is the most secure, often met even my initial question with a narrative—one I was certain had been told many times before. It was a narrative with a point; it said it better than even the woman could have.

When we read the orally delivered "life stories" of women preachers, then, we need to listen for what lies there that identifies them as individuals and what identifies them as traditional storytellers. It is impossible for me to know whether each of these women would tell this same "life story" if she were narrating to one of her neighbors. I suspect it would happen if the narrator were trying to maintain some kind of religious stance—if she were reinforcing her religiosity or her right to be the kind of woman she was. Certainly, to me, the researcher come to interview her as a woman preacher, it was important to give the "spiritual life stories."

While the women preachers of this study decry the feminist movement and deny that they have chosen a strong, feminist stance against the dictums of their world, they have, nevertheless, clearly chosen for themselves an alternative lifestyle, even against the wishes of husbands, family, and friends. Feminist scholarship that deals with narrative strategies in literature can aid us in understanding how these midwestern women have chosen to "re-script" their lives.

In her discussion of twentieth-century women writers, Rachel Blau DuPlessis has suggested that, unlike nineteenth-century women writers whose characters basically could choose only between marriage and/or death, contemporary women writers are "writing beyond" those restrictive endings for women's stories.[9] In my attempt to understand both the lives of women preachers and their narrated "life stories," I should like to rely on DuPlessis's understanding of narrative strategies. It will be constructive for us to view the lives of women preachers as alternative living strategies, and the re-constructions of those lives—in the form of life stories—as narrative strategies that reinforce and validate the identity sought in the living "script." The ability to create elaborations of "reality" may stem from what Patricia Spacks has termed the "female imagination," or the "power that penetrates the inner meaning of reality but also a power that creates *substitutes* for reality."[10] The task of the folklorist here is not to determine where "truth" leaves off in these autobiographies and where "imagination" begins; rather, it is most productive for us to view the narratives as we do other oral, traditional genres: as stories with identifiable characteristics, structure, and content; stories that are dynamic and change with the storyteller and the audience; stories that embody a shared understanding of the world and transmit that worldview to others within the group. The life accounts may or may not actually reflect historical fact, but for the women who develop and recount them, they become very real indeed. As real, in fact, as the alternative life style they have chosen.

DuPlessis has suggested that the mythic quest (or *Bildung*) was unavailable to women characters [and women] in nineteenth-century fiction [and reality], that the only social script available to them was as that of the "helpmeet". To become a "heroine", the woman character had to embrace the roles of wife and mother, or die, largely because the nineteenth-century novel had to obey the "structuring dialectics" of the social and economic limits of middle class women as a group.[11] But DuPlessis perceives a re-scripting for characters in the writings of women in the twentieth century as a change that suggests a "reassessment of the mechanisms of social insertion of women through the home, the private sphere, and the patriarchal hierarchies."[12] This re-scripting of the "social narrative" calls for a reconstruction of "culturally mandated, internally policed" patterns,[13] for a breaking of the normal sequence, signaling "a dissent from social norms as well as narrative forms."[14] For some, of course, such a deviation from "codes of expected narrative" will be perceived as an act of "disobeying the novel," but DuPlessis prefers to view these "new endings or resolutions" as a re-negotiation of possibilities for women, in narrative as well as in life. For she sees narrative as:

> a version of, or a special expression of, ideology: representations by which we construct and accept values and institutions. Any fiction expresses ideology . . . attitudes toward family, sexuality, gender . . . may call into question political and legal forms . . . women may call narrative forms into question.[15]

The "social script" embodied in any narrative, she points out, will be expressed through "strongly mandated patterns of learned behavior that are culturally and historically specific";[16] therefore, to negotiate with this script is to call into question the very foundations of life [and narrative]. Any literary convention that claims to depict experience, she suggests, also interprets it!

DuPlessis sees twentieth-century women writers as inventing alternate resolutions for the lives of women characters, a new set of choices. These alternative narrative patterns help to locate ways to "neutralize the power of the standard socio-cultural script."[17] In so doing, they "take issue with the mainstays of the social and ideological organization of gender."[18] In order to do this, the writers and their characters find it necessary to move "from the center" and "toward the margins;" but the depiction of female characters with innovative, alternative life-scripts can be treacherous. When women are placed in the margins, where supernatural forces collect, their heroic, even mythic stature can be enhanced; or their capabilities can be debased. Work and independence must not be presented as a denial of or an unfortunate alternative to scenes of family and hearth or her credibility will be damaged; self-realization and ambition must be handled most delicately, or they are viewed as a crime in women. Although some twentieth-century writers who offer alternatives to female characters would insist that they are *not* feminists, DuPlessis argues that they are, in fact, "feminist" writers because they construct "a variety of oppositional strategies to the depiction of gender institutions in narrative."[19] Simply by virtue of the re-scripting, the author is commenting upon the status quo, calling it into question, expressing dissent from it. The female ceases to be "feminine" when she leaves nature, which embodies the interior space and identification with dominant values, and becomes a critic, which moves into exterior space and expresses a denial of dominant values and refutes the typical stance of female as "muted."

Aligning life with literature, what better example of the woman "re-scripting" her life and refusing to accept the stance of female as "muted" than the woman preacher? Yet, the woman who chooses this vocation— and she does choose it, all refutation aside—must work to make certain her independence and outspoken stance do not appear as a denial of the traditional female role as good wife and mother. Most especially in this vocation, her credibility must not be shaken by any suggestion that she is a feminist or that she is in any way a threat to the status quo or is making a statement about women's "rights." Within the religious context, a safe avenue exists to buffer the accusations that might arise had the young girl chosen the life of a circus star, for example. Here, the only premise for her behavior is the assertion that God has "called" her to preach; luckily, this claim suffices to keep denial at bay, although it certainly will not eliminate criticism. Since no one can be quite certain about how "God works," it remains fairly dangerous to question his motives, although a certain amount of grumbling about the girl in question is inevitable. If we follow DuPlessis's thinking, these women are feminists, in fact, simply by the act of re-scripting—both in life and in the narrative re-constructions of life. The re-scripting itself is a comment upon the status quo, calling it into question, expressing dissent from it. Ritual disclaimers such as "I'm not for ERA . . . " or "Don't get me wrong, I'm not a women's libber" insulate them from the sagacity of their life strategies, while their narrative reconstructions re-invent the strategies and validate them for others.

While we recognize that the "life stories" of women preachers are presented as "history," actually, we must understand them as created "fictions"—fictions that are best understood as alternate narrative strategies. The stories embody some of what the women actually did in their lives, which alone represents an astounding feat given the circumstances; they illustrate for us what the women perhaps wished they had done and said; and they present the women's interpretation of what has happened to them in their lives. Both the women's lives and their fictive re-constructions of their lives serve as alternative narrative strategies for women in this region. With this as theoretical foundation, I would like to move, then, to an examination of the life stories of women preachers, pointing to some of their basic characteristics and suggesting what "narrative strategies" might be operating within them. The identifiable components of these traditional narratives of "life experiences" remain surprisingly consistent from narrator to narrator. The elements that nearly always figure in the narratives include: a clear perception of difference from other young people; an often severe conviction of a sinful nature; an attraction for the religious revival and/or missionary work; a concrete recounting of the conversion and the call to preach; and a construction of an alternative life strategy.

A PERCEPTION OF DIFFERENCE

Virtually every one of the women who has related her story to me has remarked that she was born into a very poor family. Almost all were raised in rural counties in Missouri and grew up on farms or in very small towns in rural areas. Nearly all of them belonged to large fundamentalist families, usually of Baptist or Holiness background. Missouri is largely a Bible-belt state of rural thinking, staunch conservatism, and traditional values. Notions of the importance of the nuclear family, monogamy, female/male sex roles, and the importance of religion prevail and direct the daily lives of the people who live here. I stress this traditional milieu and value system because it bears directly upon the single most unusual aspect of these women's perceptions of themselves, supported by their lives and reinforced in their narratives, and that is their perception of themselves as different and their strength to act upon that perception in such a way as to reinforce and validate that difference. This is an especially important point to make at the outset. Most of these women were born into ordinary farming

69

families that had several, often many, children. The accepted roles of girls in the 1920's and 1930's in Missouri were clearly defined and inherently restricting; they were not, in fact, unlike the lives of nineteenth-century women.

Yet the life stories of women preachers hinge upon the fact that even as very young girls, they *felt* different or knew that they *were* different from other girls, from the other children in the family. Most tell that the most visible mark of their difference was that they were especially drawn to church and to religious thoughts at a very young age. Importantly, this point in a re-constructed life story—or fiction—must be recognized as part of the narrative structure and strategy; that is, whether or not this is an actual historical point, it has become an important ingredient of the fiction that is created to validate the woman as different—different enough to be a preacher.

The women find dynamic ways to illustrate how they were different. Recall how Sister Mary talks about how she was the only child chosen to accompany her mother to church: (see p. 31) "I remember she'd take me. Just me. I was only four when she had three children. And she would take me with her." This early training and church experience obviously had a strong effect on the young girl, for she took her religious inclinations very seriously and began to proselytize at school:

> I can remember back when I was in the sixth, fifth or sixth grade, I went to the principal, see, because I had some friends and they didn't understand the way I believed, you know, because I did belong to a real strict church and my hair was never cut from the time I was four years old. And Mother braided my hair and put it around my head and pulled it straight back and they made fun of me at school, but I always tried to explain to them why.

> And I remember this time I went to the principal and there was two girls that was good friends of mind and I told them, I said, 'Why don't we try to have prayer meeting during recess?' So, I said, 'I'll go to the principal and ask him if we can.' And, you know, they allowed it. And we had prayer meeting during our recess. And I led that service.

Several points should be made about this passage. As a very young girl, Mary perceives of herself as different; when she enters the school world, her difference is manifested in and reinforced by her hair and dress. Now, she really is different. What might have begun as an internal notion of difference has been projected onto "the world". Her response to ridicule, so acute as this age, is atypical. She could, of course, reject the image at this point and strive to be like the other children; but, instead, she embraces the difference, trying to "explain to them why." And, here in the fifth or sixth grade, this girl commits herself to being a leader *and* a preacher; she initiates the visit to the principal. She asks him if she can conduct prayer meetings in the school over recess—and her bravado is rewarded: he consents and she "led the service." Viewed as a "fiction", this story embodies much that Sister Mary wishes to convey about herself. It is a carefully crafted story, told as true and intended to convince. The incident happened nearly fifty years ago, yet details in the story, such as the precise dialogue, will surprise us unless we understand that it *is* a crafted fiction— a re-creation of an incident. Significantly, the narrator of the story is the only person whose exact words of dialogue are included in the story. The taunts are left out; the principal's response has been excluded, as have the words of the two girlfriends. Only the narrator speaks—and she speaks with authority, conviction; we have to applaud her aplomb, and, of course, that is the point of this story. I have heard this woman tell this story at least twice, perhaps three times, in different contexts, and it is always told the same way. It is one of the important vignettes in her life story; it sets the stage for the subsequent acts of pure impudence she will commit.

The stories of other women preachers strongly parallel this woman's story. Sister Anna loves to recall that even while still in her mother's womb she was "marked," when her mother was frightened by a snake and stumbled (see p. 44 for this story). Anna's family folklore supports her belief that she is different, that she was "marked." The incident with the snake is not interpreted here as a "sign from God," but it definitely serves to focus on the difference of this child in the family. Likewise (p. 46), she treasures the innocent prophecy of a non-believing uncle who revealed her "holy commission" long before she could even talk.

Church became a very strong force in Anna's life. She tells of walking long distances as a very young girl, devoted already to God's house and her connection with him. Her devotion is compared here to the account of Mabel Adams:

> As a very young girl, I loved the Lord with all of my heart and I went to church by myself much of the time or I would take my younger brothers and sisters. We were very poor people. But through the years Daddy was on and off for the Lord and a lot of the time he drank. And then in later years when my mother became ill, why, he stopped that. But he didn't go to church all the time. And my mother wasn't able to. But that didn't damper *my* spirit. I would go and I'd walk.

I'd go—one place we lived I'd walk a long way, I think it was two or three miles. I think it was a long way for me to walk, even by myself.

Well, more than any of my family, I was always the one that wanted to go to church. I don't know why, I guess it must have been the hand of the Lord on me all the time because I always would find *somebody* that wanted to go to church. It didn't make me any difference, you know, where; I just wanted to go to church.

(*Mabel Adams, Hooperton, Missouri*)

CONVICTION OF SINFUL NATURE

One of the strongest evidences of this early link with God was the conviction of sin. Many of these women relate their very young feelings about their own sinful nature. In fact, both the early age of consciousness here and the heavy burden of sin seem to be characteristics of the spiritual life story. They are usual components, as well, in other conversion stories. Perhaps Sister Anna's favorite and most often delivered narrative is this one about the impression a particular song had on her at a very young age (note how it appears also in her story on pp. 44–45).

> Grandpa was really a wonderful Bible teacher. And he could explain it so clear. And so I sat under their teaching and in this little church, it was really a schoolhouse, but on Sunday it became the church. But I'd been there for revivals as just a wee little girl. And when I got old enough to sit on one of those school benches, a little desk, I was so short-legged my feet wouldn't reach the floor and I'd get so tired, but we didn't dare peep a word out loud in church. But I'll never forget, they sang a song and here I was, just small, but I have used this as an illustration many times in my messages, that they sang this old song "Standing Outside the Door." "Oh, what an awful picture. Left standing outside." That made such an imprint upon my mind, that I think that's why I can preach with vividness heaven as a real place. And I can also preach with vividness that hell is a real place, too.

Compare this narrative with Mary Harris's (p. 32), and with the following:

> I was quite young, probably, maybe nine, seven years old, maybe, nine years old, maybe, just real young like that, and my mother took me and another one or two of the younger ones to a revival in Versailles, and who was holding the revival but a nine-year-old girl—and I'll never forget that. She had long hair braided way down her back

and, ah, I'll tell you that nine-year-old girl preached, oh, she preached. And when she got through, of course, I was just a child, maybe seven, eight, anyhow, she called for different ones to come to the front to pray, you know. Well, I went up front but I didn't know how to pray. I just felt led, other people were going to the altar and I just felt like I needed to go to the altar and so I did, and I knelt down, but I didn't know how to pray, I just knelt there. And that little evangelist girl came and prayed over me and with me. And I guess God planted a seed in my heart then and I've always remembered that, and I never could get too far away from it.... And there was always conviction, and I know that God planted a seed in my heart in that revival of that nine-year-old girl when I was very young.

(*Pat Roberts, Centerville, Missouri*)

Without a doubt, these young girls *were* different. They felt a motivation for their lives that was conspicuously different from the life experiences and expectations of their siblings and their peers. Perceiving themselves as different led the girls to seek outlets for the manifestation of that difference. At this age, the girls primarily reinforced their differences by manipulating and stressing the most evident signs of being a "Holiness" Christian, by conspiciously going to church by themselves, and by startling their elders and their peers with uncharacteristic religious behavior, such as holding a revival in the lunchroom. Religion easily served as the arena for their differentness.

THE LURE OF THE REVIVAL

Nearly all of the women interviewed stated that their first stirrings toward a religious life began in revivals. I think, perhaps, there is a good reason for this. Revivals were like carnivals come to town. In isolated rural areas, the church was often the focal point of activity, at least of activity that could include all members of the family. Men and boys could certainly visit and hang around the local granges, the grain elevators, and the cotton gins. And the children went to school as much as possible. But the church was an arena for all members of the family to participate.[20] The strict religious standards did not allow for exploring new places or responsibilities—with the exception of the revival and camp meeting circuit. For young girls in this context, there were all too few role models for them— their mothers, the female schoolteachers, and the occasional woman preacher. Clearly, from the interviews excerpted above, women preachers and religious leaders made a durable impact on many young women. Importantly, religious life provided the *only* opportunity for young girls to leave home and travel. No doubt the life of a missionary or an itinerant preacher was an appealing one for girls who doubted that they would, in any other way, be able to be independent and actually leave home before marriage.[21]

Sister Anna first thought she wanted to be a missionary. As she tells on p. 48, before her mother became bedfast and Anna had to become surrogate mother to her brothers and sisters, she had planned to be a missionary to Rio de Janeiro. Importantly, this desire to be a missionary seemed feasible to the young Anna at that time. Probably, too, in her community her wish to be a missionary would be tolerated with kind condescension and no real enmity. While viewing such an inclination as worthwhile, few probably saw one from their ranks ever actually being a missionary. Apparently, due to the hard realism of her own personal life, Anna also recognizes the improbability of this aspiration—so she changes it. But she understandably becomes uneasy as she begins to relate to her family and friends that she had begun to feel that God had changed the direction for her life. Now she feels a call "not to be a missionary at all, but a *preacher*."

Missionaries brought excitement and glamour from faraway places, but the revivals held in the local areas certainly provided a more tangible kind of lure for young girls such as Anna. Weeks, sometimes months before a revival was scheduled to begin, flyers would be posted on fences, at the grain elevator, on the church and grocery doors. The face of a traveling evangelist would smile down on uplifted, eager faces, reading promises of exciting meetings, singing families, and religious ferver. Just like the carnival, the revivals and camp meetings would often be set up on the edge of town. Trucks drove by bearing strange men who piled out at the site and, wielding huge hammers, set up enormous tents that would put any circus to shame. Benches, pews, logs, chairs were lined up inside, a makeshift altar prepared, a pulpit tacked together, and sawdust dumped upon the "floor". Sometimes the crew would bring the piano out from the little church and set it up front on a precarious platform. Big signs facing in all directions announced "REVIVAL TONIGHT 7:30 EVERYONE WELCOME." And those same signs might announce this protracted meeting anywhere from three days to three months. Most recollections of these events are happy ones, even humorous.

> They had a camp meeting over at Marshall, so we thought we'd go down there. And they'd pitched their tent, you know, right outside of town and then one of them carnivals came, too, you know, with a great big tent set up out there, too. And I remember Raymond had to kind of be up there with the men, you know, because they said they'd better watch the revival tent. But he came out there one night

and the carnival had moved out and they'd moved out with the revival
tent too [laughs heartily].

(*Edith Cooper, Blue Springs, Missouri*)

Back then we'd go to camp meetings all week or longer in an old
building, like an open house, it wasn't a church house. It was just like
an open barn. It was just a big building with a roof on it and it had
some sides, and they had camp meetings in it and it had a sawdust
floor. It's still standing last time I drove by there, in a field kind of
grown up, unless they've torn it down. That's all they used it for. And
I know one time a lady got happy with her accordion and she just
shouted all over the place with her accordion. What makes me remember that one of the brothers called it a piano and one night after
that he got up and he testified [laughs], he testified about seeing this
sister shout with a piano around her neck [laughs]. He meant an
accordion, you know. I mean that's just some of the memories we
have. I was probably 14 or 15 then.

(*Alice Ford, Hinkson, Indiana*)

Everyone in the family could go to camp meetings and revivals.
Young girls who could go virtually nowhere else could hardly wait to don
their best dresses and hurry down to the tent. Often, the evangelists were
young men not much older then they were—and, occasionally, they would
see and hear a woman preach. It was so easy to become enthralled, to
respond to the calls to repent, to dedicate, to exhibit the zeal of the Lord.
And respond they did. Historical accounts of revivalism always note the
enthusiastic female participation in these meetings.[22] The messages took
on a very personal appeal for these girls: they wept; they saw themselves
as blatant, stained sinners; they went to the altar and tried to pray fervently;
and some of them promised God they would live in his service. And that
is a very important thing to note—"God's Service" meant an alternate
life—a new life-script. To be a preacher meant daily doses of new faces,
travel, independence, and status. In fact, it just may have represented the
most outrageous break with tradition available without castigation—offering much more than schoolteaching, for example, in terms of mobility.
And, to make it even more appealing, if the call was "of God" and not of
the girl herself, then the decision gained divine validation. But none of
this is to suggest that just because there were women preachers preaching
was a condoned occupation for women. It was not, and still is not, in
most fundamentalist contexts;[23] at best it is tolerated only because of the
respect for and belief in divine intercession.

THE CONVERSION AND THE CALLING

One of the most important components of a woman preacher's spiritual life story is her conversion, which is usually accompanied by reference to a poignant moment, often a part of the same narrative, when the girl believes that she's been called to do and be something special. But because of the inherent dangers of pronouncing this belief, most of the stories have embedded in them a "ritual disclaimer" of sorts—a message that either states clearly or translates to say, "Look, I didn't ask for this. God called me. What could I do but obey? I tried to resist, but you really ought not try to resist God." Implied is the message that the young women did not actually wish to be called. Some, in fact, did not act upon their "calling" immediately—some waited a year or two, others as long as eight or nine years before they could actually bring themselves to make a full commitment to what they knew they wanted but perhaps feared to do. Importantly, in the oral re-creation of the "life story" a degree of hesitancy must be in evidence; no greediness, no rushing toward this life in the center stage is allowable. Subtle resistance, even a hint that the girl was holding back or resisting can be detected in some of the narratives; in others, the statement is loud and strong—"I didn't want this life, it was thrust upon me." Whatever the fact, the message embedded in the narrative is a disclaimer of intent—for personal intent would discredit the woman's legitimate claim to the pulpit. However, while the woman must disclaim any personal involvement, her stories must prove that she has, in fact, been selected by God and that she will be effective in the capacity of preacher. Her success in that arena will attest to God's preference for her.

Sister Alma stresses her own inadequacies, her unworthiness for God's attention. Predictably, she is influenced during a revival and is surprised to find herself preparing sermons in study hall. As might be expected, her own pastor discourages her. Such initial discouragement often functions as an important motif in these life stories. Such resistance, of course, provides the impetus for an even more determined stance by the young women to become preachers "against all odds," as Alma tells us on p. 40. Leah Moberly's story too exemplifies so well the hesitancy, the reluctance, and the power of God in her "call to preach" story:

> Well, the call of God first come into my life when I was seventeen
> years of age. And I went the one time; like to scared me to death and
> I said, 'Lord, I'll do what I can to help others, but leave me alone.'

And which he did. I would try to get away from it you know. I would rather not have went to preach. I would rather have set in the pews. But God slayed me under his power and I saw a vision. I saw it seemed like the earth opened and a big river of water come pouring in and in this I saw a bunch of sheep coming out through that water and I said, 'Lord, what does this mean?' And he said, 'This river of water is the river of life that I'm willing to give unto the people that is ready and needing it.' Then I saw a big field of people in this same vision. A large field and my brother who was a minister was running backwards and forwards trying to preach to all them people. And I said, 'God, what does this mean?' And he said, 'That he has got more to reach than he can possibly reach and I have called you to go and help him and my calling is without repentance.'

(*Leah Moberly, West Park, Missouri*)

Recall Sister Mary's concern when she felt in the woods that God had given *her*, a mere sixteen-year-old girl, the sermon for that evening's revival service:

And I never will forget that place because there was a big old grape-vine, it was just about this big around [makes circle with full arms], and it was just hanging right down. And when I—it just seemed like God just almost slew me, cause I got down on my back, flat on that ground and I couldn't get up. And I started praying and God started dealing with my heart and the Lord started saying, it just seemed like—not in an audible voice—but I could just hear the Lord speaking in a small, still voice, saying, 'Will you go where I want you to go? And will you do what I want you to do?' And, you know, it was hard for me because I thought, 'Now, is this me?' Because I had admired this other girl that preaches *so much*. I'd always all my life, you know, I had always thought, 'Oh, I would like to be an evangelist.' When I was growing up I used to think, and Mama always taught me that so many things was wrong, you know, that I just was almost afraid to do anything. So, the Lord dealt with me, but the thoughts came to me, 'How can I preach? How can I do anything.' But the Lord just kept dealing with me and I couldn't get up and finally I said—I just felt come to a place that I could say, 'Lord, whatever you want me to do, even though I within myself, I'm not, I know I'm not worthy of this calling. But I'll do anything you want me to do because I know that it's in your power to speak through me. And I'll go anyplace you want me to.'

Similar experiences can be documented in the life stories of other women preachers. As is evidenced in the following examples, the "proof"

77

that the calling is of God is often manifested in the recounting of a vision sent by God to convince the reluctant preacher-to-be:

> Well, we were having a state convention in Burlington and all the churches, you know, from the state, the local churches in the state there, they all came together and the Lord just spoke to me, you know, let me know that he had called me and wanted me to preach. I rebelled, I really did. I didn't feel like, you know, that I could. I was very shy and you know I'm still very shy and I don't say too much unless I'm pushed but I was one that—I didn't feel like that I could speak and I just felt like, well Lord, surely you could find somebody that could do a better job than I can. But he said, you know, "you!" So, then, my mother had cancer and so we were praying and I began to pray, "Lord, if you'll raise her up and let her live, then I'll preach." And so from that, I tried. And he did, he healed her. They operated and, you know, they said that the scars of cancer was there but there was no sign of the cancer. So God healed her. So, I feel like, you know, I have to [preach] once in a while to keep her alive [laughs].
>
> (*Mabel Adams, Hooperton, Missouri*)

> . . . inside of my heart I knew that whatever you used to be when you get it, when you come to the Lord, you need to be more, you know, and so with much crying, wanting more of the Lord and wanting the Holy Ghost. If it was real, I wanted it, you know, and so, after about two weeks of crying the Lord filled me, you know, and he filled me good, I'll tell you what. If you don't believe it ain't real with the stammering lips, you know, and speaking with other tongues. It just felt like the spirit took my hold of tongue and it was just a-flopping in my head, you know, and just a—it was just like not even con-trolling—next thing you know it was just language, just beautiful words, and, oh, it was just so good. Then, I'd say it was probably two-three months, you know, I begin to feel it [the call to preach], but I didn't let on, you know, because I didn't know what it was. I didn't know what to do, you know, because I kept—something kept reminding me of that scripture over there where a woman needs to keep silent, you know, and so I had to get victory over that and I'd cry and I'd pray and I'd say, 'Well, Lord,' you know, 'why'd this happen and why do I feel this calling when the scripture says for a woman to keep silent?' Well, I had to, the Lord had to teach me how to rightly divide the word of truth [interpret the Bible], you know, to where I could accept it.
>
> (*Pat Roberts, Centerville, Missouri*)

I married young, at 17. Then, I took "quick TB", took to my bed the 28th day of May. Was there for three months. I went to 87 pounds. My mother took care of me; I couldn't raise my head. One Saturday afternoon, it was terribly hot and I heard my parents saying that they were going to lose me. I prayed. I told God, said, 'If you will raise me up, I'll do anything.' Then, God came to my father and sent him to get a black woman preacher we knew, to bring her to pray for me, and this was just not done. But that woman preacher came, wrapped me in a sheet and put me in a chair. And that day I got healed and I saw a vision. There was a hillside, with rows of crosses, tombstones. Way at the top of the hill was a cross. And the Lord spoke to me in the air, said, 'Millions have died and never once heard and I died to save them. They are gone but there are millions left.' Scared me half to death. I didn't know what it meant. Then, one day, eight years later, I was dusting. 'Virginia, if you'll walk humble before me, I'll make you fishers of men.' 'Lord, what did you say?' Again, clear as could be, I heard, 'Virginia, if you will walk humble before me, I'll make you fishers of men.' And I said, 'Lord, because I am flesh, confirm it. Let me know this is really you. When I call my friend, I said, when I call her she's going to be reading the Bible and she's going to read this scripture to me: "How beautiful are the feet of him that bringeth good tidings..." And so I called my friend, and she said, oh, I was just reading the Bible, let me read you what I just read, it's from Isaiah 52:7, "How beautiful upon the mountains are the feet of him that bringeth good tidings, that publisheth peace; that bringeth good tidings of good, that publisheth salvation; that saith unto Zion, Thy God reigneth!" And I didn't tell anyone about that for one year. Then, in Indianapolis, there was a woman preacher, Sister Spillman, preaching and I went to hear her. And, one night, she said, she wanted anyone who had heard the audible voice of God to stand. And people started crying and standing. And I stood up and I knew then, because I had publicly acknowledged the thing, that I had to preach.

(*Virginia Richards, Rogers Ridge, Indiana*)

Well, actually, I was a very young girl when I went with my two sisters to a big tent meeting. It was so full we had to stand outside and watch from there. And when they gave the call for people who wanted to be Christians, we all three held up our hands and a woman came out to us and invited us to come in. And I was a very young girl of fifteen when I received the call to preach. It was during a revival meeting and it was being held in an old converted theatre building, you know, like they have in theatres. And I remember those lights as

I walked down the stairs and I felt a pressure on my back and shoulder, and something told me that it wasn't a person touching me. I knew it was the Lord. So, I went forward, and when I got down to the front of the church there wasn't any room for me to kneel at the altar. So, I looked around and I noticed that there was a space under the piano just in front of it, so I crawled there into that space and I just lay down and buried my head into the floor there. And I heard a voice say to me then that I would be called to preach the word. But, I just cried and cried because I did not want to preach. Why, I could hardly speak to a group without my voice breaking. I just wasn't a public speaker. So, I put off that call to preach for thirty years.

Several things finally got me to go ahead and accept the call. One was a meeting a revival meeting that was being held by a powerful woman minister—Isabel Hook—they called her Hookie. Oh, she was a powerful woman. And during one of her meetings, she announced that *I* was being called to preach and that the time was now ripe and that I ought to accept that call.

(*Edith Cooper, Blue Springs, Missouri*)

I've had to prove all of these years that a woman can be called into the ministry. And I've kept loving the people even when they've criticized me and telling them, 'Look, this wasn't my choice.' I've stood in front of the mirror lots of times and said, 'God, are you sure you know what you're doing?' I'm a wife; I'm a mother. I didn't come into this on my own. I was contented even in holding children's crusades, which wasn't nearly as difficult. It wasn't having to be the burden bearer, you know, like you have to be if you're a preacher.

(*Anna Brock Walters, Centerville, Missouri*)

ALTERNATIVE LIFE STRATEGIES FOR WOMEN

As is evidenced in many of the accounts given above, a striking number of these young women actually did have female models to follow within the context of the tent revival or the religious camp meeting. In many cases, in fact, the pivotal point of their decision to undertake the ministry revolves around a prodigious encounter with a woman preacher. Over and over, that critical point is punctuated by a reference to how a woman preacher helped her make the decision to follow "God's call." By this female association, then, the "call" was received in a context of possibility, if not probability—what they sought to do was not queer or absurd, for other women had done it, even though it might not be a course condoned by the family or the community.

Well, I know when I was just a young Christian, really before I'd ever even considered a calling on my life, I heard a lady minister, a guest minister. She was the Assembly of God and she preached a service for us in our fellowship meeting. And I was there and heard her preach and it was beautiful, oh, the way God used her, you know, and it was just like music to your ears, and just comfort to your heart, you know. And I sat there and I just—oh, it was so wonderful, and I got so much good out of that and I cried a lot, you know, I sat there and I cried. And I told the Lord, I said, 'God,' you know, 'If you've really got a calling on my life. God, I want it to be to where I can be a blessing to those that hear.' I said, 'God, I want it to be a blessing or I don't even want to be used.'

After I gave my heart to the Lord, I'm not for sure how many weeks it was, but, you know, as I would read the Bible, and I would begin, there would be just like sermons just hop up out of that Bible to me— I'd read a verse and I'd see a sermon, you know, and in the back of my mind, you know, I'd begin to think of all these things, you know, that a person could preach on, you know, from this verse, and well it was really great. And I gave all those great sermons to my brother-in-law.

(*Pat Roberts, Centerville, Missouri*)

There was Lucy Williamson. She was a lady minister. She evangelized. I don't think she ever—I don't remember her ever pastoring. But she was a person that, a lady minister, and I always thought, 'Oh, I wish I could be like her.' . . . Sister Lucy she was just, I don't know, it seemed like she stood out from anyone else. And then there was another Sister, Sister McDaniel. She was an older lady and I can remember her preaching—her children was older than myself. But she was a little, short woman. She didn't have very much waist, and she was real bow-legged. But I can remember that so much, seeing her, but, oh, she *was* a fiery preacher. She really did preach the word of God. And, she was an outstanding person to me.

(*Mary Harris, Wheaton, Missouri*)

Sometimes, these influences from other women came from total strangers, but sometimes the influences were very close to home. All the evidences of women preachers around them were useful in convincing the young woman that it was possible to become a woman preacher, but those experiences that were closest to home were the ones which would assure her that the status quo could be altered, that a re-scripting of the "normal" female life strategy did not necessitate a rejection of home and family—

but it would require new life strategies, for both women and men. It is no small wonder that the woman strongest in her commitment to both preaching and pastoring grew up hearing stories such as the following about her own grandmother:

> My grandmother was a minister for many, many years. She was Church of God-Holiness—now that is not Pentecost. And so she, Grandma, wasn't pastoring but she was an evangelist for many years and she had five children. And my grandmother was holding a revival down at a little old schoolhouse and they called it Anton, then, and there was a store there. Course my mother was about middle-ways in the family and I've heard my mother say, course she had long hair, and that Grandpa's hands were so rough. So when Grandma was out in the hills down in southern Missouri, holding revivals, why Grandpa then would get the kids up early every morning to go to school. And my mother said, 'Oh, he would braid my hair so tight, I would always shut my eyes.' So, she always hated it when Grandma was gone to revivals because Grandpa had to braid her hair. But, then, Grandma'd come home, and instead of money—about all they could give her were squirrels and rabbits or deer meat, because that's all they could give her, but she'd be so thrilled because she could bring that home—course that wasn't what she was in it for. But this is really where I got my background.
>
> (*Anna Brock Walters, Centerville, Missouri*)

This account refers to the early years of this century, in central and southern Missouri, and given the cultural milieu is a fairly amazing narrative. Obviously, the mother has cherished the account and passed it down to her own daughter, complete with the one line of dialogue—which appears to indicate her dissatisfaction with the fact that her mother seemed to be traveling about the countryside a good bit of the time holding revivals. However, the force of the narrative is not so much discomfort about her mother being gone as much as it is discomfort with her father's ability to braid her hair. Clearly, the most important message here is the matter-of-fact way in which her mother's occupation and traveling, her leaving of the five children in the care of the father, is portrayed—her leaving to preach is a given. The rest of the family, and the father, will just have to make do until she returns. And, it appears, they survived just fine. Religion makes women brave; God's business is not to be scoffed at by any man. I recall another story a woman preacher related to me about her own mother's inclination toward the church and her father's staunch opposition. He just did not want her leaving the house to go to church, and he didn't want her to take the children. But the mother always quietly resisted, rising early on Sunday, dressing the children, and heading for the door. One day, he became especially adamant, snatching the very hat off her head, saying he wouldn't return her hat because he didn't want her to leave. "Well," she said as she walked out the door, five children in tow, "then I'll just go *without* my hat!" And she did. The daughter, whom I was interviewing, delighted in this story of her own mother's bravery.

WOMEN AS PREACHERS

When Anna Brock was offered the position of pastor of the church in Millerville, Missouri, she had four small children. She and her husband lived in Kansas City and both had jobs; she had developed a good catering business of her own there, but she certainly still thought of herself as an inexperienced country girl. She said she had never even been to Jefferson City, which was in the center of the state, approximately 200 miles away. Up to the time she got this call about the pastorship at Millerville, she had worked almost exclusively in children's crusades and revivals, although that summer she had preached one or two regular revivals, which had apparently earned her a small reputation. In her reconstruction (pp. 52–53) of her call to take the pastorship at Millerville, she recounts the strict stipulations she made to God in order for her to comfortably feel she could accept the position. Her narrative reconstruction of the events of that time illustrate that she knew that God wanted her to go. The story of those days eliminates the possibility that anyone might think that it was her *own* wish to pack up and go to Millerville. She makes the move look less than a positive kind of adventure, although she certainly recognizes it as such.

> But, anyway, I went there that morning. I knew nothing about pastoring. I'd never tried out for church, and in fact, I was just filling in for them. . . . But at the close of the service one of the deacons walked up and stood right in front of the platform. 'Well, it's been a long time since we had a service like this.' And then that night, I preached again and the Holy Spirit just fell in a miraculous way again. And this other deacon walked up and says, 'Would you like for us to vote on you?' I said, 'No. I wouldn't. I've got to do some praying about this.' The parsonage was in a bad, bad shape. It leaked. It was so much smaller than our house in Kansas City. And Brother Brock [her husband] said, 'Now, you know, if you do this, you'll have to be down there all by yourself with the kids.' Well, this was a very frightening thing, cause I knew nobody. I had no relatives around. I knew

no one there. And the responsibility of three children in a new school and a church—and I'd never pastored before. So, I said, 'God, I've got to know.'

No doubt Anna herself questioned the sanity of the move to Millerville. Yet, clearly it was a conscious change in occupation—a clear re-scripting of her life. While the repercussions were not immediately available, Anna could anticipate where the criticism would focus.

Importantly, her story includes imagery that supports her role as wife and mother. She tells us her children told her they thought she ought to move to Millerville; her husband does not stand in her way, he only tells her matter-of-factly that if she makes this move she has to make it alone; and she begs God for answers as she "agonized, slumped over a basket of clothes." Her created narrative about these events carefully weaves her personal desire tightly into the threads of her domestic situation. She is no feminist, no rejector of the system. Her story (see p. 000) tells us that she put God to the test—she "made it so hard" for God to show her, so she would "know" this move was "of him" and not "of her." It stands as her record that she tested God and he "came through." The moral, then, is:

> And so, when I have these feelings, and people come against me to make me waver a little bit, I soon bounce back because I remember that God made it so clear to me.

At the risk of seeming cynical, we must acknowledge that we have no way of ascertaining where the imagining ends and "history" begins in this very private account of a "testing of God." The important thing to note is that this kind of validation is clearly a critical component of women preachers' stories. I have encountered this story in many different guises. Yet it is identifiable in structure and intent, if not content. Always, in the recon-struction of events, the narrator tells how she set up a situation in order to determine "God's wishes." Most often it takes the form this story has taken—"So, I made it really hard on God . . . I said, 'if this is truly of you, then———.'" Then, the narrator will assert that the event did occur exactly as proposed, or she will deliberately re-construct each detail of the "event," illustrating how closely "God followed" the proposition. The narrative reconstruction will close with a ritualized ending: "And so I knew this *really* was of God!" And the unstated directive to the listener is, of course: and *you* must acknowledge this as God's directive as well.

Of course not all the discomfort and criticism comes from the com-munity at large. All of these women claim to have had difficulties in their own homes with their families' reactions to their call to preach. Sister

Mary talked to me at length about how her traveling to conduct revivals all over the state put a definite strain on her relationship with her husband, who still is not a follower of her faith. While she fully recognizes her duty to be a good wife and mother, she strongly believes her duty to God is of greater magnitude. Yet, this did not necessarily make things easy at home, as she tells us vividly on pp. 37–38. Even though her husband "supported" her work, she recognized his anger when she didn't come "straight home."

Even given the solid foundation based on the premises outlined above, however, these women have met with considerable opposition and have endured incredible pain in their election to take on what is clearly described in the Bible as a male position—speaking out in church from the pulpit. Their stories about becoming preachers and pastors reveal the various levels of their difficulty and the subtleties of the reactions against them. Their own words best illustrate the frustration and anger they feel about the opposition to the re-scripting of their lives:

> It's been a real barrier, of criticism, because they've used the scripture that the women keep silent in the church, and so on. But I usually tell them—and it's usually a man, I've never found a woman being critical—I tell them, 'If you men will do what God wants you to do, we women won't have to,' and that usually hushes them.
>
> (*Alma Cotton, Smithville, Missouri*)

> We had men preachers all along. It just started in my home and when my brother was traveling I carried on. There was my brother and Reverend Bill Mullen and they were both out evangelizing, but I stayed home and preached the gospel. My brother would say, 'Sis, feed the people. Feed the saints on Sunday morning, that's their day. Feed them. And then on Sunday night give them an evangelistic message and on Wednesday night more or less a teaching message. But hang right in there and I'll be back.' Well, after his revival, maybe two or three weeks he was out and gone, he'd come back and then, of course, he was pastor. However, *I'd* been doing the work. And I love him with all my heart.
>
> (*Ruth Hatley, Murray, Missouri*)

> I have faced my difficulties. I have went through the hard places. Many times I didn't receive the offerings like they would have given a man preacher because I was a lady minister. And I've worked in the International Shoe Company here in West Park. I worked in the Overall Factory here in West Park, and I've worked in laundries here

to be able to go out there and carry the gospel to the people, to the the small churches out around. And I've been told they didn't believe in women preachers. I've told them I didn't know whether I did or not, but if the men that was called would have got up and went on maybe I wouldn't have had to. But if God could have called the rocks to cry out like he said in the Word of God, when the disciples wanted him to have them be still, all right, then I thought he could make a woman preach if she wanted to and if he wanted her to. I've told them they didn't hire me and they sure couldn't fire me. God called me; God sent me; and I'll *be there.*

(*Leah Moberly, West Park, Missouri*)

SUMMARY

The excerpts given above and the stories in the previous chapter illustrate how the "life stories" of women preachers contain parallel structures, themes, foci, and even content. These women are conscious at a very early age that they feel different from the other children in their family, from other children in the community. As girls, they recognize the limitations of the expression of that "difference." The luring arena of religion, how-ever, offers to them a haven—not at all a secure or painless haven, but a place where they can insist upon their independence. Even as very small girls, they walked alone to church; their attendance there was not ques-tionable. Their fascination with the revival circuit and its charismatic char-acters was, as well, still in line with acceptable decorum and behavior for a young woman. Then, if that life attracted them, if they felt themselves inclined toward travel and the pulpit, they knew that that, too, could be safely achieved as long as it was carefully couched and framed within the religious belief structure of the group: God called me to be a preacher; I really didn't want to do it; it scared me to death; I tested God on several occasions and he answered my prayers; I know this is "of him and not of me"; God is all powerful, neither you nor I can protest the will of God, to do so is blasphemous and "without repentance." Finally, after acting out this "alternative script" and re-directing their own lives, many of these women actually entered the ministry and undertook to be preachers for the rest of their lives; their "life stories" are a testament to that re-scripting.

NOTES

1. Especially see Jeff Todd Titon, "The Life Story;" and liner notes for his record "Powerhouse for God." Also see L. Langness, *The Life History in Anthro-pological Science*; Sandra K. D. Stahl, "The Personal Narrative as Folklore;" and William M. Clements, "The Pentecostal Sagaman."

2. Titon, "The Life Story," p. 278.

3. *Ibid.*, p. 280.

4. *Ibid.*, p. 290.

5. Roger Abrahams, ed., *A Singer and Her Songs: Almeda Riddle's Book of Ballads.*

6. Theodore Rosengarten, *All God's Dangers: The Life of Nate Shaw.*

7. *Ibid.*, p. xiv.

8. *Ibid.*, p. xix.

9. Rachael Blau DuPlessis, *Writing Beyond the Ending: Narrative Strategies of Twentieth-Century Women Writers.* See also Sandra M. Gilbert and Susan Gubar, *The Madwoman in the Attic*; and Patricia Meyer Spacks, *The Female Imagination.*

10. Spacks, p. 4.

11. DuPlessis, p. 8.

12. *Ibid.*, p. 2.

13. *Ibid.*, p. 8.

14. *Ibid.*, p. 2.

15. *Ibid.*, p. x.

16. *Ibid.*, p. 2.

17. *Ibid.*, p. 35.

18. *Ibid.*

19. *Ibid.*, p. 34.

20. For the best overview of camp-meeting religion, especially in the nineteenth century, see Dickson Bruce, *And They All Sang Hallelujah: Plain-Folk Camp-Meeting Religion, 1800–1845.* Bruce incorrectly assumes, however, that the phenomenon he has described based on historic sources does not extend into the twentieth century.

21. Compare Barbara Welter's "She Hath Done What She Could: Protestant Women's Missionary Careers in Nineteenth-Century America."

22. See Bruce, pp. 76–87 especially.

23. The Southern Baptist Convention voted in 1985, for example, to exclude women from Baptist pulpits. This extremely large and influential fundamentalist church organization based its decision upon a traditional reading of the Bible that holds women accountable for the "fall" of man in the Garden of Eden. See Michael Berryhill, "The Baptist Schism."

3

Evangelists and Pastors: Saving Souls and Mothering Congregations

By now the reader has a sense of who these women are, how and where they grew up, and what influenced them to make the decision to become preachers. In this chapter, the women move from their life situations to their place behind the pulpit. I shall be concerned here with *how* women preach; in the next chapter I will examine more closely *what* they preach. Of course, considerations of style and performance cannot be divorced completely from content. Often content, message, and intent dictate style of delivery. Nevertheless, it seems fruitful to examine styles of preaching first, before probing the themes of women's sermons.

Women preachers who are pastors of congregations preach differently from itinerant women preachers. In this chapter I compare the preaching styles of a female revival preacher and of a woman pastor. I have chosen this comparison because the revival preacher, who travels from revival to revival, camp meeting to camp meeting, has a different mandate and a different relationship with her audience than a woman, like Sister Anna, who has held the position of pastor for a single congregation for eighteen years. Therefore, for this analysis of preaching style, I am focusing on the different performance modes available to evangelistic preachers and those who pastor a home congregation.

I first encountered itinerant women preachers who traveled around preaching revivals and special services in southern Indiana in the late 1970s. One fairly well-known woman radio evangelist, Sister Grace Watson, was known to me only via her radio sermons, which were broadcast in central and southern Indiana. Late in 1980, however, I attended a revival near Hinkson, Indiana, where Grace's niece, Linda Watson, and her grand-niece, Odetta Watson, were combining

89

their talents in a Pentecostal revival. Sister Linda, the primary revival evangelist, was a dynamic preacher who could elicit much positive response from her audience. Sister Odetta was obviously serving in an apprenticeship capacity during this revival with her older aunt. Her style closely approximated that of Sister Linda's, and she talked a great deal about going out on her own in the near future to preach revivals. She must have been sixteen or seventeen years old.

Field recordings from approximately thirty women preachers and pastors in both Indiana and Missouri yielded some general characteristics and, perhaps, as many significant differences in both preaching styles and sermon content. Even when working exclusively with Anglo "trinitarian" Pentecostals,[1] such factors as geographical region, specific type of sect, and the make-up of the audience must all be factored into our analysis. While radio sermons may help us broaden our perspective, these taped recordings ought not to be utilized unless the context and the performance situation can be evaluated as well. Importantly, we must acknowledge at the outset that these women are individual, creative performers, performing within traditional contexts. Their styles of preaching differ more radically than their message does.

EVANGELISTIC PREACHING

Sister Linda Watson, a traveling evangelist who preaches predominately in revivals in the area, has one of the most dynamic, dramatic preaching styles I have observed. During her sermon performance, she clearly goes into a chanting style, ending lines with the characteristic breath punctuation "ah", which helps to punctuate and accentuate her chanted preaching style.[2] Sister Linda's role as a traveling evangelist has a direct effect on her preaching and allows her a dramatic preaching style that may often be unavailable to the woman pastor.

Sister Linda's style of preaching is close to what we have come to expect from inspired, spontaneous evangelistic preachers in general [a verbatim transcript of one complete sermon by Sister Linda can be found in the Appendix, pp. 188–205; the reader is encouraged to read that sermon in its entirety before continuing with this analysis]. She speaks quickly and, for the most part, in a loud dramatic performance style. Her rhythmic, punctuated style yields "line" formations that are balanced symmetrically, metered, and phonetically pleasing.[3] In the most clearly "chanted" portions of her sermons, she terminates every line with the standard sermon performative "ah." She utilizes simple assonance and alliteration and persistently employs "formulas" for emphasis and for transition during certain portions of her sermons. She characteristically repeats formulaic sequences for effect.

Sister Linda's favorite formulas, or clichéd phrases, are "Glory to God," "Praise the lamb of God" (Pronounced "Praise the lamb-a God"), and "Hallelujah." The first two are obviously her favorites and "Hallelujah" appears to be reserved, in general, for the most dramatic portions of the sermon. She employs "Glory to God" at least ninety times during the sermon being examined here, "Praise the lamb of God" over thirty times and "Hallelujah" over twenty times. Early in the sermon, the clichéd phrases appear to be strategically placed as markers to end a particular segment or to accentuate a particularly striking point the preacher has just made. There does not appear to be a strict linguistic rule for the use of one of these phrases over the other, nor does there appear to be any pattern for alternation in their use. In fact, in some parts of the sermon, she seems to alternate them fairly regularly; in other parts, she uses the same one exclusively five or six times. None of the expletives are utilized at the beginnings of lines; however, sometimes they are spoken so quickly that they appear to be an extension of a "line" rather than forming one alone [see transcript for examples of this]. The combinations of repeated form-ulaic phrases and use of clichéd phrases as emphasis enhance the effective and the affective aspects of her preaching delivery style. Sister Linda does become quite animated during her sermons and often breaks into tongue-speaking, shouts, and moans, especially at the end of her sermon and during the altar call.

Sister Linda begins her sermon with a "cheerleading" section in which she actively solicits the verbal participation of her audience. She literally bounces up to the pulpit and yells: "Do you love the Lord?" To which the congregation responds: "Yes!" in a thunder. She asks again: "Do you love the Lord?" and again the thunder "Yes!" "One more time," Sister Linda insists, "let's let them know out there that we love the Lord. DO YOU LOVE THE LORD?" "YES" declares the congregation. "Glory to God!" Sister Linda shouts, "I really don't need this thing" and proceeds to throw down the microphone. For, indeed, she doesn't need any am-plification, and she prefers to march and stomp across the podium and even to run up and down the aisles as she preaches her sermon. The microphone would only inhibit her.

This "cheerleading" type of revival sermon beginning is not unique to Sister Linda, but neither is it characteristic of all women preachers. Rather, it is a technique often employed by revival evangelists, to "get the crowd going." Importantly, that is the primary function of the "revival" and of the revival evangelist—to revive the spirit of the people, to incite them to religious fervor and ecstacy. Compare the following sermon beginning delivered by a male revival evangelist at a camp meeting revival in southern Indiana:

EVANGELIST:	We have to know who the Messiah is!
CONGREGATION:	Oh, yeah!
EVANGELIST:	And know his name. And can you all say that name with me?
CONGREGATION:	Jesus!
EVANGELIST:	Say it again!
CONGREGATION:	JESUS!
EVANGELIST:	One more time! Let's let Santa Claus [the name of the nearest town] know we're in here!
CONGREGATION:	JESUS!

The significant point to be made here is that the woman preacher is able to utilize the "cheerleading" format in a manner nearly identical to that of the male preacher. While it is generally the case that female preachers decline to exhibit a great deal of pulpit enthusiasm, it is important to note that there *are* women preachers who do employ a dramatic, physical kind of sermon delivery; but in nearly every case where the delivery is *excessively* dramatic the woman in an evangelist, not a pastor. Very important for this study is the fact, however, that even women evangelists who are *expected* to stir the enthusiasm of their audience carefully frame their performances in such as way as to deflect the potential for misunderstanding or criticism. This is evidenced in several lines where Sister Linda departs from the sermon proper and indulges in several instances of what we might term "meta-preaching," or preaching about preaching. Most of these comments upon her own preaching clearly deny her dramatic capabilities and her active performance, and operate within the sermon as ritual disclaimers of her abilities and intentions. Early in her sermon, Sister Linda warns her audience that all she plans is a low-key approach to this evening's sermon. "In fact, tonight, I just want to kind of tell-talk about Jesus," she tells them (ll. 33–35). Much later in her sermon, after she has begun, in fact, to get quite animated, she inserts the following:

241 Now, I know I'm not preaching tonight
Like I been preaching here every night this week.
. . .
397 It may not be what you expected tonight.
But I'm a gonna obey the Lord tonight.

Now I know this preaching's not been like it has been all week.
410 It's not been—

92

I've not been running down the aisles tonight
And I've not maybe been preaching under a *heavy anointing*
But every service cannot be the same.
God knows what we need
415 And I—I didn't know
When I come here tonight
Exactly how I was going to deliver this message
God laid it on my heart.
Maybe it wasn't just exactly the way
420 Everybody wanted it
But I know I was obedient to the Lord.

The truth is that by the end of this sermon, as evidenced in the complete transcript, this woman was clearly within a physical, exhibition type of dramatic sermon performance. She *does*, in fact, run down the aisles. It is as though the disclaimers allow her to "break into performance."[4] To "prove" her anointing, she performs the type of sermon recognized by the group as "anointed;" yet, to establish and maintain her inferior role as female, she must deny and disclaim what she is actually doing.

Davis suggests that African-American preachers must acknowledge early in their sermons that the inspiration for the sermon did not come from *them*, but rather came from God.[5] While this seems to be a standard deference to God's authority, both in male and female preaching, women preachers must pay a deeper kind of deference. Sister Linda's sermon is somewhat indicative of this; others to be given following are more pronounced. The dual key "message", not of the sermon, but of the sermon *performance*, appears to be tied in closely with the denial that she, as a woman, would really preach in a dynamic style. The flip side of that "message" is: "I am nothing. I am merely the mouthpiece of God." This can be traced back to the "call to preach" narratives many women relate, in which they insist that they rejected the call to preach, declined to follow God's orders, and only submitted when God clearly pressured them—always against their own will and wishes. From the beginning of their ministry, then, the framework for their precarious public speaking from behind the pulpit is couched in terms of their being God's "tool." They are not standing up there of their own accord; in fact, they resisted their call as long and as strongly as they possibly could, they say, until it became clear that this was "God's will" and not their own. Their personal accounts of this part of their lives are critical, for the details included in their narrations provide the evidence to convince not only themselves but others who will be skeptical of their calling. In this vein, Sister Linda told a story about coming to preach the revival at Hinkson. The very first night she told the audience:

> 131 I'll tell you what!
>   I done one of the hardest things I ever done in my life
>   Coming here.
>   And my family'll tell you
> 135 I had the awfullest battle
>   When I felt the Lord calling me down here to hold this revival
>   My family'll tell you
>   When I had to go to Hickory Grove last Sunday evening
>   Go up there and tell them
> 140 When I felt the Lord calling me down here to hold this revival!
>   I didn't want to come down here, ah,
>   It would have been so much easier, ah,
>   To have just stayed at home, ah,
>   I wrestled with him one whole Sunday morning, ah,
> 145 And George Wilson tell you what I went through, ah,
>   But the Lord come to me
>   And he said,
>   He said, "If you don't do it one more soul will be lost."
>   And that put a fear
> 150 In my heart.
>   No, I didn't want to do it.
>   And if I'd have given into the flesh
>   I wouldn't have
>   But there was something inside of me, ah,
> 155 That wouldn't let me go against what God, ah,
>   was telling me, ah,
>   To do.

To have come to Hinkson on her own, to have presumed that they *needed* her, would have been unthinkable. Her narrative, like the "call to preach" narratives, insists upon her reluctance and her innocence. God directed her to preach the revival at Hinkson; she didn't want to do it. She resisted, but God insisted. And the "fear" God put into her heart must be shared by the congregation; they, too, must be fearful of what might happen if they refuse her ministry. The directness of this kind of indirect narrative is extraordinarily effective.

Not only is Linda's presence a directive of God's (against her will, of course), but as she preaches, then, the words which come out of her mouth are not her own words, but are God's. Sister Linda is only being obedient to his will. She makes this point at several junctures in her sermon. Immediately after the cheerleading section, she frames her sermon in the following manner:

9 You know it's been good to be here, tonight,
And I think I'm going to do something
Just a little bit different, tonight.
I'm trying to obey
The spirit of the Lord.
There's been so much that's been sung
15 And said
About Jesus Christ, tonight, the Son of God,
I don't believe there's a whole lot
That I can add to it
But I do want to be obedient
20 To the spirit of God.
There's been so much said about Jesus, tonight,
And do you know what?
We could talk about him until eternity comes
And we could never talk about him
25 Enough.
We could never tell it all, tonight,
About Jesus.
Because he is the one
And the only one
30 That's ever been—
That we'll ever need.
Praise the lamb of God!
In fact, tonight,
I just want to kind of
35 Tell-talk about Jesus.

Repeatedly, as evidenced above, she makes reference to obeying the spirit. In fact, in order to emphasize her complete submission to God's will, tonight, in contrast perhaps with other nights, she declares: "And I think I'm going to do something/Just a little bit different, tonight." She needs to assure her audience that she is, indeed, "trying to obey the spirit of the Lord." She tells them that even when she arrived tonight she did not know "exactly how I was going to deliver this message," because "God laid it on my heart, and I know I was obedient to the Lord." Her message seems to be contradictory: at the same time she says she knows she hasn't been preaching this evening "the way" she has been all week, "not been running down the aisles tonight," she says she is going to "do something different" tonight because she is "trying to obey the spirit of the Lord." While all of this may *seem* contradictory, it really isn't. The "message" is the same: Tonight I am going to preach what God wants me to preach. Of course, to remain safe, she proclaims this at every service. Thus, on a different night, she tells the congregation:

35 I thought as I was beginning to read upon this
   I didn't know
   I didn't even have a message
   But I began to pray
   To seek
40 To ask the Lord—
   Ask the Lord to give me a message.

This disclaimer is similar to what Davis has observed with male African-American preachers, but the necessity for the woman preacher to demean her own capabilities seems particularly arresting and goes beyond merely giving God the credit for the inspiration of the sermon. Compare the following woman's insistence on her own inferiority. Before she began to preach, Sister Connie (see Appendix, pp. 222–46) told her audience:

   Well, I kind of hope you all aren't expecting too much.
   He kind of put me our there
   On a limb.
1 I praise the Lord tonight
   Because truly he is—
   He's been so good to me—
   . . .
   Now I want you to know
   That I never thought about these things
100 On my own.
   I prayed
   And the Lord revealed these things to me.
   I have not got
   That much sense in my own head.
   The Lord has to show me things.
105 I am not intelligent,
   You know I never went to college,
   And I don't have any education,
   Learning in this world,
110 But whatever the Lord give to me
   He just give me straight from him.
   We'll start.

Now this may be kind of like—
Teaching,
115 I don't know.
Charlie said preach it.
But you know sometimes
It's kind of hard to preach,
But maybe a mixture of both—
120 Preaching and teaching.

Sister Linda's scripture reading for this sermon is one that is very familiar to her audience; most of them can recite it verbatim. She says:

56 Let me read to you what it says in John 3:16.
Now, I'm going to use a lot of scripture.
It says, "For God so loved the world
That he gave his only begotten son
60 That whosoever believeth on him
Shall not perish
But have everlasting life," ah.
Now, you just stop and think about what he did for you!
Praise the lamb of God!
65 He come out of the splendor of heaven, ah,
To come down on this old earth to walk up and down, ah,
To walk down here among men.
Glory to God!
And he was mocked, ah,
70 And ridiculed, ah,
And all them things that he had to go through, ah,
Praise the lamb of God! Ah,

The most remarkable thing about this woman's sermon is her nearly instantaneous "breakthrough" into a performance mode immediately following the reading of the scripture verse.[6] This "breakthrough" is easy to locate even in a written transcription as she breaks from the slower, more inhibited reading style and begins to "shout" her sermon; the chanting style of delivery is most noticeably punctuated by the "ah" added to the last word of most lines. Importantly, this switch in style occurs after all of her ritual disclaimers about this not being the same kind of sermon she's preached all week. We are taken by surprise, then, when she breaks from this apologetic mode into one that is clearly everything it "ought to be" and everything they had all "expected." This was her standard format each evening: to preach a constrained first portion filled with the necessary ritual disclaimers and then to cut loose from those constraints and "really preach." By doing both, she manages to balance her audience's expectations on all levels: her disclaimers insist that she "knows her place" and is willing to demean and discredit her capabilities; yet, after presenting the disclaimers, she can proceed to preach a sermon which belies *all* of the disclaimers and secures her position as an inspired, anointed preacher of God's word.[7]

In her performance Sister Linda relies heavily on repetition. Lines, phrases, even entire segments are repeated for dramatic effect. The lines directly following the reading of the scripture parallel several lines that precede it (l.44):

> 65 He come out of the splendor of heaven, ah,
> To come down on this old earth to walk up and down, ah,
> To walk down here among men.
> Glory to God!

Not only is this almost identical wording, these lines contain important clichéd phrases, or commonplaces, that Sister Linda relies upon in all of her sermons: "the splendor of heaven," "this old earth," "to walk among men," and "Glory to God." Again, lines 87–93 are nearly a verbatim repetition of lines 44–54. In fact, the line "he knew when he left the splendor of heaven" serves as the integrating line throughout the sermon.

This sermon is an evangelistic sermon. Sister Linda is trying to save souls. She pleads with her audience to "find Jesus" to "come to Jesus." She assumes there are sinners in the congregation. It is a tightly woven sermon with little diversion and much repetition, a sermon appropriate as a hard-hitting revival sermon intended to bring her audience to its feet and cause them to shout. She succeeds in doing just that.

As is typical of a revival sermon, this sermon ends with an altar call. The purpose of the altar call is to get people to come to the front, by the altar, and pray, or "tarry," for the spirit of God to come upon them. This experience is believed to be essential as proof of one's salvation. In Sister Linda's sermon it is not all that clear where the altar call begins; actually, this, too, is characteristic of revival sermons. The "altar call" can be as long or longer than the actual sermon. In some ways the "message" is headed in that direction from the beginning of the sermon. She begins to call people forward when she says, "Now is the time for salvation." Her pleas, then, are for people to come forward to "be saved;" her style is formulaic:

> 423 If you're here
> And you're lost
> And you don't know Jesus

Now is the time to accept him as your Lord.

. . .

442 LET ME TELL YOU!
You'll not find a greater life, ah,
Glory to God!
Than the one you'll have with Jesus, ah.
Walk with him, ah,
And let him walk with you.

. . .

469 If you're here tonight
And you're troubled
LET ME TELL YOU!
This JEEEEESUS will calm the troubled sea.
Glory to God!

At this point, after her solemn disclaimers about preaching what God wanted her to preach, and apologizing for not "running down the aisles," Sister Linda begins to shout, dance, moan, and speak in tongues. Her performance takes another significant turn as she yells to her audience:

Glory to God!
LET ME TELL YOU!
You'll not find a greater life, ah,
Glory to God! [tongue-speaking here]
445 Than the one you'll have with Jesus, ah.
Walk with him, ah,
And let him walk with you.
Glory to God!
There's peace and contentment there
450 And there's LOOOOVE
That I can't even begin to tell you about.
Glory to God!
There's LOOOOOOOOOVE
That Jesus places in our hearts,
455 Glory to God,
When we give our hearts to him, ah,
Praise the lamb of God!
OOOOOOOHHHHHHHHHHHH!!!!
GLORY!!
460 There's a LOOOOOVE
That nobody else can give us tonight.
GLORY TO GOD!

> And there's a joy, ah,
> And a peace WITHIN
> 465 That we cannot receive, ah,
> Glory to God!
> Praise his holy name!
> Hallelujah!
> If you're here tonight
> 470 And you're troubled,
> LET ME TELL YOU!
> This JEEEESUS will calm the troubled sea.
> Glory to God!
> HEEEEE'S the ONE tonight that can meet your needs.
> 475 Glory to God!
> HEEEEE'S the ONE that can save your soul.
> Glory to God!
> I can remember just as well tonight
> As I could eleven years ago
> 480 When Jesus dealt with my heart
> And I come to an old altar of prayer
> Glory to God!
> It was in an old-time tent revival
> Up in Brown County,
> 485 Glory to God,
> And we had SAWWWWWWDUST on the floor!
> Glory to God!
> That's what we had, ah,

Remarkably, here, in the altar call, Sister Linda recounts her own conversion story. For the recounting of this narrative, she does not, however, break out of the shouting, chanting mode she has entered for the altar call. She utilizes her own conversion narrative to encourage the audience to "feel Jesus" as she did. Her own enthusiasm has made her quite breathless and sweaty, flushed and agitated by this point in the service. She tells the audience she feels Jesus in the room, and then she tells about her own experience of first speaking in tongues. She relies on her own experiences to suggest to non-believers what they can expect if they will but try to seek the Holy Ghost. There follows an extended period of shouting and intermittent tongue-speaking by both Sister Linda and members of the congregation.

The animated, verbal audience response to her preaching during the second half of this sermon attests to the appreciation of her style and abilities. But Sister Linda remains careful until the end; for after nearly

100

half an hour of shouting performance, and following a period of tongue-speaking, she offers this quiet, modest comment:

> Praise God.
> I want us, I want—
> I just want to talk about Jesus.
> 645 I want to tell you about this Jesus.
> I don't know what I'd do without him.
> I don't know, Sister Margie, how I'd—
> I don't know how I'd make it without Jesus.

She stumbles a bit here because, in fact, what she is saying is incongruous with her preaching performance. But the plea is sincere; she even adds some direct address to a fellow "sister" in the audience—"all I really wanted to do here, intended to do here, Sister Margie," she seems to be saying, "was talk about Jesus."

THE SERMONS OF A PASTOR

In rural towns such as Centerville, Missouri, the pace of life is decades behind that of metropolitan Kansas City or St. Louis. Television and religion provide the basic forms of diversion; there is no theatre here, no bowling alley, no roller rink, no public library, no swimming pool. The town sports several small, locally owned cafes, garages, and – "quick-stop" grocery that provides staples and fishing paraphernalia and licenses. Many of the streets in town are unpaved, and houses can still be purchased for $20,000–$40,000 or less. Jefferson City, the state's capital, is 30 or 40 miles away and provides the facilities Centerville cannot supply. Numerous residents rarely, if ever, travel to "the city," however, remaining perfectly content to live out their lives within the context of Centerville. A local park attracts Sunday families; here, too, local truck farmers hawk their summer produce and chat with friends in the shade. In many ways, the lively Pentecostal services provide the most excitement of the week. Certainly, revivals are anticipated eagerly and attended by the entire town. There are at least five churches which are Pentecostal of one sort or another.

One thing became apparent in nearly every church included in this study. If the pastor was woman, she invariably also served in the church as a Sunday School teacher, as evening devotional leader, as Tuesday night youth leader, as Wednesday prayer meeting leader, often as pianist or song leader, as Thursday night visitation leader, as nursing home visitor, shut-in visitor—the list seemed endless. Rarely, in churches pastored by men, have I observed the same evidence of total leadership and responsibility as is the case with a great many of these women pastors. Speculation would lead to several suggestions about why this might be true. It is possible that the women are suffering under the pressures to be a "Super Woman." Without a doubt, Sister Anna suffers from this pressure. She knows that there is a great deal of scrutiny from her congregation and that any relinquishing of responsibility on her part might be interpreted as her "failure".

She is acutely aware of her own need to "show" everybody just how competent she is. She is very proud of her accomplishments as pastor of this congregation for eighteen years, and that means that she has done it all for that long as well. On the other hand, she may have some fear—warranted or otherwise—that relinquishing any responsibility at all would threaten the power and authority she has managed to amass. This sounds greedy, but the reality (or her perception of it) might be that the pastorship is an all-or-nothing endeavor and that relegating responsibilities to several different individuals would diminish the power of the central figure.

Another approach might be to consider that in many ways Sister Anna keeps and has kept this congregation alive. People are not so "religious" as they used to be; worldly pursuits have, indeed, taken over the once important place religion possessed. If Sister Anna relaxes her active direction of that church, it could very possibly dwindle to a small, ineffectual group, and she knows it. Her mission, her responsibility as she sees it, as pastor, is to keep the church activated—even if she has to do it all by herself.

At the beginning of the "sermon slot", Sister Anna, as pastor and preacher, will often begin sharply with the reading of the scriptures or read the scripture verses only after a very brief introduction to the topic. We find no "cheerleading" here; it's all business: "Turn with me this morning to Judges" and she proceeds to read the Bible verses. Clearly, the audience/congregation is able to determine very quickly what the focus of the "message", or the theme, for the sermon is going to be. Examining the differences between evangelists and pastors has aided me in understanding the difference between the initial moments of Sister Anna's sermons and those of Sister Linda's. First, the evangelist can be a total stranger to her audience. Because she is, as an evangelistic revival preacher, expected to come and "revive" the spirit of this cohesive "home" church [not *her* home church, however], the "cheerleading" is appropriate to infuse a spirit of activity and verbal responsibility for the audience at the very outset. On the other hand, the pastor, well known to her congregation, has been behind the pulpit off and on since the beginning of the service (serving in the capacity of prayer leader, testimony leader, song leader, healer, etc.) and has been talking to her audience for some time. Often during the transcribing of the services, I would mistake long spoken passages delivered by the pastor *as* the beginning of the sermon, largely because she would speak at length, the passage had a clear focus, and sometimes she even broke into an emotional, rhythmic style. Experience has taught me, however, that the "sermon slot" would be identifiable largely by the reading of the scripture verses: everyone involved, preacher and audience alike, responded to this marker with the acknowledgment that what was to follow was "the sermon." Furthermore, the reading of the scripture firmly established that what the woman was about to deliver was the inspired "message" from God. Whatever she had been saying to her "people" throughout the service prior to this moment could have been communication between her and them. What is to follow the scripture reading, however, must be recognized as sacred, inspired. Thus, when the pastor approached the pulpit for the *sermon*, she began that performance in the appropriate manner—with the reading of God's word.

Sister Anna's Sunday morning sermon on June 15, 1985, began in the following manner (the sermon can be found in the Appendix, pp. 171–88):

> We cannot change
> Ourselves.
> There's a lot of things we can do
> To help,
> 5 But there is no way—
> We're like the leopard that cannot change its spots
> And the Bible even says that we cannot
> Add to, nor take from
> One inch of our stature.
> 10 We can't do that, can we?
> So, there are some things that God has
> Set
> In motion
> That man cannot change
> 15 That we have to line up with God
> And sin is one of them.
> We ourselves have no power.
> It is the power in the blood of Jesus
> That cleanses from all unrighteousness.
> 20 So turn with me to Ephesians
> Second chapter, verses 8 and 9:
> "For by grace are ye saved through faith
> And that not of yourselves.
> It is the gift of God
> 25 Not of works lest any man should boast."
> Now we'll go over to St. John—

St. John the first chapter, verse 12:
"But as many as received him
To them gave he power to become the Sons of God
30 Even to them that believe on his name."
A lot of people are saying today
That the word sin is old-fashioned,

While it is true that she does not get to, or mention, the scripture verse until line 20, nevertheless, this is a rather formal, businesslike sermon beginning. The first few lines suggest, especially with her emphasis on "sin", that this will be a sermon about sin. It is not clear from the beginning, however, what she means when she says "there are some things that God has set in motion that man cannot change...and sin is one of these." However, her audience can anticipate that she will be able to tell them that *even though* "sin" has been "set in motion" and man is powerless to "change ourselves" that God has a plan to save us. And, indeed, by line 17, she informs them:

17 We ourselves have no power.
It is the power in the blood of Jesus
That cleanses from all unrighteousness.

In the early stages of this sermon, Sister Anna's style is a quiet, intimate one. She speaks directly to her congregation; often, her voice quivers, her voice breaks as though she will not be able to continue. In doing so, she appeals directly to the listener's emotions and relies on her own knowledge of each individual situation:

351 All those people in heaven
There in the presence of angels and the presence of God
They rejoice.
I believe that a precious Mom and Dad
355 Who have prayed long and fervent
And hard
For unsaved children
I tell you I believe
Even though they went on home to their reward
360 And they didn't see those children saved,
I want to tell you something,
I believe when that one, that child,
Bows on their knees to God,
That that Mom and Dad
365 Rejoice in heaven.

104

Clearly, the sermon of Evangelist Linda Watson is a sermon intended to revive the religious fervor and spirit of a congregation. Her performance is dramatic and intended to excite her audience. She relies heavily on hard-hitting, emphatic repetition of lines, phrases, and passages to stress her message. Sister Anna's sermon, on the other hand, relies less on repetition, although the repetition is certainly there and identifiable. She utilizes clichés and commonplaces, however, to a much lesser extent than Sister Linda. She is more likely to use an all-inclusive "we" as she speaks with *her* congregation. She speaks to their concerns, their problems. In some ways, she is, like a mother, more judgmental. Her "Let me tell you something, friend" relies on her intimate relationship with "her people." She frequently questions her audience: "Did you hear me?" She mentions child abuse, drugs, divorce, adultery, Alcoholics Anonymous, and compromise in an evil and sinful world. These are real-life, everyday issues for the people she knows so well. Poverty and unemployment are common in the lives of her congregation. Unwed mothers attend her church; young men whose wives have left them with three babies come to Sister Anna for help. She cannot be a stranger talking to an anonymous audience. She knows them too well. At one point in the sermon, she outlines her own position and aligns herself with Jesus:

453 Beloved,
  My business is to lift people UP,
455 Is to lift people—
  That's Jesus' place
  Is to lift people.
  And he came—
  He came to seek and to save
460 That which is lost

Although Sister Anna does not punctuate her sermon with formulaic phrases akin to Sister Linda's "Glory to God" or "Praise the lamb of God," she does employ repetition to make her point and she always speaks to the needs of her audience:

220 If your liabilities
  Are greater than your assets
  This morning,
  You're going to have to have help.
  If you don't have any check coming for a week
225 And you've got bills due this week
  You need help.
  If you're sick in body this morning,

No matter what it is,
And you've done everything you know to do
230 And it's not good enough,
You're going to have to seek help.

Often Sister Anna relies on a formulaic pattern such as this one that enables her to expand a thought, to make a point.

317 If the sinner refused to sin, People,
Then there wouldn't be the problem because you see,
If Satan couldn't get you to yield to sin
320 He couldn't do his dirty work.
Did you hear me?
If he couldn't get you,
To yield to sin
324 Then there wouldn't be anything he could do.

Images of Satan and hell bring Sister Anna toward the end of her sermon. As she becomes distressed with the graphic image of hell she is portraying, her own visions of heaven and hell inspire her to preach faster and with a great deal of emphasis. She wants her audience to understand the import of her words. This hell she has been describing is real, she says, very real. Yet, she feels it necessary now to place it well within the familiar experience of her audience and to point out that by the time they get to hell, it will be too late to change things. Not only will they literally be burning in torment for the rest of eternity, they will not be able to enjoy any of the amenities of this life. Here her lines are forcefully presented; the repetition and rhythm are apparent as tools to punctuate her emphatic message:

550 Just as sure as there is a heaven,
There is a hell.
And people [crying], it's—
It's thickly populated
Thickly populated.
555 And I believe it's burning today.
I believe it is a literal lake.
I believe it is a literal flame.
That's what my Bible says.
. . .
601 In hell there is no rest,
Day or night.
Forever hence.
In hell is torment.

106

605 In hell you will cry out
    For a drink of water,
    But there'll be none.
    There will be no relief
    From your torment.

Without a doubt, Sister Anna has been preaching a sermon. And she has preached a very powerful, emotional, graphic, "old-fashioned" sermon. Yet, the lines directly following this forceful delivery bring her and her audience back to reality. She must deny that she is *really* a preacher. Yes, she directly referred to herself as a preacher in the sermon, but just in case she has offended someone with the vigor of her presentation, she quietly submits her disclaimer, one so reminiscent of Sister Linda's:

625 I know this is not a shouting message
    But it's a message from God's word
    And it's real.
    God put this upon my heart
    This past week.
630 A plain, simple message
    On salvation
    We cannot change ourselves

Sister Anna then asks her people to submit to God and to place themselves in her care:

636 Will you lift your hands and let Jesus
    Have the opportunity of changing your life?
    Will you just lift your hand
    So I can see it?
640 And God can see it?
    And say "I'm sick and tired
    Of the way I'm living.
    I need your help."
    God will see it
645 And I will see it,
    And I will pray for you.
    Yes, I see your hands.
    Yes, I see your hands.
    . . .
658 I'm going to give you the opportunity—
    Let me lead you to the altar
    And we'll pray together
    Asking Jesus

> To forgive you
> . . .

> 687 People, we're going to make this just as easy for you as we can.
>   Will you come?
>   We love you.

Sister Anna spends some time pleading with audience members to come to the altar. She concludes with the simple reassuring thought: "God is not willing that any should perish." But she emphasizes that Jesus Christ will not push for their repentence; each individual must make the move on his or her own. She asks other women of the church to come up to the altar to help out when people come forward: "People, we're going to make this just as easy for you as we can." It seems significant in light of her emphasis on family and close bonding that she asks the women of the church to be up front, available to those who might wish to convert. The image of the mother as loving, consoling, available, sympathetic would operate successfully in a situation where sinners are expected to publicly reject their wild life and accept in its place the morality demanded by the Pentecostal religious stance. Furthermore, they are there to cry with the penitent ones, hug them, hold them, physically touch them, caress them, "mother" them. And Sister Anna stands at the front of the pulpit, down on the level of the people, ready, too, to embrace anyone who will walk down the aisle and offer their arms to her.

The conclusion of this altar call bears mention, for Sister Anna skillfully employs her talents to conclude the sermon and the entire service in a powerful manner. Immediately following her declaration that "God is not willing that any should perish," a woman from the congregation begins to speak in tongues. This is a common occurrence in these services; both church members and the pastor occasionally burst into "tongues" at appropriate segments of the service. In this case, a woman "speaks in tongues" for several minutes, and then Sister Anna "interprets" the tongue message. In this church Sister Anna is the only person I have ever heard interpret tongue speaking. The congregation very obviously defers to her superior powers in this delicate undertaking (some churches have abandoned the "interpretation" of tongues because they feel the risks of *mis*interpreting God's message through the tongues is too great). Her "interpretation" is an excellent example of the suggestive/manipulative power of words, given that we keep in mind the sermon she has just preached. The "interpretation" is perceived to be a somewhat literal translation of the tongues themselves. This is what God said through this tongue speaker, according to Sister Anna:

Behold. I stand at the door and knock,
But will you let me in?
Will you not let me have entrance into thine heart
695 Where I am called unto thee?
Yea, I've called unto thee
I've spoken to thee,
I know thee by name
And I have called you come unto me
700 Come unto me all ye that are weary and heavy-laden
And I will give you rest.
Take my yoke upon you,
For my yoke is easy
And my burden is light.
705 Come, I say, oh, Come,
Oh, the door's open.

Several points demand explication here. Sister Anna, in this "interpretation", has taken the imagery of the door to heaven that she has relied upon during the sermon and, actually transposed it here to the "door of the heart" where *Jesus* stands awaiting admittance. Her "interpretations" typically have the flavor of Biblical language, as evidenced by the use of "yea" and "thee", or contain verbatim Bible scripture, as this one does also. Her "interpretations" are carefully framed by her switch into the first person—clearly identifiable as someone *other* than herself, especially as it is introduced by the "Behold". The audience knows immediately that this is no longer Sister Anna speaking. If she performs this role correctly, her audience will understand that the voice is that of God. This works to bring Sister Anna and God in very close juxtaposition—closer even than when Sister Anna was preaching only words *inspired* by God, when she was God's tool, when she was God's "mouthpiece". Now, for a moment, she *is* God; these are not words inspired by God, directed by God—this is God speaking. Anna and God overlap (as Anna and Jesus did earlier) as the "interpretation" ends with "Come, I say, oh Come, Oh, the door's open," and Sister Anna resumes her normal role with the words, "Come, come, won't you come, He thinks so much of you."

NOTES

1. See explanation of "Oneness" and "trinitarian" in Chapter 1, Note 1.
2. Compare Rosenberg, *The Art of the American Folk Preacher,* and Davis, *I Got the Word*. See also Peck, "Your Daughters Shall Prophesy."
3. "Lines" here are recognized as the transcriber's need to render orally

performed words into printed ones. Again, refer to both Rosenberg and Davis for transcriptions of verbatim "performed" sermons.

4. Dell Hymes has explained how performers "break through" into a performance mode that is characterized by a distinctive stylistic presentation in his "Breakthrough into Performance."

5. Davis, pp. 67–74.

6. Cf. Hymes.

7. Cf. this disclaimer stance with both Rosenberg and Davis.

4

Sacrifice and Salvation: Themes in Women's Sermons

W hat *do* women preachers preach about? It seems that is the first question people ask me. Often, the second part of the question is, do they preach differently from men? In the preceding chapter I have discussed styles of women's preaching in varying contexts, and the structural frameworks of women's sermons. But legitimate questions remain. What are the moral and religious concerns of women preachers? Is it possible for us to generalize, to categorize the foci of their sermons? Is it a fair sort of inquiry to compare women's sermons with those of men? Although hard and fast rules about any of the characteristics of women's sermons or of females preaching should be avoided, certain characteristics do emerge as evident and important to our understanding of the phenomenon. In terms of the content—that is, what women preachers preach about—there are some recurrent themes and sub-themes that tend to appear in all women's sermons, to a greater or lesser degree, and which seem to reflect the concerns of women who are accustomed to passivity, submission, fear, and feelings of unworthiness and inadequacy.

Much of what the women preach about is, I believe, firmly entrenched in the same "maternal" imagery and female point of view that has been discussed earlier in the context of the woman preacher's role in the community and the tenuous position of the female in the pulpit. Carol Gilligan's thesis that women's perspective is much more inclined toward connection and community is reflected in the rhetoric of these women:[1] they are concerned for their own souls and those of their "people." Their upbringing, as women, in contemporary American society is mirrored in their approach to religion and salvation. While the themes of their sermons are identifiable, the lines between them are often fused. Also fused are style and content in the presentation of themes. It seems incongruous to me to isolate themes in sermons without placing these themes within the framework of their delivery. Therefore, in the following analyses, I will attempt to explore the favorite themes of the women preachers but will do so by illustrating how those themes have been presented to their audiences.

Most often, women preachers preach sermons that pivot around one of two identifiable themes, or a combination of the two. These are broadly:

1. The absolute necessity for one's total, absolute sacrifice to God and his wishes, and
2. The singular importance of repentence for salvation and a concern for "making it" into heaven

These two broad foci for sermon messages allow the women to explore several sub-themes that are directly related to the broader issues and that seem to hold a particular appeal for women in general. These include sub-themes related to #1 above:

- one's own lack of self-worth or importance and the need to be humble at all times
- the intricacy and infallibility of God's plan for our lives
- the need for us, as mere humans, to trust God's will, not our own
- to trust that God does have a plan and even when we cannot understand it to trust him to know what he is doing
- to know that if we totally "give up" ourselves to God and his plan, then Jesus will, in return, "walk by our side" and help us through our days

And related to #2 above:

- there is a clear plan of salvation outlined in the Bible
- salvation relies upon total submission to God and repentence of sin
- we must realize that we all do sin and need to be forgiven by God for those sins
- we have no power to save ourselves, only God can do that after we have submitted and repented
- no one else can save us, only our own repentence and submission will guarantee our individual salvation
- heaven is a real place and that this life must be endured in order to prepare ourselves for the next, much better one
- sacrifice, clean-living, and removal from "the world" are the best ways to insure our salvation and insulate us from the lure of the evil in the world
- Satan is very real and deals with us daily in his attempts to get us to sin and "join the world"

- hell is a very real place and people who go there literally burn for eternity without respite
- we can never be sure about our salvation and, in the end, we may, in fact, be left out of heaven

These themes and sub-themes might appear at first glance to cover all the possibilities for religious sermon-making, but of course they do not. In women's sermons, rarely are any of the sub-themes the major focus of a sermon. Most sermons clearly focus on one of the two major themes—sacrifice and salvation—and these topics appear to be religiously gender-specific.[2]

We can rely on information provided in the preceding chapter to begin our examination of content. Full sermon transcriptions are given in the Appendix.

Referring to Sister Anna's sermon (Appendix, pp. 171–88) we notice that Anna says she is preaching a sermon about *sin*. But this sermon is not going to focus just on the fact that sin is very real and that people do it all the time; actually Sister Anna is worried about making it into heaven. By line 76, the focus of the "message" is clear:

76 And God's word still speaks very plain
About SIN,
And as sure as the angel with the flaming sword
Throwed out Adam and Eve out of the garden because of their
      sin
80 There'll be no one that will be able
To enter the gates of heaven
With sin in their lives
Because God has not changed his mind
About sin.

The "message" of Sister Anna's sermon will be "getting into heaven" and how people with sin in their lives are not going to make it "in." The underlying message in this sermon is that belief in sin, belief in the Bible as the infallible, inspired word of God, belief in the "Christian walk," and belief in the reality of a heaven and a hell are "old-fashioned." Significantly, Sister Anna identifies herself with these "old-fashioned" beliefs; she states emphatically (ll. 189–91): "But I want you to know that I'm an old-fashioned preacher today, With the old-fashioned Word of God," She defines what being an "old-fashioned" preacher means to her:

247 Lots of preachers don't even preach any more
That there's going to be a rapture.
They don't even preach of the second coming of Jesus.

113

250 They might want you to believe
    That things are going to get better.
    But I tell you they'd better hurry up and start
    Because as the days come and go
    We see sin
255 Covering,
    And rampaging our nation
    Like never before.
    I almost feel like sometimes,
    Lord,
    I believe that all hell has broken loose
260 But it hasn't—
    But it keeps spewing out a little bit more
    As the days go by.

Importantly, nearly everything Sister Anna says is firmly couched in terms of "God's word." We recall that she cannot present these directives as her own, but she must indicate that she has derived them from the word of God, from the Bible. Thus, we hear her repeat:

7 And the Bible even says that we cannot
    Add to nor take from
    One inch of our stature.
    . . .
72 And God's word still declares that
    We're in a sinful and
    Adulterous
75 Generation.
    And God's word still speaks very plain
    About SIN
    . . .
133 And I declare to you today that
    God's word
135 Does not change.
    Maybe sin is an old-fashioned word,
    But so is the Bible an old-fashioned Bible.

The fundamentalist approach to individual salvation via confession and repentence might be termed "old-fashioned," too, but that is clearly at the heart of Sister Anna's sermon:

    You've got to have a mind-change.
210 You have to change your mind.
    You'll have to make up your mind first of all

114

I can't change
Myself.
I've got to have help.
215 And *then* you begin to look
To the source
Of your help.

This thread runs throughout her sermons and is related to the important sub-theme characteristic of women's sermons—"we are nothing" without God. We cannot change ourselves; we are powerless; God must change us; we must recognize his power to do that. Total submission is required for God to take over one's life. Sister Anna's opening lines are echoed in some of the final lines of her sermon as well and illustrate how she has come full circle in the course of her spontaneously delivered sermon:

632 We cannot change ourselves
But we can come to one
Who can change us.

Other sub-themes characteristic of women's sermons can be isolated in Sister Anna's sermons on nearly any occasion in which she preaches. In this particular sermon, because her theme is "making it into heaven," she can explore two of her favorite sub-themes: Satan is very real and hell is a very real place. She speaks often of Satan in her sermons and in her conversations. She has often encountered him in her house and has had to ward him off with persistence and belief in the power of God. She can describe what it feels like when he is in the room with her; she can both "feel" him and "see" him. In this sermon she speaks as a mother to her children, as a mother would speak to her older children addressing them with deference but with motherly concern:

Satan has no mercy on you, Sir.
Satan has no mercy upon you, young lady.
275 If he can get you to drink yourself to death until your body
Is so, uh,
Dilapidated,
If I can use that word,
Until your liver is consumed,
280 And your kidneys can no longer function right,
He'll laugh you into hell if he can do it,
If you'll let him.
If he can get you
To play with sin
285 Until you look like a haggard old person

> When you're in your twenties or thirties,
> He will dance with glee.
> He will laugh with glee.

Her descriptions of hell are "old-fashioned," too, and her sermon here becomes, surprisingly reminiscent of early "hell-fire and brimstone" preaching. At first, her references to hell are subtle and very general, enticing her audience to think about the possibility of hell as a very real place without actually threatening them:

294 Now, I know a lot of people today
   That don't believe in hell, either;
   That's an old-fashioned word.
   But there *is* a hell.
   It's a funny thing
   A lot of preachers don't preach on hell anymore,
300 But they can sure talk about heaven.
   But here's one that wants to tell you today
   Just as sure as there's a heaven
   There is a *hell*.
   Just as sure as God is preparing
305 A banquet table
   And a marriage supper of the lamb
   And mansions in heaven and all the refinery,
   He has had to create a hell
   For the devil
310 And all of the fallen angels
   And all of those
   Who reject
   The blood of Jesus Christ.
   Sin isn't going to make it into heaven
315 So there has to be a place
   For the sinner.

In this passage, Anna clearly identifies herself with a fundamentalist concept of religion;[3] she contrasts herself with preachers who are currently reluctant to preach about hell. She sees this as a mistake, to preach only about the joys of heaven—for, she says, first people must be made to realize that there is, indeed, a hell where people are going to burn for all eternity. When people realize this, she believes, then they will choose the other route. But preaching the joys of heaven, alone, is not enough, she says, to turn the lives of people around. She is, in fact, responding to what she perceives to be the current direction of religious focus: the religious life on earth and the anticipation of heaven. It is old-fashioned to preach "hell hot" as she puts it.

Interestingly, however, for all her rhetoric about preaching about hell, she actually turns now to a vision of heaven. It is a vision of heaven with an earthly perspective, however: she describes heaven as a scene of loved ones waiting anxiously to know that their children on earth will come to be with them. This is not a vision of streets of gold and mansions for everybody. In providing this image she appeals to the listeners' emotions and to their shared concept of family; this is a vision of a community in heaven.

> 351 All those people in heaven
>   There in the presence of angels and the presence of God
>   They rejoice.
>   I believe that a precious Mom and Dad
> 355 Who have prayed long and fervent
>   And hard
>   For unsaved children
>   I tell you I believe
>   Even though they went on home to their reward
> 360 And they didn't see those children saved,
>   I want to tell you something,
>   I believe when that one, that child,
>   Bows on their knees to God,
>   That that Mom and Dad
> 365 Rejoice in heaven.

These few lines embody much of the fundamentalist concept of the inter-related nature of heaven and earth. Persons unfamiliar with Christianity, especially fundamentalist Pentecostalism, may not realize just how personal a religion it is. Salvation is an individual matter and God woos each individual sinner into his circle of "saved ones." Conversion demands "taking Jesus Christ as your personal savior." God is perceived as all-knowing and all-caring. He knows the number of hairs on one's head; he even knows all our phone numbers, Sister Anna likes to say. He knows our every thought, he watches our every action, and he is surrounded in heaven by the angels and by all the dead loved ones who have already died. And they are all watching. There really is no concept of a vast universe out there; rather, the fundamentalist perceives of earth as the focus of God's attention and imagines an umbilical relation with an ethereal celestial sphere not really all that far away. It's up there and they are peering down.

In terms of immediate images important to Sister Anna and to her congregation, Moms, Dads, and children, the concept of family, the importance of the mother and the father loving the child and rejoicing in heaven when the "child" is saved—these are the images Sister Anna utilizes to contrast with her image of hell. Here she swells the emotions of her audience and they, thinking of their own Mothers and Dads already in heaven, openly weep in the service. But to make this reunion possible, Sister Anna believes she must graphically illustrate how horrible the alternative is. She reads Luke 16:24:

> 384 "And he cried and said "Father Abraham,
> Have mercy on me and send Lazarus,
> That he may dip the tip of his finger in water,
> And cool my tongue;
> For I am tormented in this flame."

She then tells the congregation that no matter how many years have gone by, that man is still being tormented in hell—and the message is: that man might be someone's son, someone's husband or father. And he'll never make it home. At the dramatic peak of her sermon, Sister Anna tells her people that she believes in hell because it's in God's word. She tells them hell is "thickly populated." She tells them that in hell "there is no rest, day or night, forever hence." And, for a moment, she puts them in hell, so they know what that might be like:

> 604 In hell is torment.
> In hell you will cry out
> For a drink of water,
> But there'll be none.
> There will be no relief
> From your torment.

In order to illustrate that the major themes and accompanying themes which I have suggested here do, in fact, operate consistently in women's sermons, I shall examine sermons delivered by some of the other women who have figured in this study.

One Sunday in 1984, Sister Mabel Adams preached two sermons in her tiny Church of God-Prophecy church in Hooperton, Missouri—one in the morning service and one in the evening. Sister Mabel does not preach full time, but most often preaches when her very busy, traveling husband is out of town. At these times, however, she is responsible for the church and does all the preaching. Her sermon in the morning service focused on how we must follow God's plan for our lives to the letter. She admonished her congregation to never "boast of yourselves, for by doing so you may provoke the anger of God and then he will cast you out!"

God has a plan and we *must* follow God's plan (not that of *ourselves!*). *We are nothing* without God.

48 You know, all along,
   God is wanting his people
50 To come out of captivity.
   All along life's road,
   God is wanting you and I
   To be free,
   To worship him in spirit and in truth.
55 And we find so often that, ah,
   When we look around and see so many things, ah,
   That people get into their minds, ah,
   They'd like to do this,
   They'd like to do that,
60 Even without asking God.
   That that is not always the plan of God
   For our lives.
   God knows what is best for us.
   And we know the story of how the children of Israel . . .
65 But Moses cried unto the Lord.
   And, you know, it's good to have someone
   That will cry out in our behalf.
   That is exactly what Jesus is to you and I . . .
   You know, ah,
70 When we look back on the children of Israel,
   How that they were just carried away from this, ah,
   And carried away from that, ah,
   And God met them in the wilderness, ah.
   There was nothing that God did not want them to have.
75 He wanted them to have the very best.
   And so he wanted them to go, ah,
   Over into the land, ah,
   Flowing with milk and honey.
   And so we find this morning, you know, ah,
80 So often it's in the hearts
   And in the minds
   Of men and of women
   To rebel against God.
   That's just human nature.
85 Sometimes we feel like—well, Lord—
   We don't say it, but we act it out.

We say it within ourselves-
—"Lord, I know what's best for me
Now, you just take your hands off
90 And I'll make my own way."

. . .

255 But are we still going towards heaven?
Are we still doing the things that God wants us to do?
Are we living in the place that we're, ah,
Being instruments in his hands,
That he can use us?
260 That he can bless us?
Are we going after the ways of Balaam?
Or are we going after the ways, ah,
That the children of Israel went?
Or are we going in our unbelief, ah?
265 Or are we trying to do the things that we want to do
Instead of staying in the plan of God?
And, folks, there's times that we *are*
268 Out of the plan of God.

. . .

287 And, so, therefore, we must always remember,
That if he didn't spare the natural branches,
That we have to be careful.
290 Because it just takes one time, ah,
Getting out of line with God, ah,
And he might become angry with us,
And might, ah,
Cast us aside!

. . .

329 But let me tell you folks, ah,
The very minute that we get out from under, ah,
The power of God,
And get out from under the things, ah,
That God wants for our life,
Get out from under the plan that God has for you and I,
335 Then we're in big trouble with God.
Why?
Because God takes his hand off, ah,
And then *Satan* can come in and use us.

. . .

371 And the only way, ah,
That we can make it into heaven, folks,

Is going by the way of God,
Going by the plan of God.
. . .
386 "And every one that has forsaken houses, or bretheren,
Or sisters, or father, or mother, or wife, or children, or land
For my name's sake,
Shall receive an hundredfold,
390 And shall inherit everlasting life."
Now, folks, that's what we need to be working towards
This morning.
We have to give up everything.
We have to be willing to give up everything,
395 That we might gain life everlasting,
Gain the inheritance set before us.
If we want an inheritance from God,
If we want a place in the kingdom of God,
If we want righteousness,
400 If we want to live peaceable in this life,
Then we have to give up all these things.
. . .
408 And you know over in Jude,
It tells us in the first chapter
How that God wants us to look to him,
And to be worthy of all that he has done for us.
. . .
518 And so, folks, this morning,
This is not a bed of roses.
520 It's not a one-way street.
There's many things today that you and I have to give up.
There's many things we have to quit doing,
There's many things we have to leave off,
To serve the Lord.

This is not a full transcription of Sister Mabel's morning sermon. However, enough has been included to illustrate several characteristics of her preaching style, as well as point to her theme(s). During the course of the sermon she told several long narratives, all based on Biblical stories. She utilized these narratives as *exempla*—or illustrative narratives used in a sermon to make a point or draw a moral.[4] Approximately thirty lines into the sermon, she uses a transition that gets her into the story of the journey of the children of Israel, the beginning line of her first *exemplum* and one which she utilizes as the general frame of the sermon, returning to it several times: "And we all know the story of how the children of Israel . . ." She preaches about the children of Israel and how they failed to recognize all that God was doing for them. God told Moses—"I want you to go and lead my children out of Egypt, out of bondage." Appropriately, the *exemplum* ends with a moralization or a point made by the preacher in reference to the illustration: "You know, all along God is wanting his people to come out of captivity."

The rest of this portion is given verbatim above. At length, Sister Mabel tells her own version of the story of the children of Israel, complete with dialogue and her own interpretation of their actions and the consequences of their actions, and several times as she preaches she leaves the "frame" of the *exemplum* to exhort her own congregation not to do as the children of Israel had done, which is the identifying characteristic of the story: "And so often we find this morning we do like the children of Israel" or "And so this morning we ought not to boast about the things we have accomplished" or "And so often we, too, get ourselves into trouble." It is important to note that Sister Mabel's mode of transition from the narrative example back to the immediacy of her congregation is often to say "And, you know, this morning . . . ," for both the familiar "you know" and the time referent "this morning" serve to move her words into the context of the present situation. Similarly, she often uses the familiar address form "Now, folks . . ." when addressing her congregation. When she tells her audience they will "get into trouble with God" if they do not follow His plan, she plunges into another narrative.

218 You know, when old Balaam started out, you know,
His dumb ass knew more than he did because, ah,
220 The donkey along the way, ah,
He could see an angel with a flaming sword,
Standing there in front of them,
And he wouldn't dare move because he knew
That it was the angel of the Lord.
225 And old Balaam he got so determined that he, ah,
Was going his own way,
Until he began, ah,
Began to beat the mule.
And the mule turned around and
230 Began to speak to him, he said—
"Why are you beating me?"
Said, "I am the beast, ah,
Who has carried you many a mile,
So why are you beating me?"

235 Then God opened, ah,
   Balaam's eyes and he looked
   And he seen the angel standing there.
   But before he did he got into trouble,
   Didn't he?
240 He got his foot smashed against the wall.
   And so often we get ourselves
   Smashed up against the wall
   Because of our disobedience,
   Because we get unruly,
245 Because we'd rather go in our own way, ah,
   Than go in God's way.

This story, as does the one about the children of Israel, illustrates disobedience and the consequences of disobedience. Sister Mabel uses the
narrative to make her point: "So often we get ourselves smashed up against
the wall because we'd rather go in our own way than go in God's way."
One hundred lines later, she illustrates her point with yet another story,
this time one about Paul—actually about Saul before he became Paul. Her
transition into this story is particularly smooth and relates this narrative
with the other one:

452 And, you know, in the very beginning
   God created them
   To be his chosen people [referring to the children of Israel].
455 And he came to them and they received him not.
   And therefore he turned to the gentile,
   And Paul was the first to go to the gentile.
   He was a preacher to the gentiles.

But she goes back in time, then, to tell the story of the blinding of Saul
on the road to Damascus as he set out to persecute the Christians. And
she describes, complete with her own dialogue, how Ananias was sent to
heal Saul's eyes and tell him God's plan. According to Sister Mabel, "God
told Ananias, he said—Paul, I'm going to use and I'm going to show him
the things that he's going to have to suffer for my sake." And the moral:

518 And so, folks, this morning,
   This is not a bed of roses.
520 It's not a one-way street.
   There's many things today that you and I have to give up.
   There's many things that we have to quit doing,
   There's many things that we have to leave off,
   To serve the Lord.

Without ever using the word "sacrifice", I think one could argue that this sermon really is a sermon about total sacrifice—total sacrifice of oneself to God through complete obedience. Sister Mabel tells her congregation that they must be willing to obey God's plan and not their own—hers is a message of passive submission. She admonishes them to not boast for their own accomplishments for that is sure to provoke the wrath of God—and the ultimate consequence of disobeying God's plan and inciting his anger is to not make it into heaven. Sister Mabel perceives herself—and others—as "children" of a threatening and powerful "Father."

Embedded here is the message that life on this earth is not a particularly pleasant one; even compliance with "God's plan" does not guarantee a "bed of roses" she says. The passive obedience outlined here strikes me as a female stance "appropriate" for women in this context; there is not much explanation, no real rationalization for this total submission to "God's plan" and the total denial of one's own capabilities and accomplishments, yet complete compliance is expected, even demanded. The only explanation given is that disobedience is bound to provoke the wrath of God and result in the loss of one's place in heaven. We shall see how this "theme" is duplicated in other sermons.

Interestingly, the evening sermon delivered by Sister Mabel on that same day begins with a focus on the sub-theme "Jesus sticketh closer than a brother," and, yet, in many ways this sermon convolutes back to the same themes as her morning sermon. Again in this sermon she presents her theme and then illustrates it with several stories, largely from the Bible. We can see certain characteristics of her sermon style and her message focus early in the sermon:

87 And you say, well, how do we know?
Does God really care for us?
Does he really care?
How can we tell if he cares?
. . .
Now, he didn't say that we, ah,
Were going to have a bed of roses
All the time, ah.
He didn't say that we were going, ah,
115 Through this life, ah,
Easy when we give our hearts to him.
He didn't say that we weren't going to be left alone,
That Satan wasn't going to come in, ah,
Every dark day that he could,
120 And do everything that he could against us.

124

He didn't say, ah,
That we were going to have an easy route.
But he did say that he would make a way of escape
Where there ought to be one
125 And, you know, folks, every day
That God looks at us
And he sees that we're, ah,
About to make a misstep
He will nudge us and say—
130 "Not that way, child,
There's a better way"

Sister Mabel illustrates her point with several elaborate Biblical narrative examples, but the underlying question appears in the first lines and is repeated throughout: "you ask, how do we *know* that God cares?" And her concluding "moral" is: "just like God took care of Daniel and the three Hebrew boys in the fiery furnace, he will take care of us." She tells us again that this life is not going to be a "bed of roses" and that in order for God/Jesus to be pleased with us "at the end of this race" then we have to "take the trials and the tests along with the goodness." The picture of life on this earth painted by this woman is duplicated by other women preachers—life is tough, often unpleasant, full of trials and tribulations. And Satan is an ever-present, living, identifiable force who lurks around every corner awaiting moments of weakness, ready to pounce.

Not long after I heard Sister Mabel preach, I heard Pat Roberts, from Centerville, Missouri, preach a sermon on sacrifice. (This sermon is included in the Appendix, pp. 205–22.). On a hot, muggy July Sunday, Sister Pat preached to her home congregation about being a "living sacrifice". She, too, chose to illustrate her theme with the Biblical story of the children of Israel.

4 God is very plain
To make mention of what kind of *sacrifice*
That he wanted the children of Israel to offer unto him.

. . .

15 We think we got it hard today
In the way God's got a sacrifice
Set up for you and I today
So many people think that's hard
I can't do it.
20 Even the sacrifice of coming out to a service sometimes
It's hard for people.
But it's not hard.

It's not hard what God's got set up for us today!
Just as smooth as can be.
25 You know he don't ask for much,

. . .

79 So, the sacrifice was
That God had for the children of Israel—
He said, "Hey!
You go out
And begin to bring forth of your herd
Or of your flock
85 Unto me."
And the sacrifice is on the altar—
They was to sacrifice animals.
That's the ordinance that God had in those days
For a sacrifice.
90 He said, "Hey!
I want nothing but the best of what you've got!"
And you see it *was* something of a sacrifice.
And he said, "Hey!
I don't want something that's maimed or nasty out there!"
95 He said, "Hey!
I don't want you to go out there
And pick out a little old RUNT
Because you know that thing's gonna die anyway
Bring it in here and put it on the altar to sacrifice to me today!
100 Hey!
I want you to show me that you LOVE ME
WITH THE BEST OF WHAT YOU HAVE!"
And that's what they did in those days
Was go out there amongst the herd
105 And, "Hey!
Pick out the best
That you've got."
And, you know, it was sort of like God said,
"Hey!
110 I'm gonna see if you really love me
As much as you let on."
Like a lot of people say,
"Hey, God, I love you.
Hello, I love you!"
115 But you know they don't love him enough
To live for him like they should

And they don't love him enough
To be for him what they really should be,
Or they wouldn't live their lives
120 Like they live.

. . .

276 Now we get on down to the good part—
The sacrifice for you and I today.

. . .

362 How do we sacrifice
Unto our Lord?
We don't go out
365 To our herds.
We don't go out
And check the flock
And bring in
A sheep
370 Without blemish.
No!
We don't do that.
Jesus done did that.
But he says, "Hey!
375 I've got an ordinance I want you to do!
I've got a sacrifice I want you to do for me."

. . .

393 You know the only thing
The only thing I've got tonight?
You know the *only* thing I've got to give?

. . .

420 You know the only thing I've got tonight
Is *ME!*
Myself!
WHEN IT'S ALL BROUGHT DOWN TO IT
YOU MAY THINK THAT YOU'VE GOT A LOT
    TONIGHT
425 BUT THE ONLY THING THAT'S *YOURS*
THAT YOU HAVE CONTROL OVER
IS *YOURSELF!*
AND I BELIEVE THAT'S WHY THE LORD SAYS, "HEY!
You must present your body
430 A living sacrifice."
Amen?
Me.

This is something I can give tonight.
I won't have to go over and ask permission
435 Of my husband.
I don't have to ask permission
Of my children
Or my mother-in-law—
Thank the Lord I don't have to ask her.

. . .

But you see
445 I've got myself.
And, you know the Lord knew that.

. . .

472 But the Lord said, "Hey!
I want a sacrifice without blemish.
I made it plain that I want to see
475 If they truly love me!"
So he said, "Hey!
Jesus was a sacrifice for you."

. . .

489 Now!
The Lord says, "Hey!
You love me?
What do you give
As sacrifice?"
I believe the Lord says, "Hey!
495 You—A-Number One You—
The only thing you've got
Is yourself!"
Amen?

. . .

616 You reach down to pick a rose
And you're gonna get a thorn if you're not real careful.
Amen?
But you know what?
620 I find myself picking those
Rose bouquets anyway.
Amen?

. . .

630 Sometimes that seems hard, you know,
Somebody's swiped the rug out from under you.

. . .

You know maybe Satan's having him a hey-day today

650 The Bible says that he is the God of this world.
But I want you to know that MY GOD
REIGNS SUPREME.
. . .
679 We know what God wants—
Our *lives*,
Amen!
A-Number One—Ourself.
God knows ourselves,
That's why he said, "Present your bodies."
685 I believe that's an A-Number One *sacrifice*!
Cause really that's all we've got!
That's all I've got!
All any one of us has got,
Amen?

This woman's preaching style, her "Hey! God wants you—A-Number
One You!" is remarkably different from Sister Mabel's "Now, folks, God
has a plan." Yet, there is much in these two sermons that is similar. Sister
Pat, too, talks about God's plan. She tells us that "God has a sacrifice for
you and I today" and her message is closely aligned with Sister Mabel's:
we must obey God's orders. For Sister Pat, our sacrifice must be ourselves—we must present ourselves to God as a "living sacrifice". This has
to be the same kind of passive submission that Sister Mabel insists upon.
In fact, in light of some of Sister Pat's *exempla* utilized in this sermon, the
analogy of presenting ourselves as a "living sacrifice" is quite gruesome.
When she says she is thankful that God no longer requires the sacrifice of
animals she illustrates it in the following manner:

I'm glad that God changed it
Because I'd never be able to—
280 I don't think I'd want anyway—
I couldn't do it—
It's hard for me to envision
It'd be hard for me to go out and kill those animals
And bring them in.
285 I can remember when my mom and dad
Used to butcher chicken, ah.
You know, I'd run away just as far as I could go.
You know, wrung them heads off, ah,
And them chickens would hop around,
290 You know, without any heads on, ah,
Just literally scare me to death.

> And I'm glad that I'm living in today
> My sacrifice is a lot easier than what they had in
>   the days of the Old Testament.

The sacrifice she says is required of her (and everyone) is that they be, in this life, on this earth, a "living sacrifice" to God. Like Sister Mabel, she does not think of life on this earth as particularly pleasant; in fact, she, too, likens it to a rose and points out that if you try to pick the beautiful rose, it is likely to prick your finger. She sees life as tough, like "somebody swiped the rug out from under you." She says her own body is the only thing she has any "control over." How telling it is that in this single arena where she feels she has power, she is required to give this over to God as a "living sacrifice." However, this passive submission theme is often interpreted as a means to gaining "freedom" and we need to try to understand how it is interpreted in that way. I recall a young woman's testimony from a service in Indiana that is repeated almost verbatim in Sister Mabel's sermon. The young woman said:

> I am free—I am free from everything that goes on in college. I am free from all the temptations of the discos and the boyfriends and all that stuff. I am free. I'm going to be graduated in December. I am free of the fear of going out into the business world because I know that Jesus is with me. He gave me the right to say it, but you have to let him. You have to let him make you free. You have to give him your life and you have to live for him every day, every hour, every minute. He loves me and he's made me free. And I'm so happy, and I just want to praise him for it.
>
> (*Patsy Hope, Bloomington, Indiana*)

Similarly, Sister Mabel says:

> 1 Do you know God is just as close to us
>   As we let him be?
>   He's just as close as we let him be.
>   . . .
> 8 But you know I learned a long time ago
>   That I needed him every day,
>   Every minute of the day
>   And in everything that I did
>   I needed his help and his guidance.

The equation of "passive submission equals freedom" is one I am proposing as peculiar to women. If we recall from an earlier chapter an examination of why young women would, in fact, want to become ministers, one of the suggestions was that complete submission to God does, in fact, bring with it a kind of "freedom" from the pressures of the rest of the world. Women preachers who insist that God has called them to be preachers can "use" that argument to provide for themselves a modicum of freedom even from the expectations of their husbands and their children. Likewise, Sister Pat announces that in giving herself *totally* to God she is, in a way, defying the hold that her husband, children, and mother-in-law may feel they have on her. It seems an act of defiance to say "my body is my own, and I am going to give it ALL to God! And I don't have to ask permission!" That she associates this defiant act to her position as preacher is illustrated by the following lines near the end of her sermon:

> 637 Can you do it tonight?
> Can we do what God want us to do?
> It's not hard
> 640 And it's the most rewarding work.
> YOU WANT TO KNOW WHAT I THINK OF BEING A
>   MINISTER TONIGHT?
> It's the most rewarding thing there is—
> Is to think that you stand pleasing
> Before God
> 645 The Almighty
> The one that reigns supreme
> Over the world.

She has managed, here, to turn her sermon in her own favor, to use the theme of this sermon to support her own position behind the pulpit: she has given her all to God; he required of her to be a minister and she has obeyed. Her "total submission" to his will has given her the freedom to do what she wants to do—that is, stand behind the pulpit and preach to the people. To deny God's directives is to place oneself at the mercy of Satan, whom she calls the "God of this world."

Sister Pat's message may at first seem to isolate the individual, extracting persons from their familial and community bonds; yet the *exempla* she employs in her sermon, in contrast to Sister Mabel's which are all Biblical, are largely from her personal experiences (other than the important frame of the children of Israel story, which is itself a "family" story). They serve to align her closely with her family; otherwise, her message might appear too strong. This woman often refers to her congregation as her "babes in Christ" and, although she is only 42 years old, she speaks endearingly of her grandchildren as her "grandbabies." She begins one personal anecdote, "And I thought about my little old granddaughter, you know, this morning . . . " Later in this sermon she illustrates what it is like to cull out certain cattle from the herd with an anecdote about her own father.

> 188 My daddy raised black angus cattle
>   And I'm telling you!
> 190 Oh, they were mean
>   But I want you to know, ah, when he began to corral those bulls
>   To ship them off to market
>   When he began to sell off maybe those heifers, ah,
>   It took TIME for him to go out there and sort them off
> 195 From the herd.

In this case, then, the *exempla* serve to emphasize connection and community in this world, while her message focuses on connection with/to the next world. Salvation demands individual commitment, and total sacrifice to God will result in eventual re-communing with family in heaven.

This notion of heaven as the embodiment of eternal family and connection is a central theme in women's sermons. As illustrated above and earlier in this work, Sister Anna's sermons are always filled with the imagery of heaven as a place full of old friends and family members, all blissfully communing with God and the angels. Sister Anna herself has long had a dread and fear of possibly *not* being included in this picture—of being alienated, left outside the door. One of her favorite oral stories appears as well in her hand-written autobiography:

> How well I remember sitting through Sunday School in the Card Class, swinging my little legs that were too short to reach the floor. Our church was the School House and we didn't have fancy pews, but the children sat at the school desks too and we knew to be quiet; no matter how long the sermon was and some could be very long in those days. I wasn't school age but I still remember some of those old time sermons that made me weep for fear I'd be left behind. They preached hell hot and I remember they sang a song about "Standing outside the portal, standing outside the door, oh! What an awful picture, standing outside." I would cry because I sure did not want to be left behind when Jesus comes. Thank God for the teaching I had as a little child. Those early impressions etched so deeply in my young mind has helped me and kept me in the straight and narrow way . . .

Quite astonishingly, the sermon Sister Anna preached on July 1, 1984, in her home church, began with references to the children of Israel and how they had backslidden, gone away from God—astonishing because

the two women preachers described above also used the story of the
children of Israel as the "frame" for their sermons. Without any hesitation
or doubt, I can state that I know that none of these women have heard
each other preach, at least in all the time I have known each of them. Like
the other preachers, Sister Anna is concerned with the actions of the
children of Israel and the possible analogues to her own people:

95 And they forsook the word of God their Father
Which brought them out of the land
Of Egypt,
And followed other Gods
And the Gods of other people
100 That were round about them,
And vowed themselves unto them
And provoked
The Lord
To anger.

Patterns do emerge. The dreaded fear of provoking a God of anger through
disobedience emerges in Sister Anna's sermon. She talks about how the
children of Israel did not stand together for God, and illustrates the point
with a story about World War II Danes who aligned themselves with the
Jews by wearing yellow arm bands and frustrating the Nazis who were
trying to identify only the Jews. Her story is one of connection and
community, help and alliance.

And you know what happened?
150 The Danes put on the yellow arm band, too.
They said—we will be identified with them.
They suffer, we suffer, too.
Oh, people, I remember when that happened,
And I think, God,
155 Are we,
As Christian gentiles,
Willing to be identified with God's chosen race,
The Jews?
I know it's not a popular thing to say
160 I know that I'm living in a day and time when
It could really go hard
But you are going to have to learn, people,
To stand
To stand and let people know
165 "I'm on God's side."

For Sister Anna, the "rules and regulations" that God laid down for the Jews still hold, and God's wrath will be just as great today as it was then. Her message is clearly in line with those of the other women preachers: if you invoke the wrath of God, you may forfeit your right to heaven.

245 God laid down certain rules and regulations.
 You will do thus and so
 And you will not do the other,
 Or *else* you will invoke
 My curse upon you.
250 I will bless your coming in and your going out,
 If you keep my commandments.
 I'll make you the head of the kingdom,
 If you keep my commandments.
 And on and on he gave his blessing.
255 But if you *don't*,
 The curse will be upon you.
 It has always been that way,
 And it will always be that way until *God*
 Gives . . . his call
 . . .
281 There will be those before the throne of God
 Who are crying,
283 But there's no free rides to heaven,
 Friends.
 I say there's no free ride to heaven.
 There will be no hitchhikers in heaven.
 You're not going to hitchhike
 A ride.
 And listen,
290 If you grab Mom or Dad or Grandma's coattail
 And think you'll hide
 And sneak in that door,
 I've got news for you.
 Everyone's going to pass
295 The guard
 One by one.
 One by one, friends, that's right!
 And if you don't have,
 Hallelujah,
300 The evidence of the blood of Jesus Christ
 On your ticket,

134

You'll be *turned away!*
There'll be no—
There's no back door to heaven,
305 There's no back door, there's just
One door
You'll not sneak in the back way.
We're living in such a permissive society today
That just about anything you think of
310 The devil can make it seem right
In your own eyes.

. . .

346 It is wonderful, I'll tell you,
To have brothers and sisters in the Lord
Who will stand before God.
But I want to tell you something,
350 Brother and Sister,
You need to know how to pray yourself,
You need to know how to get through the gate
To the very throne of the living God,
To make your position known unto him.
355 That's what I'm to do—
My business is to tell you . . .

Sister Anna's God is, in many ways, the God of the Old Testament—a
wrathful, vengeful, jealous God. Certainly, she preaches Jesus as a daily
friend, but the thrust of her rhetoric, the fervor in her preaching comes
from her fear of this potentially angry God.

He's the same God today
475 I serve the same God
That can still the storm
That rolled the waters back of the Red Sea
I serve the same God
That locked the jaws of the lion that protected Daniel
480 I serve the same God
That went into that fiery furnace with the Hebrew children.
People, I serve that God
This morning—

. . .

560 God's a jealous God
And he will not share his sovereignty with anything
And the Jews didn't get by either
And the gentiles won't get by either

And the nation of Israel didn't get by
565 And America won't get by
I'll tell you what
We're headed for the judgement of God
I said we're headed
569 For the judgement of God.

. . .

621 If you're here this morning
And you've rebeled against God
In *any* way—
I remember the song
625 That used to make me tremble
In the old school.
We'd sing it,
When we'd come to church.
And everytime they'd sing it as a little girl,
630 I'd tremble.
And I made up my mind then and there,
No, I'm not going to be left standing outside.
And that was the song,
"Left standing outside,
635 Almost persuaded,
Almost made it,
Even up to the door,
Left standing outside."

Sister Anna's sermons are rich in imagery that describe both heaven and hell. She calls herself an "old-fashioned" preacher because she "preaches hell hot." Over and over in her sermons, we find a concern that she (and her "people") will be "left standing outside." Her message is clearly that we (she) must obey God's will, follow God's plan, submit one's life to him. For she, like other women preachers, tells her congregation "we can do nothing to change ourselves; we must look to God to change us." We can trace these same themes and elements in the sermons of the other women preachers described here. Just how pervasive is this approach to religion from the pulpits of women preachers? And can we characterize this religious worldview as particularly female? Allow me to describe yet another sermon by a woman preacher. Virginia Richards is a co-pastor in a rather large Pentecostal Assembly in Indiana. In the sermon I have chosen to explicate, she begins her sermon in a very pleading manner, telling the congregation that "we're not home yet. The door is still open and you're *not in yet*." This image of the "door" to heaven is reminiscent of Sister Anna's concern. Many, many women preachers focus on this image of the door to heaven, open for a time but eventually to close, never to be opened again.

Sister Virginia's message hinges solidly on the same kind of feelings of inadequacy that characterize other women's sermons. She focuses on two words, she says, that she cannot stop thinking about. She is obsessed with the fact that she might stand before God at the gates of heaven, in front of everyone, of course, and be "found wanting," that is, found to be "lacking" in her spiritual demeanor. Of course, the punishment for being "found wanting" is rejection by God. And the God she envisions is not a particularly understanding God.

150 [Reads scripture]"... God hath numbered thy kingdom
    And finished it. Thou art weighed in the balances
    And art found wanting."
    When I awakened early this morning, very early
    This was going over and over and over and over in my heart
155 "Found wanting" "found wanting" "found wanting"
    And the words "found wanting"—
    The word "wanting" means to be lacking.
    . . .
188 OHHHHHHH, Beloved, let me tell you
    It will pain you to ever come before God
190 And be found wanting.
    . . .
205 You will never have any excuses
    When you stand before God Almighty
    . . .
211 When he calls your name
    You won't have a barrel of excuses
    You won't have a hundred things to say about it
    You'll stand before God
    Naked
    . . .
222 If you're going to hear him say well done,
    If you're coming in with the church,
    You must be borned again ...
    . . .
240 You say you're going to heaven without it?
    I'll tell you God said you *won't* without it.
    I'm not going without the borned again spirit.
    You're not going without it.

But the door is open
245 ———right now, yesssssss———
The door is open

This "old-fashioned" view of a vengeful God, a jealous and angry God, is repeated over and over in these women's sermons. Those who sin [i.e., disobey God] are not going to make it into the gates of heaven but will be left "standing outside." Recall these lines from Sister Linda's sermon (Appendix, pp. 190–91, 196):

97 Now you stop and think about it tonight, ah,
Glory to God, ah,
ETERNITY is for *ever* and *ever* and *ever*, ah,
100 And now we're talking about heaven in eternity
But I want to *tell* you something
There's another eternity, tonight, ah,
. . .
There's going to be another eternity
110 Praise the lamb of God!
There's a heaven and a hell tonight,
. . .
124 You got heaven on one side to gain
Or hell on the other,
And it's your choice!
. . .
Just like God told Noah to build the ark
315 And the people laughed
But when GOD shut the doors on the ark
It was over.
It was over,
And they couldn't believe it.
320 Tonight Jesus Christ is our ark.
Glory to God!
He's a crying out to people.
He's a standing before with arms outstretched
Wanting them to accept him.
325 Glory to God
But I'm going to tell you something
It's not always going to be that way.
One of these days—
One of these days
330 It's all going to be over.
No more Jesus.

138

No more time.
All the time's *all* going to be gone.
You're not going to have a chance
335 To come face-to-face with him
And give your life to him.
You know why?
Cause the day for judgement's coming
And just like the ark in Noah's day
340 The door's going to be shut
And it's going to be all over
Praise the lamb of God
It's going to be over!
Praise the Lord.
345 And I know the devil's telling you,
"Ah, you've got plenty of time!"
But you don't have plenty of time
You don't have plenty of time.
Glory to God.

Implicit here in these lines from a woman preaching 400 miles away come the very same themes and images. Her sermon is a message of "get in before it's too late." Her God is a God of judgement, sitting on his throne ready to reject those who have not repented of their sins. Those who have not made it "right with God" will be banished to an eternity in a burning hell. And, like all the other women, she relies on the image of the door— the door that is open right now, but which, when shut by God, will never open again.

Most of the women who preached these sermons became quite emotional before their sermon was completed. Their fears are genuine, heartfelt, the urgency they preach is an urgency they truly believe. Their fear is for their own salvation; without a doubt Sister Anna has a dreadful fear of being left "standing outside" the door when it is shut. No matter how "good" she is in this life, she, nevertheless, retains a subliminal fear that at the final moments they may shut the door and she will not get in. But their tears are also for their congregation. They believe this message that time is running out and they are sincerely worried for their fellow men and women. The truly happy image they have of heaven is one big happy family, a major reunion of friends and family members who have gone on before. Their concern is to get as many of these wayward "children" saved before it is "too late."

At this point it seems useful to compare women's sermons with those of male preachers. Although I have heard hundreds of men preach sermons,

139

both in my youth and during my fieldwork, I have tape recorded very few, for that has not been my focus. Of course, that has not been the focus, either, for very many other scholars. But a few folklorists have been studying the sermons of male preachers and I turn now to their published transcriptions for a minor excursion into comparison.

Unfortunately for this comparison, most published sermons come from the Afro-American tradition and may, for cultural reasons, pose problems in comparison of themes according to the sex of the performer. For example, Gerald Davis in *I Got the Word in Me and I Can Sing It, You Know,* talks at length about the "weighted secular" factor that he identifies in African-American [male] sermons and makes the point: "the African-American preacher's principal mission is to speak to the contemporary needs of his congregation."[5] Preachers "bend the churchly sermonic form to an expressly political end, the spiritual and physical liberation of African-Americans."[6] With this as our foundation, can we then, successfully compare the sermons of the African-American male preachers studied by Davis with the sermons by Anglo women in the Midwest? Perhaps it is a futile and nonproductive kind of comparison, but it may be telling that in approximately fifty pages of transcribed sermons, not one of Davis's preachers preached the kind of eschatological sermon characteristic of these women preachers.

What *do* African-American preachers preach? One preached about not being "ready" to accept the help that God stands ready to provide. This preacher tells his congregation—"The fault is not in the Lord, You're just not ready ... " And Davis's "weighted secular" factor seems clearly evident in this sermon. He talks about all the furniture, the cars, the down payments, the vacation clothes that people cannot pay for and have to have their paychecks garnisheed to cover. The preacher pleads with his congregation to just give up the worry about all of these things (not the things themselves) to God. Another of Davis's preachers preaches a sermon that admonishes the congregation to trust Jesus to make their life a better one. He preaches a world torn with people "laboring night and day, can't rest and sleep, troubled and confused and perplexed, torn, aggravated and agitated, filled with anger and hate, lust and pride and greed, haughtiness and covetousness, doubts and fears." He preaches:

76 Oh, everybody tonight who calls himself a Christian
    Dedicate your lives to God
    Man we'll have this thing cleaned up
    Before twenty-four hours
    . . .
151 As old Jesus say

"If you love Me, keep My word"
If you love Me and don't keep your word, I say
    you're a liar and the truth's not in you
My God, if God done turn this world over
155 Every man in here done hypocrite if you don't
    think with God
You done fooled around and lost out with God
And now God done turned the whole thing over
    to fakes and phonies
Nobody can't believe nothing hardly nobody
    says
Everybody's a front and a put-on and a put-up
160 A make-up and a make-out
White-washed and not washed white
Glory to God
And nobody have no confidence in nobody[7]

These preachers are preaching life on this earth. They are preaching that life on this earth can be a richer and better life with belief in God and Jesus. Life here can be easier if you trust in Jesus and leave things to God rather than trying to handle them yourselves. Life's confusing and heart-breaking, and you're a fool if you don't "think with God." In not one sermon by these men can I find a reference to "making it into heaven." This preacher calls men liars and hypocrites: "you done fooled around and lost out with God . . ." While that might be perturbing—"done lost out with God"—it, nevertheless, seems more analogous to "you're foolish" than the fear inherent in the women's message that disobedience will cause the door of heaven to shut for eternity. None of these preachers claims to "be nothing" or to be "worthless" without God; if fact, if anything, given the important socio-cultural task of the African-American preacher, it would be counterproductive for him to preach the kind of passive subservience that is in evidence in the women's sermons. The political message Davis refers to which must strive for the "spiritual and physical liberation of African-Americans" will not be served by declaring the con-gregation to be "worth nothing." Likewise, the messages of complete obedience, total self-sacrifice, passive rejection of one's abilities, and the image of a vengeful, wrathful, and angry God simply would not function to serve the needs of the African-American community.

   In contrast at least to African-American male sermons, the women's sermons considered here can be characterized to a very large extent as being concerned with making it into heaven. With this as a major focus, their messages deal primarily with life on this earth in terms of: complete

141

obedience to God's will and God's plan for their lives; total sacrifice of their being while on this earth and complete passive rejection of their own intrinsic worth and capabilities—all with a view of the possibility of being rejected in the end. Their religious worldview includes an omnipotent, vengeful, wrathful God who will become angry at disobedience and who will "cast you out" if provoked. This God must be approached on his terms and at the appropriate moments; he is quite capable of rejecting late pleas for help. These women consistently preach what they recognize as an "old-fashioned" message complete with hell-fire and brimstone. They preach the devil as a "real being" who lurks around every corner, ready to tempt them and tell them they need not be so careful. And they preach about making it into heaven; they preach about approaching the terrifying judgement at "heaven's gates." They preach about guards at those gates and about standing before God's throne to be judged; they fear they will fail the test; they fear they will be left "standing outside."

Women raised in fundamentalist American religions are acutely aware of the equation of "man's fall" with Eve's transgression in the Garden of Eden. They are fully aware that most men in these religions blame Eve for the banishment from the Garden and equate their own life's tribulations, especially those concerned with birthing children, as punishment for "woman's" sin. They blame Eve, too, and basically, it seems, they cannot rid themselves of their eternal state of transgression. They feel worthless, inept, full of sin, and, no matter what kind of life they have led, they are certainly not convinced of their own salvation. They appear to be obsessed with the notion that they will be "found wanting" and a wrathful God, still angry at Eve, will be provoked and cast them out. This patriarchial Supreme Being emerges from their sermons as a definitive "Father" figure; the women are children. They are afraid and it shows. Perhaps they became preachers to save their own souls. Perhaps that seemed, to them, to be the very closest they could walk with God. To serve him constantly might just offer a modicum of assurance for an entrance into "the door."

NOTES

1. See Carol Gilligan, *In a Different Voice* especially pp. 24–63.

2. Compare these themes with those isolated by Davis, *I Got the Word in Me*; Rosenberg, *The Art of the American Folk Preacher*; and Peck, "Your Daughters Shall Prophesy".

3. For a current, readable look at contemporary fundamentalism in America, see Carol Flake's *Redemptorama*; see also James Davison Hunter, *Evangelicalism: The Coming Generation*.

4. For an historical account of *exempla* see Elaine J. Lawless, "Narrative in the Pulpit: Persistent Use of *Exempla* in Vernacular Religious Contexts."

5. Davis, p. 62.

6. Davis, p. 63.

7. Davis, pp. 123–26.

5

Reproductive Images and the Maternal Strategy of the Woman Preacher

In her introduction to the volume *Women in American Religion*, Janet Wilson James begins: "An exploration of women's part in the history of religion soon encounters two constants: women usually outnumber men; men exercise the authority."[1] James goes on to point out, however, that the "shock waves of the sixties" have weakened the "familiar authority structures" and women are flooding the religious scene and searching out the "liberating promises of scripture to revise theologies," contending for the "right to be ordained and to exercise sacerdotal authority."[2] Importantly, the present study of women preachers in the Pentecostal faith does not illustrate how women have weakened authority structures or sought the "liberating promises of scripture to revise theologies." The significant number of women preachers and, especially, women pastors that I have located and interviewed, followed around, and come to know within a rather small geographical area in central Missouri (and which could, I am certain, be replicated in nearly any similar area in the Upland South) belies the contention that men always exercise the authority, but ironically, in no way represents a large number of women striving for "liberating promises" or supporting efforts toward a "new theology" or a "new ethics." Oddly, even in the face of their obvious heresy, it is the strong connection these women maintain with a conservative fundamentalism that enables them to acquire the position of power and authority in a church *as* pastor and provides the means for them to maintain that position. The maternal and reproductive images they employ as religious strategies serve to strip their presence behind the pulpit of its most threatening aspects.

Firmly entrenched in Pentecostalism is the tension between the God-given inferiority of women submissive to men and the belief in individual

145

equality before God. The traditional Christian belief in the inferiority of women is based on the story of Eve's submission to the wiles of the devil in the garden of Eden and her seduction of Adam to join in her disobedience of God's orders. Paul's directives to the Christian church have remained the clear directives of God, stemming from "the fall:" "Let your women keep silence in the church: for it is not permitted for them to speak: but they ought to be subject, as also the Law saith. And if they will learn any thing, let them ask their husbands at home: for it is a shame for a woman to speak in the church" (1 Cor. 14:34–35). And later, to Timothy, "Let the women learn in silence with all subjection: I permit not a woman to teach, neither to usurp authority over the man, but to be in silence" (1 Tim. 2:11–12). Yet, in 1 Cor. 11:3–5 he states: "But every woman that prayeth or prophecieth bareheaded, dishonoreth her head." This seemingly contradictory statement has fed the feud between the feminists and the anti-feminists for decades: if women are not to speak in church, then why the regulation about women who "prayeth or prophecieth . . . "?[3] Given the scriptural foundation for the muted subjection of women in Christian religions, how is it that women in the strictly conservative Pentecostal religion come to be selected to the chief post of church leader, and via what strategies and images are they able to authenicate both their religious power and their church authority?

Woven throughout this examination of the life and art of women preachers are the threads that come together to rationalize and justify their positions in the community as preachers and, more specificantly, as pastors. The women focus their own narratives on their spiritual call to preach as a directive from God, God's own re-affirmation of that unusual calling, on their own hardships as women preachers and God's support for their work, and on their reiteration that if men were only doing their job effectively during these important "last days," then the women wouldn't have to be doing it. But none of these foci, nor even the totality of their inferences, can clearly answer for us how they have acquired and how they maintain their power and authority. Both religious history and feminist theory and criticism, however, can guide us toward a more textured understanding of this unusual but not unique phenomenon. By firmly basing their role as preacher and pastor within the very frameworks that support a traditional, fundamentalist religiosity, these women pastors are able to employ the system to their advantage. It appears, however, that much of the mythology that motivates this reality may be operating for both the congregation and the pastor in subliminal and largely unconscious ways— a fact that is often true of living mythologies.

Most important to the members of a congregation with a woman pastor is the perception of that woman as "Mother" to the congregation. When group members are asked to say why they think a particular woman is a good pastor, they will answer: "She takes good care of us," or "She's just like a mother; she cares for everybody." Women pastors themselves recognize the importance of acting out the role of symbolic mother to their congregations:

> Women have a special gift of compassion, don't you think? A real caring, loving compassion. Maybe it's because God made us mothers, you know. We know how to comfort our babies, you know, when they're little, and they need attention. And I think it's a special love God puts into the heart of a mother, and gives her such tender love for her family, and then, naturally, why couldn't he use that tender love that he put there to begin with, you know, he made the Mamas. He made them Mamas, you know, and he put that love in their hearts to be Mamas, and so it is a special love so why can't he use that love out of a woman to relate to the people, that need encouragement from him? I believe it's that motherly quality of love that God puts in a mother to bring up that baby and the special love that it has to have, that God puts within a woman—a motherly love. And I believe the people can feel that—that goes along with this guy I worked for, even though he didn't believe in women preachers, he did say to me, 'I believe that ladies can have more compassion to minister than the men do.'
>
> *(Pat Roberts, Centerville, Missouri)*

> I think a woman has more of a tendency to mother the people than lead them you know, like a shepherd does. And it's hard [for a man] to follow a woman [be the next pastor]. Because they don't take a firm stand on things, it's more or less, 'yes, honey, I understand,' you know, like that.
>
> *(Alma Cotton, Smithville, Missouri)*

Sister Anna told me a lot about the influence of another woman pastor she had known well:

> Oh, this lady would just thrill your heart. Her whole life is based upon the Word, and it's beautiful. In fact, she was my spiritual mother. You know, like we would go, when we first got saved, we'd go clear out of our way to pick her up and take her to church and when service was over, we'd take her home, you know, and a lot of times, you know, being new Christians, we didn't understand a lot of things, you know, or maybe we'd be a little bit down in the dumps or what-

ever, but seemed like she could always pick them up—she was such a blessing. God told me, "I've chosen you. I've put you in the furnace of affliction that others can identify with you." Because I had prayed "Lord, give me compassion. Like you feel compassion for people." And you can't feel that with people unless you've gone through what they have. Unless you can walk in their shoes. But I'll tell you one thing. Here's one preacher that will sit and listen when somebody is ready to, needs somebody to listen. I've been told a number of times, "Sister, I believe it's because you're a mother. I feel a compassion that I don't feel in men."

These quotes are filled with the implications of what a "Mother" is likely to do for her "children." Several of these women pastors speak of their congregation members as their "babes in Christ," especially new converts who have just joined their ranks. Traditional "motherly" images include caring, compassion, empathy, the ability to be a good listener, cheerfulness, understanding, loving, and comforting, and most of these capabilities are offered as positive attributes of the woman pastor and are often offered in contradistinction to the attributes of male pastors, who are more often characterized as fine leaders or strict disciplinarians. Sister Alma clearly juxtaposes a male pastor as shepherd who gives firm directives against the woman who will mother the congregation and tell them "yes, honey, I understand." Her point is that future male pastors will have difficulty with congregations who have been "spoiled" by the mothering of a woman pastor and will be less likely to take to the man who "takes a firm stand against things."

Long before the issue of women in the pulpit became obstreperous, young women were being recruited for the mission fields. Barbara Welter has examined Protestant women's missionary careers and suggests-"women's entry into certain fields represented less a victory than a strategic retreat by the opposition."[4] She argues that men had lost interest in the mission field largely because they were frustrated that they often did not have access to the large religious female populations that "control the home and home devotions, had charge of rituals and idols, and influence on their husbands and children."[5] Furthermore, it became apparent that work in the mission field was unlike the kind of centrally located church authority men could acquire in the states. Rather, Welter points out, "like women's work, the work of the conversion of nations was never done, until the last day. Christianity required submission of the will and intellect, and all for love. Love, 'patient, self-denying, self-sacrificing,' must, on the missions, be the love of a mother for her children, however sickly, fretful, wayward, and self-conceited they might be."[6] It became apparent that women were better suited to the demands of missionary work than the men had been. In terms of the missionary role as a new and different script for a young girl to embrace, Welter points out that "the ability of women to love was the theme of many nineteenth-century novels; her search for a fitting love object was the theme of as many lives. The foreign missions provided a dramatic setting where that perfect love, all other loves excelling could be acted out . . ."[7]

To complete the image of the pastor as the "Mother" of the church, the women know that in addition to "mothering" the congregation they serve as pastor, they must be biological mothers themselves as well. Their sermons are often filled with references to their own children, to the raising of their children, to the family as a unifying image. Adrienne Rich, in her examination of motherhood, focuses upon society's need for women to be mothers: "Women who refuse to become mothers are not merely emotionally suspect, but are dangerous. Not only do they refuse to continue the species; they also deprive society of its emotional leaven— the suffering of the mother."[8] An unmarried woman, rejecting the life of wife and mother, would pose a serious threat to the equilibrium of a fundamentalist congregation. A woman preacher's own maternal experience becomes weighted and must be foregrounded in order to minimize the threat that her position "in front of" the church is a rejection of her "natural" role as wife and mother. The following remarks from several different women pastors reflects the image they convey of themselves first as wives and mothers and only second as pastors.

> When my own kids were little, I'd hold two kids and preach, you know. They'd be crying without me, you know, so I'd hold them and preach. I've always said I've got more sermons over the ironing board and the dishpan than I ever did on my knees.
>
> (*Ruth Hatley, Murray, Missouri*)

> I've had to prove all of these years that a woman can be called into the ministry. And I've kept loving the people even when they criticized me and telling them, "Look, this wasn't my choice." I've stood in front of the mirror lots of times and said, "God, are you sure you know what you're doing?" I'm a wife. I'm a mother. I didn't ask for this.
>
> (*Anna Brock Walters, Centerville, Missouri*)

> Two or three months [after being saved] that's when I begin to feel it [the call to preach], but I didn't let on. You know, I didn't know what it was. Really, the most I felt it was, like, when I was home

alone, just me and the Lord. Like when I'd be at home with, just reading my Bible, and you know, maybe the babies playing or something at my feet. I enjoy what I'm doing. I enjoy just what God's made me do. I enjoy being a lady. I enjoy being a wife, a mother, a grandma. I just love being a grandma. I just love it.

(*Pat Roberts, Centerville, Missouri*)

That the sexual threat is never completely eradicated is evidenced in the following comments from a male preacher who greatly resented women preachers and points clearly to the sexual implications of their role:

A woman can't pull a church together. People won't go to hear a woman preach. . . . Old men *will*. Just to be honest with you, the way a woman might act, squatting around, men *would* go. Some of them old men are just crazy about women preachers. . . . Now, why would some men go to look at a woman, a pretty woman? But I'm not looking at you for that. Just looking at you! [laughs]

(*William Bird, Bedford, Indiana*)

In light of the mothering capacities of women preacher, it seems no coincidence that almost every woman I have interviewed had an invalid mother of her own.[9] In nearly every case, these women had to take on the duty of "mothering" their siblings at a very young age and forfeit their own education and aspirations to care for an ailing mother and carry the responsibilities of the household. Sister Mary did not finish high school until she was an adult because she had to care for her family:

See, when I was a sophomore, right before I was called to preach, when I was fifteen, my mother got real sick and she miscarried, had a stillborn baby. And I had to quit school, cause I was the oldest.

(*Mary Harris, Wheaton, Missouri*)

Sister Anna's story of how she had to quit school and care for her family similarly illustrates how she developed her virtuous maternal inclinations at such an early age:

When I was nine years old, my mother's health began to fail and when I was almost ten my mother gave birth to my youngest brother, Danny Joe, and she later had pneumonia and took strong medicine and her heart began to bother her. So more and more responsibility fell upon my shoulders. I had to learn to cook and Mama would tell me to put a dash of this, a pinch of that, and this is how I cooked for the family when Mama was bedfast. . . . My responsibilities grew and it was very difficult to care for a bedfast mother and five younger brothers and sisters. And I helped my dad and two older brothers milk and do

150

usual chores on the farm. There was water to carry and I would heat it on the wood cookstove to wash clothes for the family. The night before I would pick up chips and bring in dry corn cobs. They made it easy to start a good hot fire in the morning. My dad felt he didn't have a good start for his day if he didn't have biscuits and gravy along with his ham or bacon and eggs. . . . At night I would light the coal oil lamp and turn out the electric lights and while everyone else slept, many nights I've rubbed my mother's back and I marvel now as I look back, she never had a bedsore in all of her time of being bedfast. This was a nervous strain upon young shoulders. She was in and out of the hospital so much before she died at the age of 37 years.

Sister Anna does not remind us, in this portion of her narrative, that she was born with severe scoliosis of the spine. Doctors tried to get her family to take her to St. Louis for surgery and remedial treatment, but the family's finances and their unfamiliarity with urban centers, which seemed to exist in a faraway world foreign from their own, prevented them from seeking the help that young Anna needed. A local doctor insisted that she needed to be placed in a corrective brace and some sort of traction to try to bring her spine back in line, and he warned her father then that Anna would never be able to bear chlidren. But, later, Anna seemed to sense the importance of her own maternity and she denied the doctors the last word on that matter!

But I prayed and prayed to get pregnant. I just pleaded with the Lord. And I lost my first one, but, I don't know, maybe it's stubbornness, God has given me a lot of something—God has given me a lot of determination and will-power. I have three [children] now. They fixed a support and I would go and they would adjust that support every month, then, for me to carry my children . . . I was suffering so bad during the time I was carrying my children and each time, of course, it spread the spine more and crippled me a little more, so God was so good to me.

The female pastor is expected to be tough. She must possess stamina and display the fierce, tenacious tendencies of a mother likely to protect her young. Many of the women speak of the determination God gave them to survive the hardships of being a woman preacher. They speak of the criticism, heartaches, and ostracism they have encountered both in their families and in the community. The accounts they give of their experiences come to sound very much alike: " . . . I've thought alright, then, I thought he could make a woman preach if she wanted to, if he wanted her to. I've told them they didn't hire me and they sure couldn't fire me.

151

God called me, God sent me, and I'm here!" (Sister Mabel Adams). Sister Ruth Hatley recalls that there have been moves to oust her from her post, but she says: "They did not hire me and they can't fire me. So, I got God to answer to. . . . I've got a determination that I am not going to give up. When God has something for us to do, he means for us to do it." This image of the woman as tough and hardy, able to withstand the threats of both men and devils, can be readily reconciled if understood within the imagery of the "natural" mother, strong enough to protect her own chidren and her position.

Within the religious community there exist clear directives for female pastors: they must be compassionate, caring, loving mothers for their congregations, and they must be biological mothers as well. As pastor of a church, a woman's strength in that capacity will lie in her ability to apply all the maternal aspects of her female being to the care and guidance of her symbolic family, or as one woman pastor puts it, her "babes in Christ." Much of what the women preach about is, I believe, firmly entrenched in the same maternal imagery. As outlined in chapter 4, Carol Gilligan's thesis that women's perspective is much more inclined toward connection and community is reflected in the rhetoric of women preachers,[10] the most common foci of women's sermons being variations on the themes of sacrifice and "making it into heaven." We can readily recognize the theme of total sacrifice as a maternal concern. The concern with the reunion of the "family"—both biological and religious—in the community of heaven is a natural extension of Gilligan's hypothesis.

These women must be loving and tough, but they must deny that they have or seek equal footing with men. The "Mother" of the church must not be confused with or made the equivalent of being the "Father" of a church. This is due largely to the maintenance of a strict hierarchical power structure in the home and in the community, a hierarchy that is expected to prevail in the religious context as well, even with a female at the helm. The forceful role of men in the homes, recognized by the believers as God-given, is mirrored in the context of religion: even when a woman is the pastor, much of the organization of the service is determined by males, and the governing body of the church is made up of male deacons. The women know that their position must not suggest an attempt to usurp what the congregation believes to be the God-given authority of men. One rationale often offered by the women for their position as pastor is the insistence that if men were only doing their job, women would not have to. Recall Sister Alma's angry words:

> It's been a real barrier, of criticism, because they've used the scripture
> that the women keep silent in the church, and so on. But I usually

tell them—and it's usually a man, I've never found a woman being critical—they've never spoken to me. Now, they might have, in their hearts, but never said anything—but it's usually a man, and I tell them, "If you men will do what God wants you to do, we women won't have to." And that usually hushes them.

(Alma Cotton, Smithville, Missouri)

The scriptural directives that insist on female silence in the churches are not taken lightly by either the women or the men in the congregation. This fundamentalist Pentecostal sect takes the Bible literally, and Paul is quite clear on the issue of women speaking out in church. Most men would, in both theory and practice, agree with the following man's assessment:

They [women preachers] are handmaidens. They should wait upon the [male] ministers of the church. A handmaiden to Christ. A woman's got no right. She is over the house. She is not over a man. A man is over the woman and Christ is over the man, over the church. Now, she's got a place in the church as a Sunday School teacher or maybe as advising to the women. But she can't stand up in that pulpit and tell people what to do because that makes her over the man and that's not according to God's word.

(William Bird, Bedford, Indiana)

The women most often justify their position behind the pulpit by agreeing that they are merely "handmaidens of the Lord" going about the business of saving souls in these the "last days." They point to Joel's prophecy in the Old Testament, which is repeated by Paul in Acts 9:16 and 17, after a group of both men and women experienced tongue-speaking together. Paul asserts that, indeed, these are the last days and that Joel's prophecy has come to be:

And it shall come to pass afterword, that I will pour out my spirit upon all flesh; and your sons and your daughters shall prophesy, your old men shall dream dreams, your young men shall see visions; And also upon the servants and upon the handmaidens in those days will I pour out my spirit.

(Joel 2:28,29)

The implied authority given in these verses to women to "prophesy" is always repeated by women preachers as evidence of their own right to speak in church. Ritual disclaimers act to remove from the situation some of its threatening potential. The women are most accommodating. The following was spoken from the pulpit by the female co-pastor of a fairly large congregation:

153

I am only there to edify the pastorship. He is the head of the church and I am only there to edify him and build him up in front of the church. I always present myself as a handmaiden of the Lord. Let the men take the part of the ministry and the government of the church because they are the head. The Bible clearly says we are the weaker vessel. Sometimes I'm called to a church and I run into a hard spirit at first. I say, "Relax, I don't call myself a preacher. Let the men do that; it's all right. But you have got to give me the right to be a handmaiden of the Lord and he has poured out his spirit unto me and he has called me into his work and I'm here."

(*Mary Harris, Wheaton, Missouri*)

Interestingly, the Bible verses that are being interpreted to allow women to speak in the religious arena are verses that give voice to "your daughters" and to "servants and handmaidens." It is understandable, I think, that the women focus on the term *handmaiden* rather than on the term *daughter* to justify their role as pastors. *Handmaiden* is yet another term to characterize the woman as caretaker. As wife and mother and daughter, she is recognized as "over the house" and is, in fact, a servant to the needs of her *family*. Women preachers refer to themselves often as "handmaidens of the Lord," a phrase that acknowledges both their servant status and their subservience to God and man. Most of their ritual disclaimers downplay their own abilities and acknowledge that some people may be more comfortable if they distinguish between women "preaching" and women "teaching," as with Sister Connie's statement: "I kind of hope you all aren't expecting too much. I want you to know that I never thought about these things on my own. . . . I have not got that much sense in my own head. I'm not intelligent. . . . Now, this may be kinda like teaching, I don't know . . . maybe a mixture of both, preaching and teaching" (from Appendix p. 225).

The expectation that a woman pastor will be a biological Mother, as well as kind and loving, like a "real" Mother to her congregation (her children), allows her to focus on her own stamina and to display with pride the fierce tendencies of a mother likely to protect her young. The women preachers pride themselves on this particular attribute—as much it seems to be as on the fact that they are loving, kind, and generous. Many of them speak of the determination God gave them to survive the hardships of being a woman preacher. They speak of the criticism, the heartaches, the ostracism they have encountered both in their families and in the community. All of them have faced reluctant, even angry men. One male minister told me: "I don't believe in women preachers. God didn't have any. He told the *men* to go out and preach the gospel. He never told a woman to do that. Lord told his disciples, 'I send you amongst wolves.' Now, do you think I'd send my wife out amongst a bunch of heathens? Sinners don't care what they do. They'll string you out. They don't care." But the women embrace that aspect of their work, as well. Sister Anna sees herself as fearless and, in her narrative re-enactments, paints that image as well. See p. 53–54 for a good example. She relates the hard hearts against her as a direct influence from Satan. She perceives him to be behind all of the bitterness she must fight; but against him, she is immutable:

> I've felt it right in this room with me. Some time ago when I was in bed, it woke me up. His presence was so strong that it woke me. And I knew—I felt that same eerie cold darkness there that I recognized as Satan. And so I said, "Devil, in the name of Jesus, get out of here. Leave me alone." And I literally felt him go. I went back to sleep. He woke me up for the *third* time. Finally, the third time I said, "All right, devil, I am tired of you. I need my rest. You get out of here, leave me alone. I am going to put this Bible under my arm. And I'm going to sleep on the promises of God and you're not coming back in here to bother me any more." And with that, I reached over and got the Bible and laid it under my arm. And I went back to sleep.[11]

Maternal and reproductive imagery helps us to understand how a woman functions within the role of pastor more than it aids us in understanding how she got there in the first place. To understand that, we must probe much deeper into the various levels of human mythology— the mythology of male/female characteristics and the prevailing religious mythology as well. Further, we must ground our analysis solidly in an understanding of fundamentalist Pentecostalism.

Barbara Welter has argued that during the nineteenth century a "feminization" of American religion developed because the conceptions of sex role divisions of labor stipulated that men were out doing the "important business," while religion became categorized as an "expendable institution" and one that eventually became the property of the "weaker members of society which . . . generally meant women."[12] This re-allocation of religion to the women's sphere, Welter suggests, determined that it became "more domesticated, more emotional, more soft and accommodating—in a word, more 'feminine.'"[13] Traditional religious values, therefore, became associated with femaleness and weakness. Welter looks to the large numbers of women in mainstream churches as evidence of the "increasing softness and flexibility" which, she suggests, necessarily followed the general male disinclination to submit to religious demands. Welter correctly asserts that the authority of religion did not become "feminized" at all; rather, the churches were filled with women who were subject to male control. She finds revival langauge to be "sexual in its imagery," urging the penitent to "stop struggling and allow yourself to be swept up in His love." She suggests this language was familiar to women:

> Whether in the divine or human order, woman was constantly urged to be swept away by a torrent of energy, not to rely on her own strength which was useless, to sink into the arms of Jesus, to become absorbed and assimilated by the Divine Will—in other words to relax and enjoy it. The fantasies of rape were nourished by this language and by the kind of physical sensations which a woman expected to receive and did receive in the course of conversion. "A trembling of the limbs," "a thrill from my toes to my head," "wave after wave of feeling," are examples of female reaction to the experience of "divine penetration".[14]

The Father/Husband who generated this experience was a jealous God, too, and a demanding one. He expected full submission and obedience to his will. Should he be angered, he would "cast out" his "children" without relent. Certainly, in revival religion or mainstream Protestanism in America, unlike the Shakers and Transcendentalists which Welter studies in depth, there has never been a hint of a Mother-Father God, nor a suggestion of a female Savior. Protestants have maintained a firm notion of God the Father. The large number of women involved in revival religion saw Jesus as Friend and Helper, mediator between not only the religious woman and her earthly life and problems, but, to some degree, mediator between women and an awesome, fearful Father. Jesus was the husband their own husbands could never be: kind, loving, sympathetic, empathetic, and merciful.

In an earlier article, Welter outlined the perceived differences between male and female characteristics and tendencies prevalent in the nineteenth century. These included contrasts of man/woman; truth/love; knowledge/wisdom; head/heart; action/re-action; justice/mercy; mind/soul.[15] These dichotomous ideals are echoed in the work of Sherry Ortner. Ortner's suggestions about the heavily laden dyadic nature of male and female images in contemporary culture help us to texture these images even further.[16] The dichotomies that relegate the female to the arena of hearth, home, and religion also relegate the male to the arena of culture, politics, and the "outside world." Perceptions of men and women, their affinities, and their roles in society may arise from distinctions based on broad stereotypes that identify man as the hunter/provider and woman as the procreator/nurturer. The various aspects of these polarities in terms of the perceived male/female spheres and attributes include culture/nature;

public/private; active/passive; dominant/submissive; producer/reproducer; and rational/spiritual.

Large numbers of women in the churches have helped to support the argument that religion appeals to women more than it does to men, that women respond more eagerly to religious zeal, that women need religion more than men do. This correlation of the female with the religious makes it possible to see how the notion of the religious came to be aligned with the sphere of the domestic—the home and the hearth. The woman's zest for the religious and the spiritual combined nicely with her assumed instinctual interest in the moral upbringing of her children and her concern with the household.

The maternal imagery discussed here clearly derives from a perception of the woman's "natural" role as mother. Because of the various fluid-emissions that flow from the woman's body (such as blood and milk), her cycle of menses, her ability to carry a child until she "bears" it, childbirth itself, and her perceived maternal instincts to nurture and protect the child, the female is both consciously and unconsciously seen to exist in a state that is close to nature than the world of men.[17] This "natural" world in which the woman operates has been relegated by men to the domestic sphere because the home is the seat of the family, the reproductive lair, the safe haven for the rearing of the children, the escape for the husband. Mother and children are safely ensconced in the private sphere of the home while the male goes out into the cultural and political arena.

While it is true that males have argued that their arena is the more important and sophisticated, they have, nevertheless, never lost sight of the importance of the female reproductive capacity. Azizah al-Hibri, in a recent article on the roots of patriarchy, has suggested an important connection between reproduction and immortality.[18] She argues that men have always envied women their ability to reproduce themselves, to bear their own likeness that will live on after their death. While men recognize their own contribution to the act of reproduction, she says the latent desire still exists on the part of males to give birth. On the other hand, all people, men and women alike, long for the ability to insure immortality. Since man has not been able to construct a means for gaining immortality, he perceives a reproductive ability to be the next best thing. The ability to reproduce oneself and leave that "product" behind when he dies, she argues, comes about as close to "immortality" as he has been able to get.

In the technological (man-made) world, al-Hibri and others have noted, man's ideas become his "babies"—he conceives them, nurtures them in their fetal stages, "births" them, cares for them until they are successful, and takes pride in them when they operate in the world on their own. Consider the introduction to a recent folklore volume: "This book was given life with the help of many individuals and institutions." The editor thanks his "helpers" for "giving advice, sharing knowledge, and lending support and assistance. They helped me through the labor pains."[19] Similarly the editor of a new scholarly journal writes: "Tradition demands that an editor of a new scholarly journal perform the ritual gesture of justifying the birth of the new academic child. . . . those of us assisting at the delivery feel strongly that in this case the proverbial claim that the new medium 'fills a gap' really does contain a modicum of truth."[20]

Al-Hibri argues that while women were caring for the young, men began to announce that the progressive, the "civilized," the "business" world that existed outside the home was the important sphere where battles were fought, decisions concerning the entire group were made, and a complex network of intricacies about interactions was developed. Man talks at length about his creations and convinces the world that these creations are the most important kinds of creations. He constricts the world of women and babies in a protected cloister and determines that this domestic world is closer to an "animal" world, necessary but messy, and more instinctual than intellectual. He designates the man-made world as the logical, rational, reasonable, predictable, and controllable world— surely more appealing than the world of birthing and nurturing. Control, in fact, comes to carry increased importance and becomes synynomous with power. Man believes he can, at all times, control the world he has created, and in order to further enhance his newly acquired sense of power, he designates himself as controller of the domestic realm as well.

In such a view of the roots of patriarchy, women were, at first, quite content to play out their "natural" role of mother; their aspirations did not go beyond the "lair" because they were not frustrated— yet.[21] Frustration and jealousy pushed the male out of the domestic scene into the public arena where he was obligated to produce something analogous to the female's production of offspring. She just wasn't watching when he decided to take in the domestic scene as part of his domain. He began to execute his domination by violent force upon women who were often physically weakened and burdened by the biological aspects of pregnancy, childbearing, and childrearing. His feelings of alienation, frustration, inadequacy, jealousy, and hostility toward the female then became manifest in the cultural rules he set about to develop and enforce—rules that determined that women could be "owned" by one man; that all the children she would bear would be "owned" by that man; and, in recent times, that his technology for the birthing and nurturance of the children was superior to the mother's "natural" birthing techniques and his superior man-made liquids must replace her milk.

Imagery current in the culture came to refer more and more to the womb as an "incubator" and sperm as "life-force." In significant ways, then, man managed both in symbol and in reality to undermine and minimize woman's role in reproduction. He came to dominate all worlds: the public, the private, and the natural. He wielded power through domination, and while he could not gain immortality through reproduction, he could dominate the reproductive powers of women and feel superior. By designating himself as ruler of the domestic world, while insisting that it was of lesser quality and needed to be ruled, as well as pronouncing himself controller of the technological world he had created, man reached a new apex in his perception of his own importance. Yet, for all of this noisy proclamation and domination, the male never forgot the seat of woman's essential and irrevocable power—her access to immortality. No matter what he does, this fact may become obscured but it can never be obliterated.

This inability to come to grips with the seat of female power may, in fact, underlie the seemingly contradictory stance males have taken toward the hearth and toward women and religion. Certainly, the male has worked hard to dominate these spheres, yet men seem to hold the two, also, in humble reverence. The "home" comes to symbolize the importance of the family; the sacred hearth becomes almost akin to "heaven on earth." In his own ritual disclaimer, man denies his quest for power through technology and claims to be struggling in the public arena only for the sake and support of his family. And his off-hand dismissal of things spiritual points to several concerns. Dismissing these unusual or potentially dangerous aspects of life is easier than confronting them; relegating "moral upbringing" to the mother removes his own inadequate self from the scene, but also serves to reinforce the importance of those aspects. The "little wife" is seen as advocate of the upright and protector of the Christian ethic. This view, of course, removes him from responsibility—and allows him freedom to enter and participate in the secular world—but it also creates an uncomfortable tension.

By dominating the domestic world and isolating it from "the world," man attempts to render it ineffectual and unimportant; yet, by relegating morality and even salvation to the sphere of women he also risks enhancing their status. Writing about the Puritans, Mary Dunn comments that "Feminine virtue became a family affair. Indeed, it is through the family that the Christian community would be preserved. To be a good woman was to be a good Christian."[22] Welter notices the same tendency in the Mormon church where only men can be conferred with the "Priesthood," yet heaven is only attainable by a man *and* his family.[23] Welter, examining the attitudes of males toward wife and mother, found that women embody all the values men profess to hold so dear—family, home, purity, and piety. She proposes that as the world becomes more and more unstable, "true womanhood" (and all that it apparently signifies) becomes the one stable element.[24] Man, faced daily with "the world," has come to defend, even irrationally, the home and the woman's place in it. Here piety is valued; hence, her religiosity is encouraged—it is her strength: " . . . and the vestal piety lighted up by heaven in the breast of woman would throw its beam on the naughty world of men."[25] Woman's economic dependence on her man led to the image of the frail woman, full of grace and beauty. Religion was exactly what a woman needed, "for it gives her that dignity that best suits her dependence."[26]

Spiritual power, as opposed to church authority, was permitted the woman because it did not detract from her natural feminine delicacy; it made her, in fact, even lovelier by stressing her attributes of holiness, and it encouraged her to maintain her position in the home, submissive to her husband. Woman was held to be stronger only in her defense against the evil of the world, and often held up as perfect as well. Woman, dressed in garments of holiness and told she was pure and selfless, was given the responsibility of rearing the children. She ran the risk of becoming a self-fulfilling prophecy.

During the great revivals of the eighteenth and nineteenth centuries, spiritual ferver swept the country. Women were noted to have participated in great swelling numbers in these emotional religious camp meetings and revivals.[27] Mary Ryan makes a clear connection between women's religious roles and the rise of American revivalism and enthusiastic religion.[28] She notes, "At the time of the first revival [Utica, 1814], women constituted 70% of the church population. The mothers, in other words, firmly planted the families' religious roots on the frontier. Women certainly claimed a maternal role in the first revival, for 12% of all the converts of 1814 appear to have been pregnant when they professed the faith."[29] For Ryan, the large numbers of young women, both married and not married, who joined churches during revivals did so independently of their family, suggesting they "exercised a degree of religious autonomy during seasons of revival."[30] In fact, although there is little evidence of women actually preaching in these revivals, women were forming important female alliances that supported religious/maternal structures. Ryan notes that through the development of the "Female Missionary Society" and the "Maternal Association," the historian can "see women weaving the social and familial ties that ran through the revival."[31] By 1827, she notes, the "Female Missionary Society" was absorbed into a masculine organization and essentially eradicated. But the first "Maternal Association," established in 1825, focused on the women's own children and family hearths rather than on missionary work. It "formalized a longstanding network of neighborly advice and consultation . . . [and was] concerned with public morality, children's souls, and the assaults of a secular and individualistic culture."[32] Early issues of *The Mother's Magazine*, first initiated by the Presbyterian Maternal Association in 1833, "depicted women guiding children and husbands toward salvation . . . [while] the typical reference to clergymen was a polite rebuke for the failure to foster Maternal Associations within their congregations."[33] Pointing to the disassociation these women felt from the official church and from the clergy, in 1835 the female editor of *The Mother's Magazine* wrote: "The Church has had her seasons of refreshing and her returns of decay; but here in the circle of mothers, it is felt that the Holy Spirit condescends to *dwell*. It seems his blessed 'rest.' "[34]

But revivalism is an unwieldly thing; spiritual power reigns and too often that power is seen exhibited by women or by men who are willing to submit to a "feminine" kind of religious experience. Thus, as the revival spirit waned, men in mainstream American Protestanism renewed their control of the religious scene, constructing important denominational distinctions and stressing anew the ruling hand of the "Fathers." Religion came to be defined and molded by educated males who went about the "business" of religion in much the same way they conducted their other business endeavors. They took religion from the domestic sphere and placed it squarely in the public arena. Religion became a hierarchical, political affair; rules and regulations became standardized, written down, codified, rationalized; membership became solidified in influential numbers; aspiring young males went to Bible Colleges to become preachers and train for the pastorship. In essence, American religion lost its spiritual, "feminine" demeanor and became, instead, secularized by men, especially as some males capitalized on the possibilities of the church's becoming a political entity. Men became associated with "civil religion" while women remained concerned with the world of the sacred.

To clarify this point, it must not be assumed that this argument presupposes that more men than women are now filling Protestant American churches or are being more religious. Rather, one man per congregation becomes more "religious," that is, becomes interested in religious matters especially as they allow for him a public, ruling chair. The congregations, however, remain largely female in numbers and, as always, the moral and spiritual aspects which may be recognized as "religious" continue to remain within the women's sphere, clearly associated with home and hearth and with the rearing of the offspring. Women have always been perceived as the "keepers of the covenent," the "protectors of the mission,"[35] but the church may become a public, political, secular arena. Religious leaders become community powers; their authority often crosses various public and political boundaries. Their control over their congregations makes them important pivotal figures in the intersections of the public and the private, the political and the domestic. Sermons become political diatribes, essays on civil living, manifestos for appropriate social interactions, and might easily be perceived as public documents aimed at an audience far beyond the walls of the church. Denominations have flourished; separate ideologies based on infinite hair-splitting theological differences have led to splits and bad feelings. The male position of "Father," as pastor of a church congregation, replicates the patriarchical inclination that has been painstakingly developed within the culture. The "Father" perceives his congregation, much as he does his offspring, as "property"—and his role corresponds to the historical emphasis on the rights and duties of the father in the patriarchical family, rather than to the role of the caring, responsible mother.

How does all of this help us to understand how women might come to have the power and authority of the pastorship of a Pentecostal congregation? The answer seems to lie in the recognition that fundamentalist Pentecostalism has resisted secularization, most likely because its constituents are more comfortable within the spiritual world of traditional religion than they are in the unfamiliar secular world.[36] The central concerns of Pentecostalism rest firmly in the sacred, spiritual realm, one that rejects outright the secular world. All aspects of the "the world," as they refer to any arena not connected to the spiritual world, are shunned and perceived as sinful, evil, uncontrolled, and inspired by Satan. Humans are safe, they believe, only within the confines of the sacred world. The power the woman is able to utilize in her quest for the pulpit and in her ability to procure and maintain religious authority stems from the most conservative, traditional roots of this twentieth-century American denomination. Pentecostals are committed to a denial of the secular and strive to embrace the sacred. If the woman can assure these fundamentalist Pentecostals that she will keep the religion closely connected to the spiritual realm and the family-based community, and as far away from the secular as is humanly possible, then she has a better chance of gaining the pastorship than a man who seems bound to take the congregation into an interaction with the secular world. Her disregard for the public arena and her inclination toward the hearth, the home, and the family represent everything the congregation holds dear. By making a clear commitment to these central configurations and pronouncing her intention and ability to keep the church within the domestic/spiritual sphere, she can win their confidence. And, further, if she "mothers" the congregation, cares for them, nurtures them, empathizes with them, counsels them, and can pray their souls into heaven, then they are all that much more likely to allow her to fill the slot of pastor. It is, after all, her ability to confer with God's spirit that has made her a more spiritual being; therefore, she must utilize this perception of her natural powers in order to assume a position of authority within the church. She is, they recognize, a spiritual being who can reproduce herself; she is close to nature and close to God and his spirits. Unleashed, her power could be dangerous, but employed for the guidance and nurturance of men's souls she might prove beneficial. At least for this conservative, fundamentalist religion, her guidance in the spiritual realm is viewed as more favorable than a possible move toward secularization and the evils "the world" has to offer.

As for the longstanding arguments based on Paul's directives against women speaking in the church, most congregations are inclined to accept the women's insistence that God has called them to preach. The women's personal narratives about their spiritual encounters with God and their testing of his intentions seem much more immediate to them than Paul's writings. These are a millenial religious people who believe "the Rapture" will come any day "in the twinkling of an eye," and the saved in Christ will be held accountable for those who have not heard the Word. Therefore, the urgency of the present situation in these last days becomes more imperative than the Biblical writings which they admit may have been addressed to specific situations in the early Christian church. It is not unusual at all to find that, in many of the churches which have a woman pastor, the ruling board of deacons is made up entirely of men or that the business meetings of the church are held with only men and the woman pastor present. In general, women are not granted equality in authority in the Pentecostal religion, but the weight of the call of God to preach is profound, especially as it stems from that most critical prerogative of the feminine nature—her relationship with the spiritual.

Anna Walters and her sister Pentecostal pastors do not represent a flood of women "searching out the liberating promises of scripture to revise theologies" or taking strides toward a "new theology" or a "new ethics." Within this milieu, such a stance would be deadly and would only have the opposite effect. Even more than in the more liberal mainstream churches these most conservative, fundamentalist American religious sects would deny seekers of sexual equality a platform—or a pulpit. Yet, the young girls who dream this most impossible dream and "re-script" their lives to fit this unusual and difficult mold are liberated. They are not liberated from all the prejudices and restrictions that hamper women in general, and most particularly women in this conservative fundamentalist milieu, but they are liberated from the standard script of cloistered wife and mother. The penalties are high, however, for they must be "super-Moms" in the greatest possible extension of that term. "Re-scripting" actually means scripting *in* extra parts for themselves and indicates the imperative of cautious and superlative performance at every level. The girl who wishes to be a pastor must also be a wife and mother, and she must extol the virtues of those capacities at every opportunity. She must declare her "motherly" nature, exclaim her delight in being a wife and mother, her joy in her children, her home. And she must deny her sexuality as a possible temptress while at the same time she must acknowledge her inferior status as woman and submit herself to all men. The role is a complex one, full of pitfalls and possible infractions. The woman pastor clearly has to balance her life on a tenuous pivot—any move too far in any direction could cause her to lose her hard-earned position of spiritual power and religious authority.

The poignant story of Sister Anna continues. In the following epilogue, the precariousness of her situation becomes evident. The price she has had to pay for her pastorship has been a high one. Anna is in constant physical and mental pain; yet, she sees her suffering as a testament to God's attentions and as proof of his mission for her life. If it were an easy path, she thinks, it might not be a celestial one.

NOTES

1. Janet Wilson James, ed., *Women in American Religion*, p. 1.
2. James, p. 1. This "flood" actually began in the nineteenth century, as Donna Behnke has so clearly shown in *Religious Issues in Nineteenth Century Feminism*.
3. See Introduction in Behnke.
4. Barbara Welter, "She Hath Done What She Could," p. 111.
5. Welter, p. 113.
6. Welter, p. 113.
7. Welter, p. 113.
8. Adrienne Rich, *Of Woman Born: Motherhood as Experience and Institution*, p. 164.
9. I am particularly intrigued with the notion of these mothers being "invalid" for their daughters; we should pay close attention to notions of "invalidity" and illness in women's experience.
10. Carol Gilligan, *In a Different Voice*.
11. Note the similarities of Sister Anna's experience with those of witch-riding beliefs in Patricia Rickel's, "Some Accounts of Witchriding," and in Maxine Hong Kingston's, *The Woman Warrior*, pp. 80–88.
12. Barbara Welter, "The Feminization of American Religion, 1800–1860," p. 84.
13. Ibid.
14. Welter, "Feminization," p. 93
15. Welter, "Feminization," p. 77 [from "Woman," *The Present*, I (Dec, 1843), p. 165].
16. Sherry Ortner, "Is Female to Male as Nature is to Culture?"

17. Mary Douglas, *Purity and Danger*.

18. Azizah al-Hibri, "Reproduction, Mothering, and the Origins of Patriarchy." pp. 81–93.

19. Simon Bronner, ed., *American Material Culture and Folklife*, p. xii.

20. John Foley, "Introduction."

21. Al-Hibri admits to the simplicity of her model, yet her argument is a valuable one.

22. Mary Maples Dunn, "Saints and Sisters: Congregational and Quaker Women in the Early Colonial Period."

23. Welter, "Feminization," p. 11.

24. See Welter's, "The Cult of 'True Womanhood'."

25. Welter, "Cult," p. 22.

26. Welter, "Cult," p. 23.

27. See Dickson Bruce, *And They All Sang Hallelujah: Plain-Folk Camp-Meeting Religion, 1800–1845*, for accounts of female participation in early revivalism.

28. See Mary P. Ryan, "A Women's Awakening."

29. Ryan, p. 101.

30. Ryan, p. 101.

31. Ryan, p. 104.

32. Ryan, p. 104,

33. Ryan, p. 110.

34. Ryan, p. 110.

35. Dunn, p. 34.

36. Compare William Clements, "The American Folk Church."

Epilogue: A New Script with a Familiar Ending

It was September 15, and I had not intended to drive to Centerville that Sunday morning. In fact, all of my husband's family had crowded into the house to visit with us, but something drove me to the car and down the road to see Sister Anna. She had recently had some serious medical problems, and had called me late one night when she could not sleep to talk about this latest in a long line of physical and emotional problems. Basically, Anna feels as though she has given this life for God the best try she possibly could, and yet her life has been fraught with pain and tribulation; she feels singled out for hardship and problems and she just cannot understand why.

The leaves had not begun to turn, but that southern drive told me that the natural world knew fall was on its way and just around the corner— something in the air, combined with signs for melons and pick-up trucks hawking tomatoes, cucumbers, zinnas and colored popcorn. I always have a sense of mixed anticipation as I drive toward any Pentecostal service, for I know too well the intensity, the frenzy of the services, the emotional impact the event will have on me. But I was not prepared for what awaited me this particular Sunday morning.

I arrived at 10:30 and joined the group of adults gathered in the musty basement for the Sunday School class. The teacher was, of course, Sister Anna. I knew she had already conducted an entire service at one of the local nursing homes before she came to the church. I am forever amazed by her stamina, so surprised when I see again her tiny, frail frame.

I sensed immediately that something was wrong. She stopped the lesson to acknowledge my presence, greeting me warmly with "Welcome, Elaine, come on in and sit down." But her voice cracked, her face was puffy, as though she had been crying for a long time. I could tell she had lost weight. She was talking about hatred and how we ought not to hate

167

others or hold grudges. We should, she was saying, turn that hardness in our hearts over to God or it would devour us, consume our very being. She could not, for example, hate her husband for what he had done, she must forgive him and let it go or it would destroy her. What had happened? My mind raced. I felt the air in the room; it was somber and sticky, like a wake. The people around me had been crying, too, I realized. They all looked so sad; some shook their heads in dismay. Then, somehow, I knew. She had tried to warn me, or warn herself, some weeks ago in the car as we slogged through the August heat on the back roads of her area. She knew something then or had glimpsed the end in a moment of frightening revelation. "If this marriage does not work out, Elaine," she had told me, "what will my people think? My congregation, what will they do? He is jealous of my time away from home. He doesn't want to share me with anybody. He is jealous of all the men, even the young men, in the congregation. Yet he swore to me upon our marriage that he would never stand in the way of my ministry. But he doesn't like it. We have terrible arguments about the amount of time I am away from home, where have I been, who have I been with. He yells at me. He hates it. So many meals interrupted, evenings away from home, so much praying in my living room with my flock, the hospital calls and emergencies day and night. I do them so naturally. They are just a part of my daily life. I've *never* spent my days at home. But it hurts him and I don't know what to do." But, then, she seemed to shrug off the impossible, the preposterous. Her church did not "believe in divorce" she said. She didn't believe in divorce. Besides he could never do that to her, for he knew what it would mean. It could mean the end of her ministry. He wouldn't do that. Would he?

As Sister Anna finished her Sunday School lesson, the memory of that conversation flashed across my mind and I knew what had happened. "Elaine," she confirmed what I suspected, "he left me yesterday, while I was gone to the Post Office. He cleaned out his closet, and he left me a note. He couldn't share me with God. He *thought* he could, but it was too much and now he's left me. I came here this morning to tell my people what has happened." She put her arms around me and openly wept. Other women hesitantly came toward us and soon we were both wrapped in the arms of women who needed to tell Anna what I needed to tell her—that we felt her pain.

Anna Brock Walters proved her mettle that September morning. She conducted the Sunday School; she led the singing; she called for the ushers to come forward for the offering; she blessed the offering and prayed for the sick. She sang a song about God being bigger than any mountain that we can or cannot see and only on the last verse of that song did her voice crack. Her shoulders shook while another woman finished the song for

168

her. Yet, she stood, then, in the pulpit and preached a sermon and brought her message around to her own trouble and told her people the whole story. She told them her husband had gone, knowing full well what the consequences of that might be. But in the spirit of a true minister and pastor, she turned her own story of heartache and shame into a prayer for all those in the congregation who felt they had somehow failed God and perhaps felt he was not near enough in their lives. She ministered to her flock:

> While every head is bowed, and every eye is closed. Is there one here who desires my prayers? If you are lonely, or hurt, or discouraged, you can be strong with God's help. I am strong, but only because I have God on my side. If you want God on your side, won't you just raise your hand? God already knows who you are, but I don't. Let me help you, pray for you. God bless you. There's a hand. And another. No one's watching but me and God—ah, yes, God bless you.

In the benediction, a young man of the congregation asked for God's care and protection over Sister Anna; the congregation murmured their prayers for her. Then, I watched every single man, woman, and child in that church go to the back and envelop that tiny woman in their arms. With tears in their eyes and voices trembling, they assured her that they loved her and that they would pray for her. She wept openly, grasping the arms desperately for proof of their love and their devotion.

Yet, even though her people expressed their love and concern for her on a personal level, both Anna and her congregation knew that a divorce for her was out of the question. Even if they could in their own hearts make an exception for this exceptional woman, they knew the rules and the rules would dictate that she could not stand behind the pulpit a divorced woman.

Several weeks later I was not surprised to get a call from Anna telling me that her husband was back; she had taken him back in. I still do not know fully what the terms of that reconciliation are, but I do know that taking her husband back was the only way Sister Anna could maintain the position of pastor of her church and hold onto the power and authority she had worked so hard to acquire. I also suspect that by taking him back, she had to relinquish some of her freedom. She had to trade her independence for the right to retain her role. She was reined in by this man. From the privacy of the home, his home, came the message loud and clear: we have a "monster" on our hands. This woman has clearly overstepped her bounds. You must support my effort to put her back in her "place." She must submit, first, to my will—then God's. In my house, I am Lord, and I will not be subject to my wife. She must obey me. I will allow her to be your pastor, and you can love and respect her. But you can keep her only if she first heeds my will. If she does not bend, then I will divorce her. And you will throw her out, because you know you agree with me.

Appendix: Texts of Sermons

Sister Anna Brock Walters
Centerville, Missouri
June 15, 1985

We cannot change
Ourselves.
There's a lot of things we can do
To help,
5 But there is no way—
We're like the leopard that cannot change its spots,
And the Bible even says that we cannot
Add to nor take from
One inch of our stature.
10 We can't do that, can we?
So there are some things that God has
Set
In motion
That man cannot change,
15 That we have to line up with God,
And sin is one of them.
We ourselves have no power.
It is the power in the blood of Jesus
That cleanses from all unrighteousness.
20 So turn with me to Ephesians,
Second chapter, verses 8 and 9:
"For by grace are ye saved through faith
And that not of yourselves.
It is the gift of God
25 Not of works lest any man should boast."
Now we'll go over to St. John—

St. John the first chapter, verse 12:
"But as many as received him
To them gave he power to become the Sons of God
30 Even to them that believe on his name."
A lot of people are saying today
That the word sin is old-fashioned,
That it really doesn't have
The meaning that
35 We are
Saying that it does have,
That it's not as bad
As some of us proclaim it to be,
In spite of the fact
40 That we see more open sin today
Than we did ten years ago.
I—
When I was a little child
And growing up
45 Even
When I had my children,
Very, very seldom did you ever hear the word child abuse.
Even when my children were young,
Which hasn't been—
50 It's not been that long ago,
But at the same time, ah,
I knew nothing
About
Drugs being so common
55 As they are today.
You didn't hear
Of the many divorces
Just even ten years ago
As you do today.
60 And yet
Society is saying that
The word sin
Has no meaning,
That we are blowing things out of proportion.
65 But I want to tell you something, friend,
Sin
Has always been *sin*,

And it's a strange thing,
If sin no longer has any meaning
70 Then God hasn't heard about it,
Because God still punishes sin,
And God's word still declares that
We're in a sinful and
Adulterous
75 Generation.
And God's word still speaks very plain
About SIN,
And as sure as the angel with the flaming sword
Throwed out Adam and Eve out of the garden because of their
sin,
80 There'll be no one that will be able
To enter the gates of heaven
With sin in their lives
Because God has not changed his mind
About sin.
85 If you've ever had any dealing with Alcoholics Anonymous,
You will know that this is one of the first
Steps
That they take—
The principle of Alcoholics Anonymous
90 Is—
They have to admit—
In fact, this is the first step towards sobriety
That once their own individual life
Has become
95 Unmanageable—
They bring those people to the place where they realize
That their own life is unmanageable and
That they themselves
Find out
100 That they cannot change
Their habit.
They have no control over it.
And this is the reason they set up
The AA.
105 And I'm not picking on alcoholics,
I just used that as an illustration.
Anything,

Any other kind of habit
That gets out of your control whether it's
110 Drugs—
Child abuse can come under that—
Do you realize that unless
A child is healed of his hurts
They will grow up to be a child abuser too?
115 Almost—
Well, the biggest percent of them will.
They don't understand it,
But that's the way it goes.
But friends,
120 There is victory
And there is deliverance
And there is healing
And what AA can't do, God can do, ah,
And what the church itself can't do, ah,
125 God can do.
For what we ourselves cannot do,
There is still victory
There is still deliverance,
Because the blood of Jesus Christ
130 Cleanses us from all
All
Unrighteousness.
And I declare to you today that
God's word
135 Does not change.
Maybe sin is an old-fashioned word,
But so is the Bible an old-fashioned Bible.
The Christian walk
Is still old-fashioned.
140 And it really disturbs me—
My youngest sister and I was riding along in Springfield the
    other
Friday—
I guess it was or Thursday evening—
And she said,
145 "You, know, it really disturbs me and I cry out to
God—
'God, when I see so many Christians compromising,
Please help me not to compromise.' "

Maybe you don't think about it,
150 But I see it.
I see a lot of God's people
Compromising today,
Settling for something less
Because it's just too much work,
155 It's too hard to pray through today
So they settle for something less.
We can't afford to.
I, for one, believe
That the coming of Jesus
160 Is so very near at hand
And there is not time to avoid church
And there is not time to settle and say
That Sin
Is an old-fashioned word
165 That has lost its meaning.
It has not.
But neither has
Repentance.
That's an old-fashioned word, too.
170 Did you hear me?
If sin is old-fashioned,
So is forgiveness.
So is forgiveness.
But it's still the only way
175 To heaven.
It's the only way to salvation—
Is to repent—
To have a godly start.
Now a lot of people today have the idea
180 That, ah,
Repentance is
Just remorse,
Just
Sorry,
185 Mostly because they got caught,
Not really because
They are sick and tired
Of the sin that they've committed.
But I want you to know
190 That I'm an old-fashioned preacher today

With the old-fashioned Word of God,
And I know that you can't just turn over a new leaf.
You can't just decide,
"I'm going to quit alcohol,
195 I'm going to quit drugs,"
And just walk away from it.
That isn't good enough, People.
It is not good enough
Just to turn over a new leaf
200 And quit drinking.
You're still not saved.
It isn't good enough
Just to quit another habit
That you're doing.
205 It isn't enough even to come and sit in a pew in church.
You've got to repent.
You have to be sorry with a godly sorrow
And vow you'll turn that faith around.
You've got to have a mind-change.
210 You have to change your mind.
You'll have to make up your mind first of all
I can't change
Myself.
I've got to have help.
215 And then you begin to look
To the source
Of your help.
I'll guarantee you one thing,
If the stack of bills is higher—
220 If your liabilities
Are greater than your assets
This morning,
You're going to have to have help.
If you don't have any check coming in for a week
225 And you've got bills due this week,
You need help.
If you're sick in body this morning,
No matter what it is,
And you've done everything you know to do
230 And it's not good enough,
You're going to have to seek help.
But I want to recommend

Someone to you this morning.
He is the source
235 For the supply
Of every need that you have—
And that's Jesus Christ
And him crucified
And resurrected
240 And sitting on the right hand of the Father
And ready to come back
At a moment's notice
When God gives the order—
He's coming again.
245 That's old-fashioned, too,
Brother Allen—
Lots of preachers don't even preach any more
That there's going to be a rapture.
They don't even preach of the second coming of Jesus.
250 They might want you to believe
That things are going to get better.
But I tell you they'd better hurry up and start
Because as the days come and go
We see sin
255 Covering
And rampaging our nation
Like never before.
I almost feel like sometimes,
Lord,
260 I feel like all hell has broken loose,
But it hasn't—
But it keeps spewing out a little bit more
As the days go by.
I told the class downstairs a while ago,
265 We were talking about
Just an incident that was in last week's paper
Concerning the two young men
That were in the Satan worship occult
And how that they took a seventeen-year-old boy
270 And literally gouged his eyes out while he was still alive
And then they stabbed him in the head so many times,
Because it was a part of their occult.
Satan has no mercy on you, Sir.
Satan has no mercy upon you, young lady.

275 If he can get you to drink yourself to death until your body
Is so, uh,
Dilapidated,
If I can use that word,
Until your liver is consumed,
280 And your kidneys no longer function right,
He'll laugh you into hell if he can do it,
If you'll let him.
If he can get you
To play with sin
285 Until you look like a haggard old person
When you're in your twenties or thirties,
He will dance with glee.
He will laugh with glee.
I believe we ought to have a revival every week,
290 I really do,
Because some people are so gullible
And believe the lies that
We hear today.
Now, I know a lot of people today
295 That don't believe in hell, either;
That's an old-fashioned word.
But there *is* a hell.
It's a funny thing
A lot of preachers don't preach on hell anymore,
300 But they can sure talk about heaven.
But here's one that wants to tell you today
Just as sure as there is a heaven
There is a *hell.*
Just as sure as God is preparing
305 A banquet table
And a marriage supper of the lamb
And mansions in heaven and all the refinery,
He has had to create a hell
For the devil
310 And all of the fallen angels
And all of those
Who reject
The blood of Jesus Christ.
Sin isn't going to make it into heaven
315 So there has to be a place
For the sinner.

If the sinner refused to sin, People,
Then there wouldn't be the problem because you see,
If Satan couldn't get you to yield to sin
320 He couldn't do his dirty work.
Did you hear me?
If he couldn't get you
To yield to sin
Then there wouldn't be anything he could do.
325 But he knows that he's always been able
To find the weak spot
In human nature
In men and women.
But when he gets you so ensnared
330 That you can't help yourself,
You're in his trap
And he is your master
And you will do what he says.
But the Bible says we can't serve two masters.
335 We're going to either
Give allegiance to one
Or the other.
We'll turn over in Luke
The fifteenth chapter
340 And the seventh verse:
"I say unto you,
That likewise joy shall be in heaven
Over one sinner that repenteth."
Isn't that great?
345 I believe that.
Well, let's read the tenth verse:
"Likewise, I say unto you,
There is joy in the presence of the angels of God
Over one sinner that repenteth."
350 I believe that that simply means this:
All those people in heaven
There in the presence of angels and the presence of God
They rejoice.
I believe that a precious Mom and Dad
355 Who have prayed long and fervent
And hard
For unsaved children
I tell you I believe

Even though they went on home to their reward
360 And they didn't see those children saved,
I want to tell you something,
I believe when that one, that child,
Bows on their knees to God,
That that Mom and Dad
365 Rejoice in heaven.
They know,
Because it's in the presence of the angels of God
That they rejoice over one sinner
That repenteth.
370 I believe over the balcony of heaven this morning
If one soul in this congregation this morning
Repents of their sin
I'll tell you what, Bretheren,
I believe he knows it.
375 I believe Brother Brock [her deceased first husband] knows it.
I believe when one sinner
Repents, ah,
In this place,
They know it and they rejoice
380 In the presence of angels
Over one sinner that repents.
And then you find
Over in Luke 16:24:
"And he cried and said, Father Abraham,
385 Have mercy on me and send Lazarus,
That he may dip the tip of his finger in water,
And cool my tongue;
For I am tormented in this flame."
Well, it may be old-fashioned
390 But it's still in existence today
And because the rich man died
And lifted up his eyes
And he was in torment he felt that torment—
He's *still* feeling that torment.
400 I don't know how many hundreds of years
Have gone by
But that rich man is in torment today just as real and as much
As he was when he went there.
And I'm here to tell you,
405 That Judas, ah,

Is still in hell because, ah,
He came to man
And, ah,
Instead of to Jesus.
410 You can confess to as many
Priests as you want to—
Don't get me wrong,
I'm not knocking any kind of denomination—
But I'm just telling you
415 You can go to as many men or women as you want to
And repent of your sin
But except you come to Jesus,
It won't do you a bit of good.
We must come
420 Through the door.
And Judas
Went back to man
And he threw the money down
Because he realized
425 He had, ah,
Committed a terrible sin.
The very best friend he had
He sold for five pieces of silver
And he said it was blood money.
430 But you know what
Not even the men wanted it.
Isn't it something, uh,
That a lot of older men
Are the ones
435 That come out and get the younger ones
Hooked on drugs.
A lot of times it's some
Old man
That will get a younger man
440 Started drinking for the first time.
When they're the ones that have been along the road
And they ought to know—
And they do know.
Some of them,
445 It's for
Money.
Others it's because

     They've sunk so low
     And they're satisfied in their own sin
450 But they want to drag somebody else down
     Even lower than they are.
     But for whatever reason it is,
     Beloved,
     My business is to life people UP,
455 Is to lift people—
     That's Jesus' place
     Is to lift people.
     And he came—
     He came to seek and to save
460 That which is lost.
     If you'll turn with me over to the book of Revelations,
     Twentieth chapter.
     Let's read
     A portion of scripture here.
465 It's not my *opinion*
     That there is a hell,
     But it's the Word of God.
     And if you're one here this morning
     And Satan has tried to sell you a bill of goods
470 That what you're doing isn't so bad
     Because you can look and see someone else that's doing worse,
     I want to tell you something.
     The Bible says
     "He that knoweth to do good and doeth it not
475 Committeth a sin."
     You know what you're doing
     Is not right.
     If you feel the least bit of guilt over it,
     Then it's wrong.
480 "And the devil that deceived them
     Was cast into the lake of fire and brimstone,
     Where the beast and the false prophet are,
     And shall be tormented day and night
     Forever and Ever.
485 And I saw a great white throne,
     And him that sat on it,
     From whose face the earth and the heaven fled away;
     And there was found no place for them.
     And I saw the dead, small and great,

490 Stand before God;
      And the books were opened;
      And another book was opened
      Which is the book of life:
      And the dead were judged out of those things
495 Which were written in the books,
      According to their works."
      Now, that's the only time
      That people that go to hell are going to get out.
      And it's just long enough
500 To stand before God in the great white throne
      And that's not going to be a picnic.
      They're not going to want to go back.
      But I'll tell you what
      I believe they would rather call out for the rocks and the
           mountains
505 To fall on them
      To hide them from the face of God
      Than to stand there
      And listen ot what God's going to have to say to them.
      Because it's the last ray of hope
510 That that sinner's going to have.
      And that isn't *any* hope!
      There may be some that will say,
      "Scan the pages again,
      Scan the pages.
515 Why, I attended Eastside Assembly of God Church."
      But God will have to say,
      "Depart from me, you workers of iniquity,
      I never knew you.
      I never knew you."
520 The only way he's going to know you, my friend,
      Is that your sins are washed
      As white as snow.
      "And whosoever was not found written in the Book of Life
      Was cast
525 Into the Lake of Fire."
      And the only way
      You can have your name written down
      In the lamb's Book of God
      Is that old-fashioned word—
530 Repent.

Repent of your sins.
Repent of your sins.
Ask the Lord to be merciful onto your soul.
I tell you that old Pharisee was too proud.
535 And a lot of people are too proud to bend their feelings.
I'll tell you something
One of these days every knee will bow
And every tongue will confess
That Jesus Christ is Lord.
540 So if you don't bow this side of the judgement,
You will bow then,
But it *will be too late then*,
Because now is the time.
Jesus said
545 That now is the time.
Today.
Today is the day of salvation.
Today.
  Let me tell you something,
550 Just as sure as there is a heaven,
There is a hell.
And people [crying], it's—
It's thickly populated
Thickly populated.
555 And I believe it's burning today.
I believe it is a literal lake.
I believe it is a literal flame.
That's what my Bible says.
And *no one*
560 Need to go there.
But, people, you have to learn to love,
Because the Bible says—
How can you say you love God when you have not seen him
If you don't even love your brother
565 Or your sister?
The Bible tells us the Pharisee said,
"I thank God I'm not as
This man over here."
But the old Publican
570 Couldn't even lift his eyes up
And he was filled with sorrow.
"God, be merciful to me."

He wanted to repent,
But it was too late.
575 Remember it was the repentant one
There
That hung on the cross
Beside Jesus,
That asked him
580 To remember him
And to forgive him.
Two thieves.
One on the left
And one on the right.
585 One went to heaven
And one went to hell.
As I look across the congregation
Only heaven knows this morning
Those in sin
590 And who repents
And those who know Jesus.
Guilt and repentance
Are the products
Of God's Holy Spirit
595 And he will walk right into your heart this morning
And you *will* know him.
I believe there is a hell
Because you read it in God's word.
I know God's word does not lie
600 But I believe tonight
In hell there is no rest,
Day or night.
Forever hence.
In hell is torment.
605 In hell you will cry out
For a drink of water,
But there'll be none.
There will be no relief
From your torment.
610 You'll be separated from
Peace
Because there'll not be any peace.
There'll not be any light
For Jesus is the light of the world.

615 You'll not hear
A sermon.
There'll be no altars in hell
And you will never hear another altar call.
You'll never have another opportunity
620 To repent of your sins
Because you see
There's no way out of there
Except to stand before God
And have him reject you.
625 I know this is not a shouting message
But it's a message from God's word
And it's real.
God put this upon my heart
This past week.
630 A plain, simple message
On salvation
We cannot change ourselves
But we can come to one
Who can change us.
635 Will you come to Jesus this morning?
Will you lift your hands and let Jesus
Have the opportunity of changing your life?
Will you just lift your hand
So I can see it?
640 And God can see it?
And say, "I'm sick and tired
Of the way I'm living.
I need your help."
God will see it
645 And I will see it,
And I will pray for you.
Yes, I see your hands.
Yes, I see your hands.
You don't want to be left out.
650 You don't want to be left out standing at the door
When the door of grace is closed.
See, if you knock at that door after God closes,
It'll be just like
People trying to get into the ark.
655 When God reached down and closed the door of the ark,
Not even Noah

Could open it.
I'm going to give you the opportunity—
Let me lead you to the altar
660 And we'll pray together
Asking Jesus
To forgive you
To wash away your sins
And you'll leave here justified,
665 As though you had never committed a sin
In your life.
He'll wipe your record clean
And he says he'll put those sins
Behind his back
670 To remember against us no more.
Would you do that this morning?
Would you just stand
And walk down this aisle?
Jesus walked all the way to Calvary for you.
675 Would you just walk
To the altar for him this morning?
He's here.
He's in this building.
He's already waiting for you right here.
680 Will you come to him?
I'm asking you to come and stand down here on this side
To wait for those who will come.
Hazel, maybe it'll give them a little more courage,
If you come,
685 To stand here,
Will you just come and stand over on this other side.
People, we're going to make this just as easy for you as we can.
Will you come?
We love you.
690 God is not willing that any should perish
But that all should come to safe knowledge of Jesus Christ.
[tongue-speaking from various parts of the room]
Behold. I stand at the door and knock,
But will you let me in?
Will you not let me have entrance into thine heart
695 Where I am called unto thee?
Yea, I've called unto thee
I've spoken to thee,

I know thee by name
And I have called you come unto me.
700 Come unto me all ye that are weary and heavy-laden
And I will give you rest.
Take my yoke upon you,
For my yoke is easy
And my burden is light.
705 Come, I say, oh, Come,
Oh, the door's open.
[This constitutes Sister Anna's interpretation of the tongue-
speaking]
Come, come.
Won't you come?
Won't you come?
710 The Holy Spirit has pleaded
In this very altar today.
He thinks so much of you.
He's made another special attempt—
Won't you come.

Sister Linda Watson
Hinkson, Indiana
August 8, 1981

Do you love the Lord?
Do you love the Lord?
One more time!
Let's let them know out there
5 That we *love* the Lord!
Do you love the Lord?
Glory to God!
I really don't need this thing—   [disposes of the microphone]
You know, it's been good to be here, tonight,
10 And I think I'm going to do something
Just a little bit different, tonight.
I'm trying to obey
The spirit of the Lord.
There's been so much that's been sung
15 And said
About Jesus Christ, tonight, the Son of God,
I don't believe there's a whole lot

That I can add to it
But I do want to be obedient
20 To the spirit of God.
There's been so much said about Jesus, tonight,
And do you know what?
We could talk about him until eternity comes
And we could never talk about him
25 Enough.
We could never tell it all, tonight,
About Jesus.
Because he is the one
And the only one
30 That's ever been—
That we'll ever need.
Praise the lamb of God!
In fact, tonight,
I just want to kind of
35 Tell-talk about Jesus.
Praise the lamb of God!
I feel like this is the way
The Lord would have me to do it.
I'm going to obey the Lord
40 And I'm going to use his Word.
Glory to God!
It talks about in the Bible
About where
The Son of Man come down out of the splendor of heaven
45 And he come down here for one reason
And one reason only
And that was
That was to come down here—
And when he come, Sister Beulah,
50 He knew that he was going to die on the cruel cross, ah,
But he come anyway, because he loved us so much, ah,
That he wanted to come down here
That we might have a way
To make it to heaven through him.
55 Praise the lamb of God! Ah,
Let me read to you what it says in John 3:16.
Now, I'm gonna use a lot of scripture.
It says, "For God so loved the world
That he gave his only begotten son

60 That whosoever believeth on him
Shall not perish
But have everlasting life," ah.
Now, you just stop and think about what he did for you!
Praise the lamb of God!
65 He come out of the splendor of heaven, ah,
To come down on this old earth to walk up and down, ah,
To walk down here among men.
Glory to God!
And he was mocked, ah,
70 And ridiculed, ah,
And all them things that he had to go through, ah,
Praise the lamb of God! Ah,
But what really impressed me
Is the fact, ah,
75 When he left heaven,
Glory to God!
He *knew* what he was going to face here on this earth.
Glory to God.
Over here the Bible says, ah,
80 Over in the fifteenth chapter of John,
Glory to God—
You just bear with me—
It says, "Greater love hath no man that this
That a man lay down his life for his friends."
85 Let me go a little bit further.
You stop and think about that!
This man from out of the splendor of heaven
Knowing what his destiny was going to be
When he got down here
90 And he come down here for one reason
And one reason only
And that was to give his life upon an old cruel cross
That we could have life in heaven
For ETERNITY!
95 Now, you—
You heard what the sister said about eternity.
Now, you stop and think about it, tonight, ah,
Glory to God! Ah,
ETERNITY is for *ever* and *ever* and *ever*, ah,
100 And now, we're talking about heaven in eternity
But I want to *tell* you something

There's another eternity, tonight, ah,
And if you don't know the Lord,
Glory to God, ah,
105 If you're here tonight,
And you're not saved
And you don't know Jesus,
Glory to God!
There's going to be another eternity,
110 Praise the lamb of God!
There's a heaven and a hell, tonight,
Glory to God!
And it's in your hands *what you do* with it.
Praise the lamb of God.
115 So it's Jesus Christ.
He come down here to walk about—
But let me tell you something.
My God won't force anything on you.
Praise the lamb of God.
120 It's in—within *our hands* what we do with it.
Glory to God!
Hallelujah!
It's all in these *hands*.
You got heaven on one side to gain
125 Or hell on the other,
And it's your choice!
It's your choice tonight.
Glory to God!
Jesus—Jesus didn't come
130 To force us into anything.
He said, "No man cometh unto me except the spirit draw him."
It takes the spirit of God tonight.
You know,
I know
135 That Jesus
Is the only one tonight
That can save our souls.
I can get up here
And everybody in this building can get up here
140 And talk
And talk and talk and talk.
But it takes the spirit of God.
But you can get to thinking about it

You think about how he walked upon this earth
145 And, oh, they made fun of him
And they tried to set traps to entrap him
To where they could imprison him
And then they did this
And they did that
150 And even one of his—
Even the kiss of Judas,
Glory to God,
He's the one that turned him in,
Praise the lamb of God!
155 But you begin to think about
I mean get your *minds* on *Jesus* tonight, ah,
Just stop and think about what he really did for you,
And what he went through
That we could have this eternal life
160 That I'm talking about.
Glory to God!
Praise the lamb of God!
Let me *tell* you!
We need to get our minds centered on Jesus Christ tonight.
165 Let that sweet spirit of his flow through this place.
We want to fix our eyes on that cruel cross
That he hung upon,
Glory to God!
While he walked here and did many things.
170 Praise the lamb of God.
Wherever he went,
Praise the lamb of God, ah,
Wherever he went he healed them
And the lame was made to walk
175 And the blinded eyes was opened,
Praise the lamb of God,
And all the while they tried
They tried to trick him
In a way that they could put him in prison.
180 Glory to God!
Well, it finally come about
But you know *all this time*, ah,
They thought that they was really doing something.
But *all this time*
185 Jesus knew all this was coming about,

Glory to God!
He *knew* before he ever left the splendor of heaven
That he was going to have to go through this,
Glory to God, ah,
190 When he come to the garden again.
Let me read this to you.
This talks about our Jesus
And what happened to him on earth.
It says, "Who hath believed our report?
195 And to whom is the arm of the Lord revealed?
For he shall grow up before him as a tender plant,
And as a root out of a dry ground:
He hath no form nor comeliness;
And when we shall see him,
200 There is no beauty that we should desire him.
He is despised and rejected of men;
A man of sorrows, and acquainted with grief;
And we hid as it were our faces from him;
He was despised,
205 And we esteemed him not.
Surely he hath borne our griefs,
And carried our sorrows:
Yet we did esteem him stricken,
Smitten of God and afflicted.
210 But he was wounded for our transgressions,
He was bruised for our iniquities:
The chastisement of our peace was upon him;
And with his stripes we are healed.
And we like sheep have gone astray;
215 We have turned every one to his own way;
And the Lord hath laid on him the iniquity of us all."
Listen to that!
"The lord hath laid the iniquity"—
That's sin!—
220 "Of us all"—
Oh!
He was oppressed, ah,
He was afflicted, ah,
Yet he—
225 Get that—
They've just taken him and nailed him on that cross
And as they stood there—

"He was oppressed and
He was afflicted,
230 Yet he opened not his mouth, ah,
He is brought as a lamb to the slaughter,
And as a sheep before her shearers is dumb,
So he openeth not his mouth."
Listen to this!
235 Listen to this!
"Yet it pleased the Lord to bruise him."
You know the Bible tell us
He said, "Forgive them, Lord,
For they know not what they do."
240 Praise the lamb of God!
Now, I know I'm not preaching tonight
Like I been preaching here every night this week.
But I do believe that the Lord's really anointing me
But I'm delivering just what the Lord's put on my soul tonight.
245 Glory to God!
I wish that we could just walk through the world
And people would just catch it off of us,
Glory to God,
But it don't work that way.
250 The only thing we can do is tell them about Jesus
And his great love for them.
That he was willing to die for them
That they could have eternal life
And reign with him in heaven forevermore,
255 Glory to God!
And live up there among the gorgeous streets of gold
And look upon his face.
Praise his holy name!
Glory to God!
260 That's all we can do tonight
We can't do any more than that.
Glory to God!
But let me tell you!
Let me tell you about this Jesus!
265 If you don't know him tonight
You don't know what you're missing.
Glory to God!
He's the man of the hour, ah,
He's the *only* one that can come into our hearts

270 And give us the joy and peace
    To help us deal with this old world, ah,
    And you may be looking all around
    To and fro and trying to find
    Something that'll satisfy this inner man, ah,
275 Glory to God,
    But let me tell you something tonight!
    You're never going to satisfy that inner man
    Until you come face-to-face with the savior,
    Glory to God,
280 Until you take him as your personal savior.
    Glory to God!
    That's where it's at tonight.
    Praise the lamb of God!
    You pray for me—my throat's getting really bad.
285 Glory to God!
    But let me tell you something
    It's Jesus! It's Jesus! It's Jesus! It's Jesus!
    He's the ONLY one tonight,
    Glory to God,
290 That can set us free, ah,
    Praise the lamb of God!
    He's not only willing to set us free, ah,
    And forgive our sins and THROW them into the sea of
        forgetfulness,
    Glory to God,
295 But he wants to walk with us,
    He wants to walk with us
    Every step of the way,
    Glory to God,
    Every step we take.
300 Glory to God!
    Hallelujah!
    Praise the lamb of God!
    When you're hurting he wants you to lean on him, ah,
    When you've got problems he wants you to cry out to him, ah,
305 Glory to God,
    That's what he wants tonight!
    Hallelujah!
    He wants to help these people,
    Glory to God,
310 He wants to walk with them,

Side by side.
Praise the lamb of God!
Glory to God!
Just like God told Noah to build the ark
315 And the people laughed
But when GOD shut the doors on that ark
It was over.
It was over,
And they couldn't believe it.
320 Tonight, Jesus Christ is our ark.
Glory to God!
He's a crying out to people.
He's a standing before with arms outstretched
Wanting them to accept him.
325 Glory to God.
But I'm going to tell you something
It's not always going to be that way.
One of these days—
One of these days
330 It's all going to be over.
No more Jesus.
No more time.
All the time's *all* going to be gone.
You're not going to have a chance
335 To come face-to-face with him
And give your life to him.
You know why?
Cause the day for judgement's coming
And just like the ark in Noah's day
340 The door's going to be shut
And it's going to be all over.
Praise the lamb of God!
It's going to be over.
Praise the Lord.
345 And I know the devil's telling you,
"Ah, you've got plenty of time!"
But you don't have plenty of time.
You don't have plenty of time.
Glory to God.
350 *Now* is the time for salvation
Now is the time to give your life to almighty God.
Glory to God!

Glory to God!
Listen to this.
355 Listen to this.
Praise his holy name.
"Ho, every one that thirsteth,"
Join me at the fifty-fifth chapter of Isaiah.
"Ho, every one that thirsteth,
360 Come ye to the waters,
And he that hath no money
Come ye, buy and eat,
Yea, come, buy wine and milk
Without money and without price."
365 Where else can you go in this world
And get what Jesus is offering you tonight
Without money and without price?
The price is *already paid*!
Praise his holy name!
370 "Wherefore do ye spend money for that
Which is not bread?
And your labour for that
Which satisfieth not?"
That's just what I was pointing to—
375 People running through this—through the world
Trying to achieve this and achieve that
Trying to set aside this inner man,
Glory to God,
In their labors.
380 It is all in the wrong direction.
It satisfieth not.
"Hearken diligently unto me
And eat ye that which is good,
And let your soul delight itself in fatness.
385 Incline your ear, and come unto me;
Hear and your soul shall live;
And I will make an everlasting covenant with you,
Even the sure mercies of David."
Listen to this.
390 Listen to this.
"Seek ye the Lord while he may be found,
Call ye upon him while he is near."
Praise the lamb of God tonight!
If you're here and you don't know the Lord

395 Listen to my voice.
　　I obeyed my heart.
　　It may not be what you expected tonight.
　　But I'm a going to obey the Lord tonight.
　　If you're here and you don't know Jesus
400 Now is a good time to find him.
　　I feel him
　　I know he's been here tonight.
　　He's been here.
　　Praise the lamb of God!
405 Glory to God!
　　Now is the accepted time.
　　Glory to God!
　　Let's all stand.
　　Now, I know this preaching's not been like it has been all week.
410 It's not been—
　　I've not been running the aisles tonight
　　And I've not been preaching under a *heavy anointing*
　　But every service cannot be the same.
　　God knows what we need
415 And I—I didn't know
　　When I come here tonight
　　Exactly how I was going to deliver this message
　　God laid it on my heart.
　　Maybe it wasn't just exactly the way
420 Everybody wanted it
　　But I know I was obedient to the Lord.
　　The most important thing here tonight is—
　　If you're here
　　And you're lost
425 And you don't know Jesus
　　Now is the time to accept him as your Lord.
　　Glory to God!
　　There's been enough said here tonight
　　That it ought to convict your heart.
430 Glory to God!
　　Whether I ever opened my Bible
　　And read a word from it
　　Or whether I ever attempted to preach anything from it,
　　There's been enough said here tonight about Jesus, ah,
435 But most of all the spirit of God has been here

And that should convict your heart, ah,
Glory to God,
To the place
That you'd want to give your life to Jesus
440 And serve him.
Glory to God!
LET ME TELL YOU!
You'll not find a greater life, ah,
Glory to God!
[She slips into tongue-speaking for two lines here]
445 Than the one you'll have with Jesus, ah.
Walk with him, ah,
And let him walk with you.
Glory to God!
There's space and contentment there
450 And there's LOOOOVE
That I can't even begin to tell you about.
Glory to God!
There's LOOOOOOOOVE
That Jesus places in our hearts,
455 Glory to God,
When we give our hearts to him, ah,
Praise the lamb of God!
OOOOOOOHHHHHHHHHHHHH!!!!
GLORY!
460 There's a LOOOOOVE
That nobody else can give us tonight.
GLORY TO GOD!
And there's a joy, ah,
And a peace WITHIN
465 That we cannot receive, ah,
Glory to God!
Praise his holy name!
Hallelujah!
If you're here tonight
470 And you're troubled,
LET ME TELL YOU!
This JEEEESUS will calm the troubled sea.
Glory to God!
HEEEEE'S the ONE tonight that can meet your needs.
475 Glory to God!

HEEEEE'S the ONE that can save your soul.
Glory to God!
I can remember just as well tonight
As I could eleven years ago
480 When Jesus dealt with my heart
And I come to an old altar of prayer,
Glory to God!
It was in an old-time tent revival
Up in Brown County,
485 Glory to God,
And we had SAWWWWWWDUST on the floor!
Glory to God!
That's what we had, ah,
Cause it was outSIDE, ah,
490 Praise the lamb of God!
Well, *let me tell you*!
God dealt with my heart to come unto him
To give my heart to him
And IIIIII didn't see a thing
495 But that altar,
Glory to God,
And it looked like it was a mile away from me, Sister Beulah,
And Glory to God,
I begin to think I was never gonna reach it,
500 Glory to God,
But let me tell you something!
When I reached that altar
I fell down upon my knees,
Glory to God,
505 And I met somebody there to set me FREE!
WHOOOOOOOO!!!! [pounds pulpit with fists]
Jesus'll set you free tonight!
Glory to God!
Hallelujah!
510 He wants to set you free.
He wants to come into your life
And make you a new person—
A new man!
A new woman!
515 A new child!
Glory to God!
Let him put something in your heart

That you'll want to tell the world about
That you'll want to SHOUT about!
520 Hurrah!
Hallelujah!
Praise the lamb of God!
I'm going to tell you something!
When I knelt at that altar
525 And I met Jesus there,
I got the *real* thing.
Praise the lamb of God!
I didn't get no imitation!
WHOOOOOO!!!
530 Hallelujah!
WHOOOOOO!!!
Hurrah!
Hallelujah!
I didn't get an imitation, Sister Beulah!
535 I got the real thing!
Hurrah!
[She is pounding the pulpit, stomping her feet,
    and shouting as the crowd is loudly
    responding]
When I got up from that altar
I knew I had *JESUS*!!
Boy, I knew I had something in my heart
540 That I'd never had before!
Glory to God!
And the same thing that I felt
When I got up from that altar
[whisper] Is for everybody here.
[Loud responses from congregation]
545 It's not just for MEEEE!
It's just not for the ones in this church
It's for the WHOOOOLE WORLD!
Glory to God!
It's for everybody TONIGHT.
550 All you have to do is to accept it
In the name of Jesus!
Glory to God.
I want to tell you something!
When I got that first taste of Jesus
555 I wasn't satisfied!

Glory to God!
The next night I hit the altar again!
And the next night, ah,
I received the baptism of the Holy Ghost!
560 Glory to God!
Well, you've heard of holy rollers?
Well, I was one of them!
Glory to God!
I had sawdust in my HAIR!
565 And I'll tell you something!
I didn't CARE!
Because I had been to JEEEESUSS!
Hurrah!
Hallelujah!
570 He had given me eternal LIFE!
Praise the lamb of God!
And you know what?
It didn't cost me a thing!
Glory to God!
575 It didn't cost me a penny!
Praise the lamb of God!
It was FREEEEE
And it's still free tonight.
Praise the lamb of God!
580 Hallelujah.
Glory to God.
I don't know about you
But I feel this Jesus tonight.
Hurrah!
585 I FEEL him tonight.
Hurrah!
He said, "Ho, everyone that thirsteth,"
Glory to God!
He didn't say, "Ho, if this one thirsteth or that
    one,"
590 He said EVERYONE.
Praise the lamb of God!
COME TO THE WATERS!
Oh, Hallelujah!
I believe he's wanting somebody to come to the
    waters tonight,
595 Don't you?

WHOOOOOOOO!!!
Hallelujah!!
Praise the lamb of God!
You want to know something?
600 I was tired when I came to church tonight,
Glory to God,
But I'm not TIRED anymore!
You know why?
I got JESUS!
605 Hallelujah!
I've got to tell you tonight
That there's nothing but Jesus.
If you don't know him
You're missing something
610 You're missing the greatest life that ever was.
If you don't know Jesus.
Praise the lamb of God!
Hallelujah!
I'm going to tell you
615 How I was raised in Pentecost
Down at the church at Aunt Grace's
From the time I was a little girl.
Glory to God.
And I seen people talk in tongues
620 They'd get up and shout and shout.
And I'd say, oh, how can there be more than that?
How in the world can there be more than that?"
Oh, Hallelujah.
Then, when I met Jesus
625 I knew it was him.
It was Jesus! [shrieks and shouts—crowd responds]
Hallelujah!
Praise the lamb of God!
And when I received the baptism of the Holy Ghost
630 I wanted to make sure I had it
I didn't even know what it was,
Praise the lamb of God!
But I sure was talking funny!
But most of all I'm glad to know I know JESUS.
635 Hallelujah!
Glory to God!
Don't you think that God is near?

Well, are you ready to have church?
I'm ready to have church!
640 Hallelujah!
I'm ready to have church!
[Slips into lengthy tongue-speaking]
Praise God.
I want us, I want—
I just want to talk about Jesus.
645 I want to tell you about this Jesus.
I don't know what I'd do without him.
I don't know, Sister Margie, how I'd—
I don't know how I'd make it without Jesus.
Glory to God.
650 I see people walking around
And they're—they're so miserable
And all they need is Jesus.
All they need is Jesus.
Glory to God.
655 And you try to tell them, you know,
And they just kinda look at you, Sister Faith.
Glory to God.
But one of these days, ah,
When it's too late, ah,
660 They're gonna want him, ah,
They're gonna WANT HIM.
They're gonna want this Jesus that we're talking
   about here tonight.
They're gonna want this Jesus
That we're shouting about.
665 Glory to God.
THEY'RE GONNA WANT HIM!
BUT THEY'RE GONNA HAVE LEFT IT TOO LATE!
They're gonna've left it too late.
Glory to God.
670 Because he's gonna have already COME
After his church.
Glory to God,
And they're gonna be KNOCKING the church
   doors DOWN
Wanting INNNNNN.
675 THEY'RE GONNA WANT WHAT WE'VE
   GOT HERE TONIGHT!

But they're gonna have left it too late.
They're gonna have left it too late.
Glory—[slips into tongues]
Hallelujah!
680 Praise the lamb of God!
Jesus loves you.
If you're here tonight,
If you're here tonight
And you don't know Jesus,
685 Let me tell you,
This'd be a good time to find him.
He'll give you peace and joy unspeakable in your heart.
Glory to God.
There's nothing like serving Jesus.
690 There's nothing like it.
Glory to God.
Let's sing . . .

Sister Pat Roberts
Centerville, Missouri
June 17, 1984

If you want to turn with me to the book of Leviticus
In the twenty-second chapter
Verse twenty-one and twenty-two.
God is very plain
5 To make mention of what kind of *sacrifice*
That he wanted the children of Israel to offer unto him.
You see back in the early days, ah,
Before Christ was ever born, ah,
And back when the children of Israel was, ah,
10 The very most chosen of God's—
You know, God's very own chosen people,
I tell you they had, uh,
Something to go by that actually wasn't too easy,
Amen?
15 We think we got it hard today
In the way God's got a sacrifice
Set up for you and I today.
So many people think that's hard
I can't do it.
20 Even the sacrifice of coming out to a service sometimes

205

It's hard for people.
But it's not hard.
It's not hard what God's got set up for us today!
Just as smooth as can be.
25 You know he don't ask for much,
But if you'll turn back to the Old Testament
And find out what God begun to speak unto the
    children of Israel
And if we're only going to try to touch the topic
Of *sacrifice*
30 Tonight—
And so
He wanted the children of Israel
To take heed
To what God had to say.
35 God said, "Hey!
You're mine!
Now, I want to see how much you love me.
I'm gonna set down some ordinances for you."
Amen?
40 God said, "Hey!
I want you to do this for me.
I want you to sacrifice unto me
And I got it all planned out the way I want you to do it."
And God had that set up—
45 The sacrifice
So he would know
Whether or not
The children of Israel
Loved him—
50 Amen?
And so you see
It comes right on down to a sacrifice today
And I don't want to jump or get ahead of myself
But God has not quit requiring a *sacrifice*
55 To see WHETHER OR NOT
YOU AND I LOVE HIM TODAY
AMEN?
No.
And so.
60 Turn with me now over to the book

Of Leviticus
The twenty-second chapter—
We're gonna read verse twenty-one and twenty-two.
Leviticus 22.
65 This was the sacrifice
And the ordinance that God had put down
For the children of Israel.
He told them—he said:
"Whosoever offers a sacrifice
70 A peace offering unto the Lord to accomplish his vow,
Or a freewill offering in beeves or sheep,
It shall be perfect to be accepted;
There shall be *no blemish therein*.
Blind or broken or maimed
75 Or having a wen, or scurvy, or scabbed,
Ye shall not offer these unto the Lord,
Nor make an offering by fire of them upon the altar
Unto the Lord."
So the sacrifice was
80 That God had for the children of Israel—
He said, "Hey!
You go out
And begin to bring forth of your herd
Or of your flock
85 Unto me."
And the sacrifice is on the altar—
They was to sacrifice animals.
That's the ordinance that God had in those days
For a sacrifice.
90 He said, "Hey!
I want nothing but the best of what you've got!"
And you see it *was* something of a sacrifice.
And he said, "Hey!
I don't want something that's maimed or nasty out there!"
95 He said, "Hey!
I don't want you to go out there
And pick out a little old RUNT
Because you know that thing's gonna die anyway
Bring it in here and put it on the altar to sacrifice to me today!
100 Hey!
I want you to show me that you LOVE ME

WITH THE BEST OF WHAT YOU HAVE!"
And that's what they did in those days
Was go out there amongst the herd
105 And, "Hey!
Pick out the best
That you've got."
And, you know, it was sort of like God said,
"Hey!
110 I'm gonna see if you really love me
As much as you let on."
Like a lot of people say,
"Hey, God, I love you.
Hello, I love you!"
115 But you know they don't love him enough
To live for him like they should
And they don't love him enough
To be for him what they really should be,
Or they wouldn't live their lives
120 Like they live.
And God says, "Hey!
I want to see if you love me
And so they go out
And I tell you I believe the *desire*
125 Is genuine in their heart
To be obedient
And bring a sacrifice to God.
I believe they looked around
And I believe they took a little bit of time—
130 Amen?
Nowadays so many people they don't—
They don't want to take a little time for God—
You know any folks like that?
WHO DON'T HAVE TIME FOR GOD?
135 TOO BUSY DOING THIS AND DOING THAT?
Just in a hurry, you know,
Get it over with.
Hurry up, you know, you're going to church.
HURRY UP AND GET IT OVER WITH!
140 And I thought about my little old granddaughter
You know she—ah,
This morning as we was setting during the Sunday School class
She said, "Grandma,

Ain't you not preach this morning?
145 Ain't you not preach?"
And you see she wanted me to hurry up
And get church over with
Because she wanted to go home with Grandma.
She wanted to be with Grandma
150 And I'll tell you like a child
You'll pay for what it is
These grown-up people
When they've not got no time for God!
And so,
155 I believe that when they begin to go out into the herds
And go out in their flocks
And they go out amongst the birds—
And they was gonna offer the birds—
I believe it took them some time
160 To go out there and make sure
THEY GOT THE BEST OF WHAT THEY HAD—
AMEN?
Give the best of what you've got—
I'm telling you!
165 When you give yourself to the Lord
Make sure you give him, ah,
All that you've got in yourself,
Amen?
Won't do a bit of good trying to hold back
170 A part and keep it yourself.
But you say, "I *have*, Sister Roberts."
And I might not know about it.
Course, I tell you I think I will
Because I have the gift of discernment.
175 I can usually tell.
But it won't do no good with God, Amen?
And so you see
I believe now it's your time.
I believe it's A-Number One that—
180 God's saying to you, "Hey!
I'm gonna see if you are taking your time
To go out there and LOOK AROUND.
Don't be in a hurry
And go out there
185 And just jerk up the first one

That'll come to you."
I know all about cows and barns.
My daddy raised black angus cattle
And I'm telling you!
190 Oh, they were mean.
But I want you to know, ah, when he begin to corral those bulls
To ship them off to market
When he begin to sell off maybe those heifers, ah,
It took TIME for him to go out there and sort them off
195 From the herd
It wouldn't do a bit of good
For that guy across the way
To come in and buy a certain heifer
And when he come to get that heifer
200 Go over there and get something else—
Wouldn't do a bit of good.
   He took TIME
To sort them out.
And so every one of us
205 How much are we giving God?
The sacrifice was in the days of old.
He said, "Go out there
And bring the sacrifice in of the animal
Bring it on the altar."
210 And there was also ordinances done
Just how to do the sacrifice on the altar.
We'll not get into that—all that—but, ah,
I'll tell you it's REAL
What God set up in the beginning is not changed
215 Unto today!
I'll tell you what!
Many times folks tries to change what God's got.
Many times you do away with the Old Testament,
Say, "I don't get it at all."
220 But I want you to know when we look at our Lord Jesus Christ
And what he's got for you and I
Is based
Upon the Old Testament
That is the foundation
225 For what we're standing on today.
No way we can understand our Lord
And our savior

210

Without going back and seeing what God wants
In the beginning.
230 Amen?
And it fits it all in so good.
Fits it in perfect
With what God's got for you and I.
He's saying, "A-Number One, You,
235 How much time you gonna take to do what I want you to do?"
Amen?
Lord,
I'm preaching to myself
Cause sometimes I don't take enough time
240 For God.
Amen?
Sometimes we got time for everything else.
Amen?
Everything else in the world
245 Gonna take up our time.
But Hey!
Have we got enough time for God?
And so, here is what God was saying unto the children of Israel.
He said, "I want you to go out there
250 And when you bring in the sacrifice,"
He said, "I don't want it to be
The worst that you've got
Or I don't want it blind
Or I don't want it broken
255 I don't want it maimed
I don't want it having no sores on it."
You know, I believe it took TIME
For them to look at them animals
And see if there was sores on them,
260 You ever think about that?
Amen?
He didn't want no *scabs*
On them animals.
That took a little TIME,
265 Amen?
Some people say, "Oh, it's foolish
To try for what God's got.
Oh, it's foolish."
It might be foolish to some people

270 But I believe it's not foolish to you and I.
We love the Lord.
LOVE what he's got for his children.
We know that LOVE
Is what he's got for you and I,
275 Amen?
Now we get on down to the good part—
The sacrifice for you and I today.
I'm glad that God changed it
Because I'd never be able to—
280 I don't think I'd want anyway—
I couldn't do it—
It's hard for me to envision
It'd be hard for me to go out and kill those animals
And bring them in.
285 I can remember when my mom and dad
Used to butcher chickens, ah,
You know, I'd run away just as far as I could go.
You know, wrung them heads off, ah,
And them chickens would hop around,
290 You know, without any heads on, ah,
Just literally scare me to death.
And I'm glad that I'm living in today
My sacrifice is a lot easier than what they had in
    the days of the Old Testament.
Many people think,
295 "Well, I may be a Christian.
But I've got no time to go to church.
I'm too busy today
Cause I got something else I gotta do
Somewhere else I gotta go, you know,"
300 And some ladies, you know,
You try to get them to go to church on Sunday—
"Oh, I can't do that, you know,
Cause I work all week,
And I got to do my laundry on Sunday."
305 Sacrifice!
Where's the sacrifice,
Amen?
Where's the sacrifice?
And so it boils down to what God has got
310 For you and I today.

First Corinthians.
It wouldn't be complete—
I couldn't even start
The second part of the sermon
315 Without doing First Corinthians,
The fifth chapter and the seventh verse.
First Corinthians,
Five and seven:
"Purge out therefore the old leaven,
320 That ye may be a new lump,
As ye are unleavened.
For even Christ our passover
Is sacrificed for us."
Oh, Praise the Lord!
325 The most perfect
Sacrifice
God himself gave
And that was
Jesus Christ—
330 Amen?
And so you see
God never quits doing things.
From the very beginning
He'll not quit until the end
335 Even if it's in the Old Testament
And you get over into the New Testament
God is still the same.
He just goes
His own way
340 Of doing what he sees he ought to do.
And so we find
When you move over to
The gentile dispensation
Over and into the New Testament,
345 Jesus Christ
Is our passover.
God begins to do a new thing
And so Christ is then our passover
And our sacrifice.
350 Then Jesus says, "Hey
Wait a minute.
I've done the sacrifice

For you.
The children of Israel
355 Had to do sacrifice for God.
Now, hey,
What's gonna be *your* sacrifice
For me?
Amen?
360 The savior of the world
The savior of our soul.
How do we sacrifice
Unto our Lord?
We don't go out
365 To our herds.
We don't go out
And check the flock
And bring in
A sheep
370 Without blemish.
No!
We don't do that.
Jesus done did that.
But he says, "Hey!
375 I've got an ordinance I want you to do!
I've got a sacrifice I want you to do for me."
Well, we're gonna read some of those tonight.
First of all in Romans twelve and one.
Here's a good one
380 Romans twelve and one:
"I beseech you bretheren
By the mercies from God
That you present your bodies
A living sacrifice.
385 Holy, acceptable unto God
Which is your reasonable service."
YOU WANT TO DO A REASONABLE SER-
   VICE FOR GOD TONIGHT?
YOU WANT TO BRING A SACRIFICE
UNTO THE LORD
AND TRULY SHOW YOU HAVE SACRIFICED
390 FROM THE VERY BEGINNING?
HE SAID, "ALL RIGHT I'M GONNA TELL YOU
HOW I WANT YOU TO SACRIFICE FOR ME!"

214

You know the only thing
The only thing I've got tonight?
395 You know the *only* thing I've got to give?
Well, I could say
I've got a husband
And I do.
He's good to me and I love him—
400 He's a dandy!
Even if he is downstairs
And can't hear me say it.
But you know what?
Lots of homes break up—
405 Amen?
Lots of women
Have a husband
Maybe one week
Not long and they be divorced
410 And alone
With children.
The Bible says you know that
Even children
They'll
415 Come against parents
They'll be a division.
Homes'll break up
Mother-in-laws against daughter-in-laws—
All this kind of thing.
420 You know the only thing I've got tonight
Is *ME*!
Myself!
WHEN IT'S ALL BROUGHT DOWN TO IT
YOU MAY THINK THAT YOU'VE GOT A
   LOT TONIGHT
425 BUT THE ONLY THING THAT'S *YOURS*
THAT YOU HAVE CONTROL OVER
   IS YOURSELF!
AND I BELIEVE THAT'S WHY THE LORD
   SAYS, "HEY!
You must present your body
430 A living sacrifice."
Amen?
Me.

This is something I can give tonight.
I won't have to go over and ask permission
435 Of my husband.
I don't have to ask permission
Of my children
Or my mother-in-law—
Thank the Lord I don't have to ask her.
440 You know what I really think?
She'd say no.
She's a dandy, you know,
She's a jim-dandy.
But you see
445 I've got myself.
And you know the Lord knew that.
How many times you know you can't depend on nothing—
But we got ourself!
What are we gonna give unto the Lord tonight?
450 He said, "Hey!
Present your body as a living sacrifice."
Well, now, I don't have to sacrifice you tonight!
Thank God!
Oh, Hallelujah!
455 You don't have to sacrifice somebody else
Because they probably won't let you,
Amen?
I'd probably sacrifice you
And you wouldn't like that!
460 And God said, "Hey, you,
You—
You can give yourself."
Thank God.
I try to give somebody else?
465 I try to give somebody else?
I'll even try to give my—
Well, you know, maybe something
Something out of my refrigerator—
You know, like maybe the electric went off
470 And it'll spoil a little
And I'd give that—
But the Lord said, "Hey!
I want a sacrifice without blemish.
I made it plain that I want to see

475 If they truly love me!"
So he said, "Hey!
Jesus was a sacrifice for you."
Did he love the Father enough to stand true?
Yes!
480 He did!
He said, "Father,
If it be possible
Let this cup pass from me."
But you see it wasn't possible
485 And he stood there
And he took
Punishment.
He was our sacrifice.
Now!
490 The Lord says, "Hey!
You love me?
What do you give
As sacrifice?"
I believe the Lord says, "Hey!
495 You—A-Number One, You—
The only thing you've got
Is yourself!"
Amen?
That's why
500 The husband cannot make
The wife go to heaven.
The wife cannot make
The husband go to heaven.
The parents cannot make
505 The children—
And I've even seen children say—
They'll go to church
And pray around the altar
Bless their hearts
510 For their mom and dad.
But that didn't make their mom and dad
Make heaven,
Did it?
The only thing you can give
515 Is yourself [whispers this].
I believe that's why

The Lord will say, "Hey!
Present your bodies
A living sacrifice!"
520 That's something I can give tonight.
I couldn't give something else
And know for sure
That I was giving whole-hearted.
I'll tell you what!
525 When I give my heart to the Lord
When I was at the age of 29—
In 1942
You all can count that up—[laughs]
I knew
530 I tell you then I KNEW
That it was REAL!
It had to be REAL!
I'm so glad that he said, "Hey!
Come unto me."
535 I believe, though, that it even goes deeper than that.
I want to present my body in a way
That the Lord wouldn't be ashamed—
Amen?
DON'T WANT TO GO OUT
540 AND PRESENT MYSELF IN A WAY THAT
THE LORD
Would be ashamed of me—
Amen? [whispers]
I'll tell you what!
Those sacrifices
545 In the old days
Wasn't allowed to be gaudy—
Like the Hebrews—
We need to be careful—
Amen?
550 With our sacrifice
That we're giving unto the Lord
A sacrifice that our Lord will understand—
Amen?
We're not living
555 As the Jews
In the days
Of the Old Testament

WE'RE LIVING UNDER THE DISPENSATION
OF *JESUS*
560 AND THE HOLY GHOST!
And the only thing we go to give
As sacrifice unto the Lord
Is our *bodies*. [whispers]
Let's be careful
565 With our bodies.
O.K. LET'S GO ON DOWN TO HEBREWS
The thirteenth chapter
Read the fifteenth verse.
Glory, listen to this:
570 "Therefore, let us offer the sacrifice of praise
To God continually,
That is,
The fruit of our lips thanks to his name.
But to do good and to communicate
575 Forget not
For with such sacrifices
God is well-pleased."
Here is another sacrifice.
I believe the Lord—
580 The idea for it he expects you and I to do—
Praise after him!
That's a sacrifice, you know what?
It is a sacrifice
To praise the Lord
585 When things is going rough,
Amen?
When things is hard
And it seems like
You offer God your praise
590 Where you're at
It's a sacrifice
To give praise unto him.
It seems like the enemy is right there
You try to put your hand up
595 And the enemy's there to pull it down.
YOU TRY TO SPEAK FORTH THE PRAISE
 UNTO THE LORD
BUT IT SEEMS LIKE THE ENEMY'S THERE
To take your words.

600 And he's got a whole bag of tricks
And he'll make you think
That God didn't like that sacrifice [whispers]
Or praise.
THE ENEMY'S OUT THERE TO BITE OFF
 ANY PRAISE
605 THAT WE GIVE UNTO GOD
But HE wants us to sacrifice and praise his name.
And truly it is
It is a sacrifice—
Not all the time
610 We know we have good times
But when we have those bad times
Just like out in the flower garden—
Prettiness there
Loveliness there—
615 Beauty of God—
But you reach down to pick a rose
And you're gonna get a thorn if you're not real careful,
Amen?
But you know what?
620 I find myself picking those
Rose bouquets anyway,
Amen?
I think it makes us more careful!
I WILL OFFER SACRIFICE
625 UNTO MY LORD.
I WANT TO BE CAREFUL
I WANT TO BE PLEASING UNTO THE LORD!
This scripture says we need to do it with *love*!
We need to do it with *love*.
630 Sometimes that seems hard, you know,
Somebody's swiped the rug out from under you
And it's awful hard to praise God
BUT YOU'RE GONNA DO IT ANYWAY
Because that's the sacrifice [whispers]
635 Unto the Lord.
Amen?
Can you do it tonight?
Can we do what God wants us to do?
It's not hard
640 And it's the most rewarding work.

YOU WANT TO KNOW WHAT I THINK
   OF BEING A MINISTER TONIGHT?
It's the most rewarding thing there is—
Is to think that you stand pleasing
Before God
645 The Almighty [whispers]
The one that reigns supreme
Over the world.
NOT IN THIS LIFE!
You know maybe Satan's having him a hey-day today
650 The Bible says that he is the God of this world.
But I want you to know that MY GOD
REIGNS SUPREME.
AND FOR ME TO DO ALL THAT I KNOW
THAT I CAN DO
655 TO STAND
IN HIS FAVOR
I WANT TO DO THAT!
AMEN?
And I believe you do too
660 Or you wouldn't be in God's house tonight.
I believe you're serious
About walking with him
And if you're not
I challenge you
665 This night
To get serious
And you won't regret it
Because
You're gonna stand before him.
670 The Bible says
Every knee
Is gonna bow
Every tongue
Is gonna confess.
675 There'll come a time
We'll have to confess unto the Lord,
Amen?
Offer them sacrifices unto him
We know what God wants—
680 Our *lives*,
Amen!

A-Number One—Ourself.
God knows ourselves,
That's why he said, "Present your bodies."
685 I believe that's an A-Number One *sacrifice*!
Cause really that's all we've got!
That's all I've got!
All any one of us has got,
Amen?
690 And I'll tell you what!
The Lord will repay,
Amen?
Himself!
Jo will you come to the piano?
695 Every head bowed.
No looking around.
I'm not gonna call for sinners
Or anything like that.
But I tell you what!
I'm really gonna call on you
700 To hear God say,
"Where's your sacrifice?
Hey, what you sacrificing unto me?
Hey, you gotta look nice
For me.
705 Hey, you gotta sing
Like you should
For me."
Oh, thank you Jesus.
God, you're filling every heart here tonight.
710 Every heart,
Every heart here tonight.
God bless you tonight.
I'm gonna ask Brother Bob to come dismiss us
in prayer.
Brother Bob.

Sister Connie Morton
Hinkson, Indiana
May 28, 1980

I praise the Lord tonight
Because truly he is—

He's been so good to me, and
You know, the Word of God
5 Is what feeds the Holy Ghost
And, ah, you can't, ah,
Without reading the Word of God
The spiritual man within you will, ah,
Soon die out
10 Because that's what feeds him
That's what takes care of him.
And I love the Lord tonight
And I love to read his word
Because it really it just—
15 It brings such a blessing to me
And it just—
I just get all excited about it
Enthused about it
There's just no other
20 It's just joy unspeakable.
You can't really describe
The feeling that you have
About the Word of God.
I know many people have told me,
25 "I don't like to read the Bible
Because I don't understand it
It just don't make no sense
To me."
But, you know,
30 Once you've been born again,
Of the water and the spirit,
And once you receive the Holy Ghost
And you read the scriptures
You just feast on it
35 It just enthuses you
Because you *realize*
And you understand it
Because it's the *Holy Ghost*
That reveals
40 The truth to you.
Now, we're going to start
Over in St. John
And tonight

We're going to do something
45 That's
Kind of unusual.
It's been about two weeks ago
That the Lord began
To deal with me—
50 Maybe I should say
Three weeks ago
The Lord began—
To deal with me
On the—
55 On the crucifixion.
And I know a lot of times,
When we think about, ah,
Jesus, dying on that cross,
It will bring tears to our eyes.
60 It will make us feel, ah,
We think about all the things
That he suffered
And it brings a sadness
To our hearts.
65 But, you know,
The Lord showed me
Something
Totally different
About the crucifixion
70 And I'd like for you tonight
To just to try to, ah,
To picture the crucifixion
In a different way.
The Lord had—
75 You know, the Lord
Had a purpose
For everything
That happened to him
There on the cross.
80 Everything is a symbol
Of something,
It's significant.
And if you *read*
The Word of God,
85 Not just look at the words,

And just say the words,
But if you'll study it
You'll *think* about it
And you'll *pray* about it
90 And you'll ask the Lord,
Say, "Lord, feed me on this,
Show me what you mean,
Let me grow,
Give me depth in this."
95 And the Lord will open up things to you, ah,
I'm sure that you've
Never thought about.
Now, I want you to know
That I never thought about these things
100 On my own.
I prayed
And the Lord revealed these things to me.
I have not got
That much sense in my own head.
105 The Lord has to show me things.
I'm not intelligent,
You know I never went to college,
And I don't have any education,
Learning in this world,
110 But whatever the Lord give to me
He just give me straight from him.
We'll start.
Now this may be kind of like—
Teaching,
115 I don't know.
Charlie said preach it.
But you know sometimes
It's kind of hard to preach,
But maybe a mixture of both—
120 Preaching and teaching.
And we're going to start reading
In St. John,
The nineteenth chapter
And we're going to start—
125 On the—
Takes a long time to find it—
On the twenty-third verse.

Now we're just going
To be jumping around
130 In the Bible
And I may not have time
To do this whole thing—
And if I don't
Maybe they'll let me
135 Finish up next week
Because it's a lot.
We're going to start on the twenty-third verse:
"Then the soldiers
When they had crucified Jesus
140 Took his garments
And made four parts
To every soldier
And also his coat.
Now, the coat was without seam
145 Woven from top throughout."
When I read this verse
This one word—
It just jumped right out at me
And that was "his coat."
150 And I looked at that
And I thought, well, Lord,
Surely there's something
Significant here.
If it wasn't significant
155 About that coat
You wouldn't have let that word
Just stand out at me.
And, you know,
I just kept thinking about that
160 And about the next word,
"Without a seam."
Hallelujah!
A coat, ah,
Without a seam.
165 Just one piece.
One complete piece.
They started at the top
And they just began to weave it
And they never left any—

170 I don't believe—
　　Left any arm holes.
　　They just went down
　　And just, ah,—
　　It was just straight
175 One piece
　　And they didn't—
　　You know, a lot of times, ah,
　　Sister Wilma she sews, and
　　She's got a pattern,
180 And she'll cut out the sleeves,
　　She'll cut out the front section,
　　She'll cut out the side,
　　And the back,
　　And we've got all these different pieces
185 And then we sew it all together,
　　Don't we?
　　Those who have sewn.
　　We sew it all together.
　　But this says that Jesus' coat
190 "Was of one piece
　　Without any seams
　　From the top
　　Throughout."
　　They started at the top.
195 Now, Sister Allison—
　　She's made
　　A lot of, ah,
　　Crochet.
　　I know, she wore one to Sunday School.
200 And she started at the top
　　And she went down
　　And she just crocheted the whole thing
　　She didn't have to sew
　　Any of it together
205 Cause it was all one piece.
　　Now then, this one piece,
　　Being without any seams,
　　In other words,
　　You didn't sew it together
210 You didn't add anything to it
　　It was one piece

Represents Jesus Christ,
The Godhead.
The Godhead is what it represents.
215 Jesus himself
The Godhead.
He is the—
There is only one God,
One God.
220 Jesus is the one true God.
You can't add anything to him
You can't take anything away from him
There is just one,
One true and living God.
225 Now I want to go over
And read just a few scriptures
In the first chapter of John
That talks just a little bit
About the Godhead
230 And lets you know
That there is no other
Besides him.
The third—well,
We'll just read the first three verses:
235 "In the beginning was the word
And the word was with God
And the word was God.
The same was in the beginning.
All things were made by him
240 And without him was not anything
Made that was made."
Hallelujah!
Now then, when we think about this scripture
We think about the creation—
245 In the beginning.
All things that were made
Every—
This earth, the stars and the moon
All these things that were made
250 Were made by God.
And who is God?
Jesus!
Because it goes on to say

That he was the Lord.
255 Hallelujah!
"He was in the world
And the world was made by him
And the world knew him not."
Hallelujah!
260 Who was it that the world didn't know?
Who was it that the Jews didn't accept?
It was Jesus Christ.
It was him.
He is the light
265 And he is the one they didn't want to accept.
Hallelujah!
Praise the Lord!
Now, then, let's go to Colossians
Two and nine—
270 And just to let you know
That I may not read all these scriptures
As I get a little further into it
But I'm going to read this one.
Sometimes people—
275 You say things and people say
I don't believe that's in there.
That's the reason why
I'm going to read this.
And we sing this song,
280 "It's all in him,
It's all in him,
The wonder of the Godhead,
It's all in him."
And we get that song
285 From this scripture,
Colossians two and nine:
"For in him dwelleth all the fullness
Of the Godhead bodily."
Hallelujah!
290 It's speaking of Jesus Christ!
Hallelujah!
Thank you Lord!
Now, we're going to talk about
One more thing
295 About this coat of Jesus.

Now, it says
It was without any seams.
It didn't have any—
I don't believe
300 It was made like any kind of coat
We have today.
I don't know,
I can't say,
It was like a robe
305 He wrapped around him
Or if it was—
Maybe it just had an opening
At the top
Where it just slipped over his head.
310 But many pictures that we've seen
Of that day and time,
They just had—
They just kinda wrapped it over their shoulders,
Wrapped it around them.
315 Whichever way it was
That Jesus put it on himself
It only had one opening.
That is the key to it.
It only had one opening.
320 There were no arm holes
Here or here
But it was just wrapped around him
Or placed down upon his head whichever way
There was only one opening
325 That could be—
Put upon him
And that signifies to mean
Jesus said,
"I am the door to the sheepfold."
330 We'll go to the tenth chapter of John
And read that.
This will give you just another
Little extra thing on his robe.
The ninth verse, seventh verse,
335 Then we'll jump down to the ninth:
"Then Jesus said unto them,
Verily, verily I say unto thee

I am the door of the sheep.
I am the door.
340 If any man enter,"
The ninth verse,
"He shall be saved and shall go in and out
And find pasture.
I am the good shepherd,"
345 Verse eleven,
"And the good shepherd
Giveth his life for the sheep."
Hallelujah.
Now, why did Jesus say that?
350 This was before he was ever crucified
But he *knew* what he was going to go through.
He said he gave his life for us.
Hallelujah!
He is the door to the sheepfold.
355 Hallelujah!
Thank you, Jesus!
Now, we'll go back to our nineteenth chapter
And continue with the scripture of the crucifixion.
And when they crucified Jesus
360 Took his garments—
Now, this is talking
About two different things now—
This is not talking about his robe.
This is talking about his garments
365 That were *under* his robe.
His robe is an outer coat.
And they made four parts
To every soldier.
Hallelujah!
370 Today, we have—
Have you ever thought about the different
Religions that we have today?
Everybody wants just a part of Jesus.
They don't want all of him
375 They just want a part of him.
And whenever I read this
The Lord brought to my mind—
There's the Catholic sect
There's the Jewish—

380 If you look up in your encyclopedia
Look up religion
You'll find basic categories
Protestant—
These are the parting of his garments
385 The different parts that thy took out
Just parts of Jesus
Not accepting the whole thing
But just parts of it.
And they parted his garments.
390 So, today, we can see this
We can see it all around us
All the time every day
All these different religions
They just want a little piece of Jesus.
395 Now, the seventeenth verse:
"Which are a shadow of things to come
But the body is of Christ."
Surely this means something.
Everything I believe means something
400 In the Lord.
If you'll search deep enough
You'll find that meaning.
Did you ever think
That as Jesus was hanging
405 There on the cross
There it was in his body.
One piece of the cross
The body of Jesus
The other piece of the cross
410 The spiritual man.
The flesh died in order
That the spirit could live.
There you have your two parts:
The flesh and the spirit.
415 The flesh dying out.
Paul said "I die daily."
And today, we have died out
We have to die out—
We have to cut our flesh out of our lives
420 We don't crucify ourselves
And kill ourselves

But each day we have to deny the things
That the flesh desires after—
We lust after.
425 We're tempted in this world
Each and every one of us.
None of us can say
That we're above temptation that—
That the devil doesn't come to us
430 And tempt us.
There are things in this world
That we have to say—
I am going to deny myself of that—
I'm going to cut this flesh off
435 And let the spiritual man live
And when Jesus died on the cross
The spiritual man
He reigned
He reigned supreme
440 Throughout all eternity.
Hallelujah!
Blessed Jesus!
Now, we'll go to St. Luke,
Twenty-third chapter, verse forty.
445 I want to talk a little bit
About the two thieves
And the significance they play
In the crucifixion.
"And one of the malefactors which was hanged
450 Railed on him saying, 'If thou be Christ
Save thyself and us.'"
Hallelujah!
There was two of them.
The first one began to ridicule
455 Jesus
Denying him of his power.
"Well, if you've got so much power,
Then why don't you get off that cross
And not only you get down
460 But take me also!"
What does that bring back to your remembrance?
Do you remember the time that Jesus
Had been fasting

And Satan come to him
465 And he said,
"If you be the son of God
Why don't you just turn these here stone
Into bread."
Didn't he?
470 Doesn't that just make you—
Just sound like Satan?
You see Satan represented here
In this thief!
And he says,
475 "If you be the son of God
Then why don't you just do this!"
Hallelujah?
But you know
The Lord didn't have to prove anything!
480 Hallelujah!
He is the supreme!
Let's read Matthew four and the fourth verse.
This is what Jesus says to him.
"And then the tempter came unto him
485 And he said, 'If thou be the son of God
Command these stones to be made bread.'
But he answered and said unto him,
'It is written,
Man shall not live by read alone
490 But by every word that proceedeth
Out of the mouth of God.'
And then again Satan took him up
And tempted him again.
And he said,
495 'If thou be the Son of God,
Cast thyself down,
For it is written he shall give his angels charge
Concerning thee and in their hands
They shall bear thee up' "—
500 Satan is quoting scripture to the Lord—
" 'Lest at any time thou dash thy foot against a stone.'
Jesus said unto him,
'It is written again,
Thou shalt not tempt the Lord thy God.' "
505 Oh, Hallelujah!

234

I praise the Lord tonight
For I know whom I have believed!
Thank you Jesus!
Hallelujah!
510 You know,
Satan always likes to get his part in
But you know the Lord
He's got people that believe on Him!
He's got children—
515 Hallelujah—
Who have not yet turned themselves
Over to the devil!
Now, let's go back to Luke twenty-three, and verse forty.
And this is what the other thief said
520 Which really touched my heart:
"And we indeed justly,
For we receive the due reward of our deeds,
But this man hath done nothing amiss."
Hallelujah!
525 He realized what he was
And Jesus said it takes *godly sorrow*
For repentance.
And this man—
He really was repenting
530 Because he said
I deserve
Dying on the cross.
I deserve this
Because of what I've done.
535 I'm not any count.
But you, Lord,
I see that you're an innocent man.
He seen and knew who Jesus was
And he knew what he represented
540 And he said unto Jesus:
"Remember me when thou comest into thy kingdom."
Oh, Hallelujah!
Jesus, Hallelujah!
    Remember *me*—
545 Oh, Yes, Lord—
    Remember *me*
    When thou comest into thy kingdom!

Oh, Hallelujah,
Thank you, Jesus.
550 "And then,
The Lord spoke to him and said,
'Verily, I say unto thee,
Today thou shalt be with me in paradise.' "
Just makes me to know
555 That when we call upon the name of Jesus
When we got godly sorrow in our hearts
When we're down and out
We call on the name of Jesus
He's not going to turn his back on us.
560 But he *is*
Going to give us that everlasting life
That he promised us.
So, the other thief,
He represents the mankind
565 That are crying out to the lord
For forgiveness—
Crying out to the lord for help.
Blessed Lord!
You know, they put a sign above the cross
570 And it said:
"Jesus of Nazereth,
King of the Jews."
And you know
It made the high-ups in the temple there—
575 It just bothered him so much
Because they put that on there.
And they said to Pilate,
"Write not 'The King of the Jews'—
But that he *said*
580 He was 'King of the Jews.'
And Pilate answered,
'What I have written
I have written.' "
You know,
585 I also think he knew who Jesus was!
You know, he questioned the Lord
And he said, "I find no fault in him.
I find no reason for him to be crucified.
This man, he's done nothing.

590 He's innocent."
But, you know,
So many times
The big religious leaders,
The ones that the world thinks is just so—
595 Have got just so much
And they've got the position—
But they don't have the knowledge—
They've got a lot of—
Maybe *influence* in the world
600 But they don't really realize
Who Jesus is!
But, you know, Pilate said,
"What I have written
I have written."
605 And he wouldn't change it
Because he *knew*
That Jesus really *was*
The King of the Jews!
And I believe also
610 That Jesus had paid the price
To have that sign put upon him.
You know, we can go out these days
And we can go to school to be a certain thing—
We can go to be a doctor
615 Or we can go to be a lawyer,
And you're going to pay a price
For what you're going to be.
Whatever you choose to study
You'll pay a price for that.
620 And, you know,
Our savior—
He paid a price
To be called The King of the Jews,
To be called the King of Kings
625 And Lord of Lords.
He gave his life.
Truly tonight
He paid a deeper price
Than any of us can ever even
630 *Think* about paying.
Hallelujah!

Thank you Jesus!
And there's more
That's interesting.
635 The thirty-third verse:
"And when they came to Jesus
And saw that he was dead already
They brake not his legs."
Now, it was a custom in that time
640 That when they crucified somebody
And if they didn't die soon off
And they didn't want to leave them hanging there,
Well, they'd break their legs
And this was, you know, this would
645 Kill them quicker.
But when they came to Jesus
They didn't break his legs
Because he was already dead.
"But one of the soldiers
650 With his spear pierced his side
And forthwith came there out blood and water."
Now, he looked at Jesus,
And I just feel like
That he had some kind of anger
655 Or he just wanted do do one more thing
To hurt the Lord
And when he just took that spear
And he pierced his side
And out of his side came
660 The blood and the water.
But you know what?
He didn't know what he was doing!
He really—
He thought he was doing just one more thing
665 To hurt the Lord
But when that blood and water
Came forth
It was just one more blessing for us!
For it is through water baptism
670 That our sins are washed away.
They are washed away
By the *blood* of Jesus.
You know, the blood of Jesus

Cannot be applied to your life
675 Except you go down in the name of *Jesus*
In water baptism.
This is a symbol
To represent water baptism
And the covering of the blood—
680 Remission of our sins,
Right here.
You see,
Sometimes Satan will pull things
On God's people
685 And even unto the Lord himself do things.
But, you know,
This just brought another blessing for us
Because it just makes us realize
More and more
690 That through water baptism
And the covering of Jesus' blood
That our sins are washed away.
Thank you Lord!
And the crown of thorns
695 That they put upon his head.
"And the soldiers platted a crown of thorns
And put it upon his head."
You know what I thought about this?
I thought about that crown of thorns
700 And how terrible it must have been
And how—
How many thorns would it take to make a crown?
It would take a lot of them,
Wouldn't it?
705 You know,
If we step on one thorn, well,
It just hurts just so much.
I know when I was a child
We lived in the country, you know,
710 And there was an old thorn tree
That grew along the fence row
And every now and then we'd get a thorn
In our foot
And there wasn't no way you could get away
715 From it because it was there

239

On the ground
And we'd always be barefooted
And we'd step on one
And Mom would have to pit it out
720 Or it would really get infected really bad.
And I think about how much that hurt
And how many thorns it would take
It would take a lot of thorns
To be woven together
725 And to be placed on Jesus' head.
And it brought the scripture to my mind:
"Many are the afflictions of the righteous."
That's in Psalms:
"Many are the afflictions of the righteous
730 But the Lord delivers him out of them."
Hallelujah!
Praise the Lord!
No matter how many times
And how many different ways—
735 And I'm telling you what
There's a lot of different things
That are going to come upon you
When you take upon you the name of Jesus—
We could go on and on
740 About the different things
And different tribulations
And different trials
That we—just as there were many, many
Thorns in that crown—
745 There's going to be many, many
Different kinds of afflictions
Come upon you in your Christian life, ah.
Isaiah talks about the stripes
That were upon Jesus' back.
750 And it shows us just exactly
What this means for us.
Each and every thing.
This is what I want you to realize tonight.
I may be going kinda slow
755 And not jumping around
And being real fiery
But I want you to realize that each thing

That happened to the Lord
There was a purpose for it.
760 "But he was wounded for our transgressions.
He was bruised for our iniquities:
The chastisement of our peace
Was upon him;
And with his stripes we are healed."
765 You know, tonight,
We can claim that healing.
We have a right to that healing
Because Jesus purchased that for us.
You know,
770 A lot of times
It is *hard*
To go to the doctor
And pay doctor bills.
I've had to go.
775 I've had a lot of sickness
And I've had to go
And I know how expensive they are.
But Jesus has already paid the price!
And all his people they have a right to that.
780 You know,
Many times the doctor will say,
"I won't let you have any credit,"
You know, "You got to pay now or I won't see you."
But you know, the *Lord*
785 Has purchased that for us.
That healing belongs to us
And we can claim it
Because he, by his stripes,
We are healed tonight.
790 Hallelujah!
Thank you Jesus.
Now, in the last part of St. John
When Thomas come to him,
He said he wouldn't believe—
795 Unless he could put his hands in Jesus'—
In the nail prints that were in his hands.
He wouldn't believe
That was Christ.
So that lets us to know

800 That truly there were spikes
  Driven into the hands of Jesus.
  And he said,
  "Look at my feet, Thomas.
  Put you hand in my thigh
805 If you don't believe
  That this is me,
  That I have risen."
  You know—
  I believe that each one of those nails
810 They had a meaning.
  And the first one that the Lord
  Showed me
  Was faith.
  In Galatians we read:
815 "But the scripture hath concluded all under sin,
  That the promise by faith of Jesus Christ
  Might be given to them that believe.
  But before faith came,
  We were kept under the law."
820 Now the law was up until the crucifixion—
  This is where the scripture comes in
  It fits right in with the crucifixion.
  In other words,
  Before Jesus came,
825 "We were kept under the law."
  After Jesus had been crucified
  The scripture goes on to say,
  "The just shall live by faith."
  Now, this day,
830 We don't *see* Jesus.
  We don't see him in a bodily form,
  Walking in a bodily form in our congregation with us,
  Preaching his ministry to us
  Like the apostles did.
835 But we walk by faith.
  Without faith it is *impossible*
  To please God.
  Now, don't you believe that faith is important?
  The three nails were
840 Faith, hope, and charity!
  You hear this constantly,

All the time,
But you think—
Well, could this really be that important?
845 What did the Lord say?
Without faith it is impossible
To please God.
And when we say *impossible*
We're saying a lot, aren't we?
850 That makes me to know
That faith is very, very important.
"For he that cometh to God must believe
That he is and that he is a rewarder
Of them that diligently seek him."
855 Oh, I praise him tonight.
Because I have believed on him.
I didn't have to see him.
I don't have to see him.
You know,
860 When the Russians went to the moon
They went out there and said,
"Well, we didn't see no God up there."
Of course, you can't see God with your eyes.
You have to feel it in your heart.
865 You have to walk by faith.
Without faith it's impossible
To please God tonight.
We'll go on to the next now,
Which is hope.
870 Colossians, first chapter.
That is a little bitty book and hard to find—
The first chapter here:
"If ye continue in faith grounded and settled."
Now, these three here are going to go together:
875 Faith, hope, and charity are going to go together.
He first began to talk about faith.
"If we continue in faith grounded and settled
And be not moved from the hope of the gospel,
Which ye have heard,
880 Which was preached to every creature
Which is under heaven,
Whereof I Paul am made a minister."
Now, I'll tell you what you may not—

It's hard to believe that the gospel was preached
885 *All over the world* at that time
But, you know, people today,
There's millions more than in Paul's time
But there are missionaries going in every direction
Going in every country
890 Preaching the gospel of Jesus.
Hallelujah!
"And be not moved away from the hope of the gospel."
Hallelujah!
Grounded in faith and not removed from that hope.
895 You know, "without a vision the people perish,"
The scripture says.
If you lose hope
And you lose your faith,
Well, you don't have anything.
900 You don't have anything to lean on.
You don't have anything to look forward to!
Romans eight and twenty-four:
"For we are saved by hope,
But hope that is seen is not hope,
905 For what a man seeth,
Why doth he still hope for?"
Hallelujah!
We've never seen him
And the Bible says eyes have not seen him—
910 We can't even imagine the beauty of it,
But we have that hope.
We're saved by that hope
That we *believe* that Jesus
Is going to take us *to that place*
915 Because he *told* us
That if he'd go away to prepare us a place
That he would come again.
And, you know, the Lord can't lie.
Hallelujah!
920 We have that hope
And we can trust in that hope
We don't have to give up
Because we know that his word is true.
Now, we'll go on and talk about charity
925 Which is another word for love.

Charity is just another word for love.
We're going to read the second verse
Of the thirteenth chapter of First Corinthians:
"And though I have the gift of prophecy
930 And understand all mysteries"—
Can you believe how smart you would be
If you could understand all mysteries?
"And all knowledge.
And though I have all faith,
935 So that I could remove mountains,
And have not charity,
I am nothing."
In other words,
Love, if I have—
940 If I don't have love—
Now, you can't separate
Faith, hope, and charity,
You cannot separate them—
Because you can't use—
945 Here Paul tells us you cannot use,
Even if you have all faith,
But if you don't have love,
You don't have it,
You just don't have nothing.
950 "Charity suffereth long and is kind;
Charity envieth not,
Charity vaunteth not itself,
Is not puffed up."
Doesn't it remind you
955 Of the humility
That Jesus had when he died upon the cross?
They said he didn't—
He was as a lamb led to the slaughter
He didn't even open his mouth
960 He was so humble.
He had charity.
He suffered long
Because he had charity.
We'll read the last verse, the thirteenth verse:
965 "And now abideth faith, hope, charity,
These three,
But the greatest of these is charity."

There's a song I've heard on the radio
So many times:
970 "It was love that helped my savior
To the old rugged cross."
How many have heard that?
Isn't that beautiful?
It was love
975 And there's another scripture that says,
"Greater love hath no man
Than to lay down his life for a friend."
And that's what I believe Jesus possessed.
Each and every one of these things
980 Jesus possessed them.
I hope that this has brought a blessing
To you tonight.
I hope that I didn't stumble around
And be too slow
985 But I wanted you to see
That each and every thing—
It may not seem like much
When you first look at it,
But if you look at it again
990 With your spiritual eye
And you try to dig in there
And study,
The Lord will reveal something to you.
Just like those three little old nails—
995 You wouldn't have thought
That would have any significance,
But faith, hope, and charity.
I love the Lord this night
And I love him because he died for me
1000 That my sins might be remitted
That I might someday be able to be with him
In Paradise.
God bless you.

Bibliography

Abel, Elizabeth, ed. *Writing and Sexual Difference.* Chicago: University of Chicago Press, 1980.

Abrahams, Roger. "Folklore and Literature as Performance." *Journal of the Folklore Institute* 4 (1967):75–95.

———. "Introductory Remarks to a Rhetorical Theory of Folklore." *Journal of American Folklore* 81 (1968):143–58.

———, ed. *A Singer and Her Songs: Almeda Riddle's Book of Ballads.* Baton Rouge: Louisiana State University Press, 1970.

———. "Personal Power and Social Restraint in the Definition of Folklore." *Journal of American Folklore* 84 (1971):16–30.

———. "Folklore and Literature as Performance." *Journal of the Folklore Institute* 9 (1972):75–94.

al-Hibri, Azizah. "Reproduction, Mothering, and the Origins of Patriarchy." In *Mothering: Essays in Feminist Theory*, ed. Joyce Trebilcot, pp. 81–93.

Alland, Alexander. "Possession in a Revivalistic Negro Church." *Journal for the Scientific Study of Religion* 1 (1962):204–13.

Allardt, E. "Approaches in the Socialization of Religion." *Temenos* 6 (1970):10–12.

Allison, J. "Religious Conversion: Regression and Progression in an Adolescent Experience." *Journal for the Scientific Study of Religion* 8 (1969):23–38.

Anderson, Robert Mapes. *Vision of the Disinherited.* New York: Oxford University Press, 1979.

Ardener, Edwin. "Belief and the Problem of Women." In *The Interpretation of Ritual*, ed. J. S. LaFontaine, pp. 135–59.

———, ed. *Social Anthropology and Language.* London: Tavistock, 1971.

Ardener, Shirley. *Perceiving Women.* London: J. M. Dent, 1975.

———, ed. *Women and Space: Ground Rules and Social Maps.* New York: St. Martin's Press, 1981.

Arnold, Matthew. "Religious Language is Moral-emotive." In *The Problem of Religious Language*, ed. M. J. Charlesworth.

Auerbach, Nina. *Woman and the Demon: The Life of a Victorian Myth.* Cambridge, Mass.: Harvard University Press, 1982.

Ayers, Robert H. and Wm. T. Blackstone, eds. *Religious Language and Knowledge.* Athens: University of Georgia Press, 1972.

Beal, J. Van. *Symbols for Communication: An Introduction to the Anthropological Study of Religion.* Assen, The Netherlands: Van Gorcum and Co., 1971.

Babcock, Barbara, ed. *The Reversible World.* Ithaca, N.Y.: Cornell University Press, 1978.

Bacon, Margaret Hope. *Mothers of Feminism: the Story of Quaker Women in America.* San Francisco: Harper and Row, 1986.

Banton, Michael, ed. *Anthropological Approaches to the Study of Religion.* London; Tavistock, 1966.

Barnes, Douglas F. "Charisma and Religious Leadership." *Journal for the Scientific Study of Religion* 17 (1978):1–19.

Bascom, Wm. "Verbal Art," *Journal of American Folklore* 68 (1955):245–62.

Basso, Keith, H. and Henry A. Selby, eds. *Meaning in Anthropology.* Albuquerque: University of New Mexico Press, 1976.

Batson, C. Daniel. "Religion as Prosocial: Agent or Double Agent?" *Journal for the Scientific Study of Religion* 16 (1977):29–45.

Bauman, Richard. "Aspects of Quaker Rhetoric." *Quarterly Journal of Speech* 56 (1970):67–74.

———. "Differential Identity and the Social Base of Folklore." In *Toward New Perspectives in Folklore*, ed. Americo Paredes and Richard Bauman, pp. 31–42.

———. *Verbal Art as Performance.* Rowley, Mass.: Newbury House, 1977.

———. "The Field Study of Folklore in Context." In *The Handbook of American Folklore*, ed. Richard M. Dorson, pp. 362–69.

——— and Roger D. Abrahams, eds. *"And Other Neighborly Names."* Austin: University of Texas Press, 1981.

——— and Joel Sherzer. *Explorations in the Ethnography of Speaking.* New York: Cambridge University Press, 1974.

——— and Joel Sherzer. "The Ethnography of Speaking." In *The Annual Review of Anthropology* 4 (1975), ed. Bernard J. Siegel. Palo Alto, Cal., 1975.

Bednorowski, Mary Farrell. "Outside the Mainstream: Women's Religion and Women Religious Leaders in 19th century America." *Journal of the American Academy of Religion* 48 (1980):207–31.

Behnke, Donna. *Religious Issues in Nineteenth Century Feminism.* New York: Whitsom Pub. Co., 1982.

Beit-Hallahmi, Benjamin, ed. *Research in Religious Behavior.* Boston: Brooks/Cole Pub., 1973.

Bell, Roger T. *Sociolinguistics.* London: B. T. Batsford, 1976.

Ben-Amos, Dan. "Toward a Definition of Folklore in Context." In *Toward New Perspectives in Folklore*, ed. Americo Paredes and Richard Bauman.

——— and Kenneth Goldstein, eds. *Folklore, Performance and Communication.* The Hague: Mouton, 1974.

Berryhill, Michael. "The Baptist Schism." *The New York Times Magazine* (June 9, 1985):90–95, 99.

Blackstone, Wm. T. "The Status of God-Talk." In *Religious Language and Knowledge*, ed. Robert H. Ayers and Wm. T. Blackstone.

Bliss, Kathleen. *The Service and Status of Women in the Churches*. London: SCM Press Ltd, 1952.

Block-Hoell, Nils. *The Pentecostal Movement*. Norway: Universitetsforlaget, 1964.

Blount, Ben G., ed. *Language, Culture and Society*. Cambridge, Mass: Winthrop Pub., 1974.

Boatright, Mody C. "Comic Exempla of the Pioneer Pulpit." In *Coyote Wisdom*, ed. J. Frank Dobie, M. C. Boatright and Harry H. Ransom, pp. 55–68.

Boggs, Beverly. "Some Aspects of Worship in a Holiness Church." *New York Folklore Quarterly* 3 (1947):29–45.

Boisen, Anton T. "Economic Distress and Religious Experience: A Study of the Holy Rollers." *Psychiatry* 2 (1939):185–94.

———— *Religion in Crises and Custom*. New York: Harper & Bros., 1955.

————. "Religion and Hard Times: A Study of the Holy Rollers." *Social Action* 39 (1972):8–35.

Borker, Ruth, Nelly Furman, and Sally McConnell Genet, eds. *Women and Language in Literature and Society*. New York: Praeger Pub., 1980.

Bourguignon, Erika, ed. *Religion, Altered States of Consciousness and Social Change*. Columbus: Ohio State University Press, 1973.

————. "Cross-cultural Perspectives on the Religious Uses of Altered States of Consciousness." In *Religious Movements in Contemporary America*, ed. Irving L. Zaretsky, pp. 228–44.

————. *A World of Women: Anthropological Studies of Women in the Societies of the World*. New York: Praeger Pub., 1980.

Bronner, Simon, ed. *American Material Culture and Folklife*. Ann Arbor, Mich.: UMI Research Press, 1985.

Brouwer, D. and M. Gerritsen. "Speech Differences Between Women and Men: On the Right Track?" *Language in Society* 8 (1979):33–51.

Bruce, Dickson. *And They All Sang Hallelujah: Plain-Folk Camp-Meeting Religion, 1800–1845*. Knoxville: University of Tennessee Press, 1974.

Bruner, Frederick D. *A Theology of the Holy Spirit*. Grand Rapids, Mich.: Wm. Eerdmans, 1970.

Brunvand, Jan, ed. *Readings in American Folklore*. New York: W. W. Norton & Co., 1979.

Burr, Nelson. *A Critical Bibliography of Religion in America*. Princeton, N.J.: Princeton University Press, 1961.

Byrne, Donald. *No Foot of Land*. Metuchen, N.J.: Scarecrow Press, 1975.

Caillois, Roger. "Play and the Sacred." In *Man and the Sacred*, ed. Roger Caillois. Glencoe, Ill: The Free Press, 1959.

Caplow, Theodore, et al. *All Faithful People: Change and Continuity in Middletown's Religion*. Minneapolis: University of Minnesota Press, 1983.

Capps, Donald. "Publishing Trends in the Psychology of Religion to 1974." *Journal for the Scientific Study of Religion* 15 (1976):15–28.

Carmody, Denise L. *Feminism and Christianity: A Two-Way Reflection*. Nashville, Tenn.: Abingdon Press, 1982.

Carr, Leslie G. and Wm. Hanser. "Anomie and Religiosity: An Empirical Re- Examination." *Journal for the Scientific Study of Religion* 15 (1976): 26–42.

Carroll, Berenice, ed. *Liberating Women's History: Theoretical and Critical Essays.* Urbana: University of Illinois Press, 1976.

Carroll, Elizabeth. "Women and Ministry." *Theological Studies* 36 (1975), pp. 660–87.

Carroll, Jackson W., Barbara Hargrove, and Adair T. Lummis. *Women of the Cloth: A New Opportunity for the Churches.* San Francisco: Harper and Row, 1983.

Catton, Wm. R. "What Kinds of People Does a Religious Cult Attract?" *American Sociological Review* 22 (1957):561–66.

Charlesworth, M. J., ed. *The Problem of Religious Language.* Englewood Cliffs, N.J.: Prentice-Hall, 1974.

Chodorow, Nancy. *The Reproduction of Mothering: Psychoanalysis and the Sociology of Gender.* Berkeley: University of California Press, 1978.

Christ, Carol and Judith Plaskow, eds. *Womanspirit Rising.* San Francisco: Harper and Row, 1979.

Christie-Murray, David. *Voices from the Gods.* London: Routledge & Kegan Paul, 1978.

Cicourel, Aaron W. "Basic and Normative Rules in the Negotiation of Status and Role." In *Studies in Social Interaction*, ed. David Sudnow.

Clanton, Arthur L. *United We Stand.* Hazelwood, Mo.: The Pentecostal Publishing House, 1970.

Clark, Elmer T. *The Small Sects in America.* Nashville, Tenn.: Abingdon Press, 1959.

Clements, William M. "The Rhetoric of the Radio Ministry." *Journal of American Folklore* 87 (1974):318–27.

————. "The American Folk Church." Ph.D. dissertation, Indiana University, 1974.

————. "Conversion and Communitas." *Western Folklore* 35 (1976):35–45.

————. "Faith Healing Narratives from Northeast Arkansas." *Indiana Folklore* 9 (1976):15–39.

————. "The American Folk Church in Northeast Arkansas." *Journal of the Folklore Institute* 15 (1978):161–80.

————. "The Pentecostal Sagaman." *Journal of the Folklore Institute* 17 (1980): 169–95.

————. "Public Testimony as Oral Performance: A Study in the Ethnography of Religious Speaking." *Linguistica Biblica* 47 (1980): 21–32.

————. "Ritual Expectations in Pentecostal Healing Experience." *Western Folklore* 40 (1981): 139–48.

————. "The Folk Church: Institution, Event, Performance." In *The Handbook of American Folklore*, ed. Richard M. Dorson, pp. 136–45.

Cleveland, Catherine. *The Great Revival in the West, 1797–1805.* Chicago: University of Chicago Press, 1916.

Cohn, Norman. *The Pursuit of the Millennium.* New York: Oxford University Press, 1970.

Collins, J. B. *Tennessee Snake Handlers*. Chattanooga: Middle Tennessee State University Press, 1947.

Collins, Sheila D. *A Different Heaven and Earth*. Valley Forge, Pa.: Judson Press, 1974.

Cone, James H. "Sanctification, Liberation, and Black Worship." *Theology Today* 35 (1979):139–150.

Cott, Nancy. "Young Women in the Second Great Awakening in New England." *Feminist Studies* 3 (1975):14–29.

———. *The Bonds of Womanhood:"Women's Sphere" in New England, 1780–1835*. New Haven, Conn.: Yale University Press, 1977.

Cox, Harvey. *The Feast of Fools*. New York: Harper and Row, 1969.

———. *The Seduction of the Spirit: The Use and Misuse of People's Religion*. New York: Simon and Schuster, 1973.

Crick, Malcolm. *Explorations in Language and Meaning*. London: Malaby Press, 1976.

Crites, Stephen. "The Narrative Quality of Experience." *Journal of the American Academy of Religion* 39 (1971):291–311.

Crystal, David. *Linguistics, Language and Religion*. New York: Hawthorn, 1965.

Culver, Elsie Thomas. *Women in the World of Religion*. New York: Doubleday & Co., 1967.

Cunneen, Sally. *Sex: Female; Religion: Catholic*. New York: Holt, Rinehart and Winston, 1968.

Cutten, George B. *Speaking With Tongues*. New Haven, Conn.: Yale University Press, 1927.

Dance, Frank E. X., ed. *Human Communication Theory*. New York: Holt, Rinehart and Winston, 1967.

Davis, Almond H. *The Female Preacher, or Memoir of Salome Lincoln*. New York: Arno Press, 1972. (First published Providence, R.I., 1843.)

Davis, Gerald. *I Got the Word in Me and I Can Sing it, You Know*. Philadelphia: University of Pennsylvania Press, 1985.

Daly, Mary. *Beyond God the Father*. Boston: Beacon Press, 1973.

———. *The Church and the Second Sex*. New York: Harper and Row, 1975. (First published 1968.)

Damboriena, Prudencio. *Tongues as of Fire: Pentecostalism in Contemporary Christianity*. Washington D.C. and Cleveland: Corpus Books, 1969.

Degh, Linda, Henry Glassie, and Felix Oinas, eds. *Folklore Today*. Bloomington: Indiana University Press, 1976.

Dieter, Melvin. *The Holiness Revival of the Nineteenth Century*. Metuchen, N.J.: Scarecrow Press, 1980.

Dobie, J. Frank, Mody C. Boatright, and Harry H. Ransom, eds. *Coyote Wisdom*. Austin: Texas Folklore Society publication 14 (1963).

Doely, Sarah Bentley, ed. *Women's Liberation and the Church*. New York: Association Press, 1970.

Donovan, Peter. *Religious Language*. London: Sheldon Press, 1976.

Dorson, Richard M., ed. *Folklore and Folklife*. Chicago: University of Chicago Press, 1972.

————. *The Handbook of American Folklore*. Bloomington: Indiana University Press, 1983.

Douglas, Ann. *The Feminization of American Culture*. New York: Avon, 1977.

Douglas, Mary. *Purity and Danger*. London: Routledge & Kegan Paul, 1966.

————. *Implicit Meanings*. London: Routledge & Kegan Paul, 1975.

Drake, St. Clair and Horace R. Clayton. *Black Metropolis*. New York: Harper and Row, 1962.

Dundes, Alan. "Trends in Content Analysis: A Review Article." *Midwest Folklore* 12 (1962):31–38

————, ed. *The Study of Folklore*. Englewood Cliffs, N.J.: Prentice-Hall, 1965.

————, ed. *Mother Wit From the Laughing Barrel*. Englewood Cliffs, N.J.: Prentice-Hall, 1973.

————, ed. *Analytic Essays in Folklore*. The Hague: Mouton, 1975.

————, ed. *Interpreting Folklore*. Bloomington: Indiana University Press, 1980.

————. "From Etic to Emic Units in the Structure of Folktales." In *Analytic Essays in Folklore*, ed. Alan Dundes, pp. 61–73.

————. "Metafolklore and Oral Literary Criticism." In *Analytic Essays in Folklore*, ed. Alan Dundes, pp. 50–61.

————. "Text, Texture, and Context." In *Interpreting Folklore*, ed. Alan Dundes, pp. 20–33.

Dunn, Mary M. "Saints and Sisters: Congregational and Quaker Women in the Early Colonial Period." In *Women in American Religion*, ed. Janet Wilson James, pp. 27–46.

DuPlessis, Rachel Blau. *Writing Beyond the Ending: Narrative Strategies of Twentieth-Century Women Writers*. Bloomington: Indiana University Press, 1985.

Durasoff, Steve. *Bright Wind of the Spirit*. Englewood Cliffs, N.J.: Prentice-Hall, 1972.

Dworkin, Andrea. *Woman Hating*. New York: E. P. Dutton, 1974.

Eliade, Mircea. *The Sacred and the Profane: The Nature of Religion*. New York: Harcourt Brace Jovanovich, 1983.

Elverdam, Beth. "Where Men and Women have Separate Worlds—How Ritual is Used as a Mechanism of Socialization." *Temenos* 13 (1977):56–66.

Engelsman, Joan C. *The Feminine Dimension of the Divine*. Philadelphia: Westminster Press, 1979.

Epstein, Barbara Leslie. *The Politics of Domesticity: Women, Evangelism, and Temperance in Nineteenth-Century America*. Middletown, Conn.: Wesleyan University Press, 1981.

Ermarth, Margaret Sittler. *Adam's Fractured Rib*. Philadelphia: Fortress Press, 1970.

Ervin-Tripp, Susan. "On Sociolinguistic Rules: Alternations and Co-Occurence." In *Directions in Sociolinguistics*, ed. J. J. Gumperz and Dell Hymes, pp. 213–50.

————. "Sociolinguistics." In *Language, Culture and Society*, ed. Ben G. Blount, pp. 268–334.

Falk, Nancy A. and Rita M. Gross. *Unspoken Worlds: Women's Religious Lives in Non-Western Cultures*. San Francisco: Harper and Row, 1980.

Farb, Peter. *Word Play*. New York: Alfred Knopf, 1974.

Farrer, Claire. *Women and Folklore*. Austin: University of Texas Press, 1975.

Fauset, Arthur Huff. *Black Gods of the Metropolis*. Philadelphia: University of Pennsylvania Press, 1944.

Fell, Margaret. *Womens Speaking Justified* (1667). Reprinted by the Augustan Reprint Society. Los Angeles: Wm. Andrews Clark Memorial Library, Pub. #194, 1979.

Fernandez, James. "Revitalized Words from 'The Parrot's Egg' and 'The Bull that Crashes in the Kraal': African Cult Sermons." In *Essays on the Verbal and Visual Arts*, ed. June Helm, pp. 45–63.

———. "The Mission of Metaphor in Expressive Culture." *Current Anthropology* 15 (1974):119–33.

Ferris, William "The Rose Hill Service." *Mississippi Folklore Register* 6 (1973):37–56.

Festinger, Leon. *When Prophecy Fails*. New York: Harper Torchbooks, 1964.

Fischer, Claire Benedicks, Betsy Brenneman and Anne McGrew Bennett, eds. *Women in a Strange Land*. Philadelphia: Fortress Press, 1975.

Fishman, Joshua. *Advances in the Sociology of Language*. The Hague: Mouton, 1971.

———. "Domains and the Relationship Between Micro- and Macro- Sociolinguistics." In *Directions in Sociolinguistics*, ed. J. J. Gumperz and Dell Hymes, pp. 435–53.

Flake, Carol. *Redemptorama*. New York: Penguin, 1984.

Foley, John Miles. "Introduction." *Oral Tradition* 1:1 (1986):7–9.

———, ed. *A Memorial for Milman Parry*. Columbus, Oh.: Slavica Press, 1987.

Ford, T. "Status, Residence and Fundamentalist Religious Beliefs in the Southern Appalachians." *Social Forces* 39 (1960):41–49.

Frodsham, Stanley H. *"With Signs Following"*. Springfield, Mo: Gospel Publishing House, 1926.

Gage, Miltalda Joslyn. *Woman, Church and State*. New York: Arno Press, 1972.

Gee, Donald. *The Pentecostal Movement*. London: Elim Publishing House, 1941.

Geertz, Clifford. "Religion as a Cultural System." In *The Interpretation of Cultures*, ed. Clifford Geertz, pp. 87–126. New York: Basic Books, 1973.

Geiger, Susan N. G. "Review Essay: Women's Life Histories: Method and Content." *Signs* 11 (1986): 334–51.

George, Kenneth. " 'I Still Got It': The Conversion Narrative of John C. Sherfey." M.A. Thesis, University of North Carolina, Chapel Hill, 1978.

Gerlach, Luther P. and Virginia H. Hine. "Five Factors Crucial to the Growth and Spread of a Modern Religious Movement." *Journal for the Scientific Study of Religion* 7 (1968):36–47.

———. *People, Power, Change: Movements of Social Transformation*. New York: The Bobbs-Merrill Co., 1970.

———. "Pentecostalism: Revolution or Counter-Revolution." In *Religious Movements in Contemporary America*, ed. Irving L. Zaretsky, pp. 669–700.

253

Gerrard, Nathan. "The Serpent-Handling Religions of West Virginia." *Trans-Actions* 5 (1968):22–38.

———. "The Holiness Movement in Southern Appalachia." In *The Charismatic Movement*, ed. Michael P. Hamilton.

Gibbons, Don and James deJarnette. "Hypnotic Susceptivity and Religious Experience." *Journal for the Scientific Study of Religion* 11 (1972):152–57.

Gibson, Elsie. *When the Minister is a Woman*. New York: Holt, Rinehart and Winston, 1970.

Giglioli, Pier Paolo, ed. *Language and Social Context*. New York: Penguin, 1972.

Gilbert, Sandra M. and Susan Gubar. *The Madwoman in the Attic*. New Haven, Conn.: Yale University Press, 1979, repr. 1984.

Gilligan, Carol. *In a Different Voice.* Cambridge, Mass.: Harvard University Press, 1982.

Gilmore, Susan K. "Personality Differences Between High and Low Dogmatism Groups of Pentecostal Believers." *Journal for the Scientific Study of Religion* 8 (1969):161–66.

Gladwin, T. and William Sturtevant, eds. *Anthropology and Human Behavior*. Washington, D.C.: Anthropological Society, 1962.

Goffman, Erving. *Encounters*. Indianapolis: Bobbs-Merrill, 1961.

———. *Behavior in Public Places*. New York: Free Press, 1963.

———. *Interactional Ritual*. New York: Doubleday and Co., 1967.

———. "The Neglected Situation." In *Language and Social Context*, ed. Pier Paolo Giglioli, pp. 61–66.

———. *Frame Analysis*. New York: Harper and Row, 1974.

Gold, Peter. "Easter Sunrise Sermon." *Alcheringa/Ethnopoetics* 4 (1978):1–14.

Goldenberg, Naomi R. *Changing of the Gods*. Boston: Beacon Press, 1979.

Goldschmidt, Walter. *As You Sow*. New York: Harcourt Brace, 1947.

Goldstein, Diane E. "The Language of Religious Experience and Its Implications for Fieldwork." *Western Folklore* 42 (1983):105–13.

Goodenough, Ward. "Componential Analysis and the Study of Meaning." *Language* 32 (1956):195–216.

———, ed. *Explorations in Cultural Anthropology*. New York: McGraw-Hill, 1964.

Goodman, Felicitas. "Phonetic Analysis of Glossolalia in Four Cultural Settings." *Journal for the Scientific Study of Religion* 8 (1969):227–39.

———. "Glossolalia: Speaking in Tongues in Four Cult Settings." *Confinia Psychiatrica* 12 (1969):113–29.

———. "The Acquisition of Glossolalia Behavior." *Semiotica* 3 (1971):77–82.

———. *Speaking in Tongues*. Chicago: University of Chicago Press, 1972.

———. "Glossolalia and Hallucination in Pentecostal Congregations." *Psychiatria Clinica* 6 (1973):97–103.

———. "The Apostolics of Yucatan: A Case Study of a Religious Movement." In *Religion, Altered States of Consciousness and Social Change*, ed. Erika Bourguignon.

———. "Altered Mental States vs. 'Style of Discourse'." *Journal for the Scientific Study of Religion* 11 (1972):197–99.

————, et al., *Trance, Healing and Hallucination*. New York: John Wiley and Sons, 1974.

Gordon, Robert W. "Negro 'Shouts' From Georgia." In *Mother Wit From the Laughing Barrel*, ed. Alan Dundes, pp. 445–52.

Gordon, Stanley, and W. K. Bartlett and Terri Moyle. "Some Characteristics of Charismatic Experience: Glossolalia in Australia." *Journal for the Scientific Study of Religion* 3 (1964):269–78.

Gould, Carol C., ed. *Beyond Domination: New Perspectives on Women and Philosophy*. Totowa, N.J.: Rowman and Allanheld, 1984.

Grele, Ronald J., ed. *Envelopes of Sound: Six Practitioners Discuss the Method, Theory and Practice of Oral History and Oral Testimony*. Chicago: Precedent Publishing, 1975.

Gross, Larry. "Art as the Communication of Competence." *Social Science Information* 12 (1973):115–41.

Gumperz, J. J. *Language in Social Groups*. Stanford, Ca.: Stanford University Press, 1971.

————. "The Speech Community." In *Language and Social Context*, ed. Pier Paolo Giglioli, pp. 219–231.

————. "Sociolinguistics and Communication in Small Groups." In *Sociolinguistics*, ed. J. B. Pride and Janet Holmes, pp. 203–24.

———— and Dell Hymes, eds. *Directions in Sociolinguistics*. New York: Holt, Rinehart and Winston, 1972.

Hackett, Charles D., ed. *Women of the Word: Contemporary Sermons by Women Clergy*. Atlanta: Susan Hunter Publishing, 1985.

Haddad, Yvonne Yazbeck and Ellison Banks Findly. *Women, Religion and Social Change*. New York: State University of New York Press, 1985.

Hageman, Alice. *Sexist Religion and Women in the Church*. New York: Association Press, 1974.

Hallpike, C. R. "Social Hair." In *Reader in Comparative Religion: An Anthropological Approach*. ed. William A. Lessa and Evon Z. Vogt, pp. 99–105.

Hamilton, Michael P., ed. *The Charismatic Movement*. Grand Rapids, Mich.: Wm. Eerdmans, 1975.

Hanawalt, N. G. "Feelings of Security and of Self-esteem in Relation to Religious Belief." *Journal of Social Psychology* 59 (1963):347–53.

Hardesty, Nancy. *Women Called to Witness: Evangelical Feminism in the 19th Century*. Nashville, Tenn.: Abingdon Press, 1984.

Harkness, Georgia. *Women in Church and Society: A Historical and Theological Inquiry*. Nashville, Tenn.: Abingdon Press, 1972.

Harrell, David E., Jr. *All Things Are Possible: The Healing and Charismatic Revivals in Modern America*. Bloomington: Indiana University Press, 1975.

Hartman, Mary S. and Lois Banner. *Clio's Consciousness Raised: New Perspectives on the History of Women*. New York: Harper & Row, 1984.

Hassey, Janette. *No Time for Silence: Evangelical Women in Public Ministry Around the Turn of the Century*. Grand Rapids, Mich.: Academic Books, 1986.

Hawkes, Terence. *Structuralism and Semiotics*. Berkeley: University of California Press, 1977.

Hawley, Florence, "The Keresan Holy Rollers." *Social Forces* 47 (1969):272–80.
Haywood, Carol Lois. "The Authority and Empowerment of Women among Spiritual Groups." *Journal for the Scientific Study of Religion* 22 (1983):157–66.
Helm, June, ed. *Symposium on New Approaches to the Study of Religion.* Seattle: University of Washington Press, 1964.
———, ed. *Essays on the Verbal and Visual Arts.* Seattle: University of Washington Press, 1967.
Hendricks, W. O. *Essays on Semiolinguistics and Verbal Art.* The Hague: Mouton, 1973.
Hewitt, Emily C. and Suzanne R. Hiatt. *Women Priests: Yes or No?* New York: Seabury Press, 1973.
Hill, Samuel S., ed. *Religion and the Solid South.* Nashville, Tenn.: Abingdon Press, 1972.
Hine, Virginia. "Pentecostal Glossolalia: Toward a Functional Interpretation." *Journal for the Scientific Study of Religion* 8 (1969):21–26.
———. "Bridge-Burners: Commitment and Participation in a Religious Movement." *Sociological Analysis* 31 (1970):61–66.
———. "Non-Pathological Pentecostal Glossolalia: A Summary of Relevant Psychological Literature." *Journal for the Scientific Study of Religion* 8 (1969):211–26.
Hoch-Smith, Judith and Anita Spring. *Women in Ritual and Symbolic Roles.* New York: Plenum Press, 1978.
Hoekema, Anthony A. *What About Tongue-Speaking?* Grand Rapids, Mich.: Wm. Eerdmans, 1966.
Holden, Pat. *Women's Religious Experience.* London: Croom Helm, 1983.
Hollenweger, W. J. *The Pentecostals.* Minneapolis: Augsberg, 1972.
Holms, Nils G. "Ritualistic Patterns and Sound Structure of Glossolalia in Material Collected in the Swedish-speaking Parts of Finland." *Temenos* 11 (1975): 43–60.
Holt, Grace Sims. "Stylin' outta the Black Pulpit." In *Rappin' and Stylin' Out*, ed. Thomas Kochman, pp. 189–205.
Holt, John B. "Holiness Religion." *American Sociological Review* 5 (1940):740–47.
Honko, L. "Genre Analysis in Folkloristics and Comparative Religion." *Temenos* 3 (1967):48–64.
——— ed. *Science of Religion.* Turku, Finland: Proceedings of the Study Conference of the International Association for the History of Religion, 1973.
Hultkrantz, A. "The Phenomenology of Religion: Aims and Methods." *Temenos* 6(1970) :68–88.
Humez, Jean M. *Gifts of Power: The Writings of Rebecca Jackson, Black Visionary, Shaker Eldress.* Amherst: University of Massachusetts Press, 1981.
Hunter, James Davison. *Evangelicalism: The Coming Generation.* Chicago: University of Chicago Press, 1987.
Hunter, Jane. *The Gospel of Gentility: American Women Missionaries in Turn of the Century China.* New Haven, Conn.: Yale University Press, 1984.

256

Hutch, Richard A. "The Personal Ritual of Glossolalia." *Journal for the Scientific Study of Religion* 19 (1980):264–81.

Hymes, Dell. "Ethnography of Speaking." In *Anthropology and Human Behavior*, ed. T. Gladwin and Wm. Sturtevant.

———. "Ethnography of Communication." *American Anthropologist* 66 (1964):1–34.

———. "Directions in (Ethno) Linguistic Theory." *American Anthropologist* 66 (1964):6–56.

———. "The Anthropology of Communication." In *Human Communication Theory*, ed. Frank E. X. Dance, pp. 1–39.

———. "Sociolinguistics and the Ethnography of Speaking." In *Social Anthropology and Language*, ed. Edwin Ardener, pp. 47–94.

———. "Models of the Interaction of Language and Social Setting." *Journal of Social Issues* 23 (1967):8–28.

———. "Breakthrough into Performance." In *Folklore, Performance, and Communication*, ed. Dan Ben-Amos and Kenneth Goldstein, pp. 11–55.

———. *Foundations in Sociolinguistics*. Philadelphia: University of Pennsylvania Press, 1974.

———. "The Ethnography of Speaking." In *Language, Culture, and Society*, ed. Ben Blount.

———. "The Grounding of Performance and Text in a Narrative View of LIfe." *Alcheringa* 4 (1978):137–40.

———. *What Is Ethnography?* Austin, Tex.: Southwest Educational Developmental Lab., 1978.

Jackson, George Pullen. "The 'Old-Time Religion' as a Folk Religion." *Tennessee Folklore Society Bulletin* 7 (1941):30–39.

———. *White Spirituals in the Southern Uplands*. Chapel Hill: University of North Carolina Press, 1933.

Jacobs, Melville. *The Content and Style of an Oral Literature*. Chicago: University of Chicago Press, 1959.

Jacobs, Sue-Ellen. *Women in Perspective: A Guide for Cross-Cultural Studies*. Urbana: University of Illinois Press, 1976.

Jacobus, Mary, ed. *Women Writing and Writing About Women*. London: Croom Helm, 1979.

Jaggar, Alison and Paul S. Rothenberg. *Feminist Frameworks: Alternative Theoretical Accounts of the Relations Between Women and Men* (2nd ed.). New York: McGraw-Hill, 1984.

Jain, R. K. *Text and Context: The Social Anthropology of Tradition*. Philadelphia: Institute for the Study of Human Issues, 1977.

Jakobson, Roman. "Closing Statement: Linguistics and Poetics." In *Style in Language*, ed. Thomas A. Sebeok, pp. 350–78.

James, Janet Wilson, ed. *Women in American Religion*. Philadelphia: University of Pennsylvania Press, 1976.

James, William. *The Varieties of Religious Experience*. New York: Random House, 1929.

Jansen, William. "Classifying Performance in the Study of Verbal Folklore." In *Studies in Folklore*, ed. W. Edson Richmond.

———. "The Esoteric-Exoteric Factor in Folklore." In *The Study of Folklore*, ed. Alan Dundes.

Jeffner, Anders. *The Study of Religious Language*. London: SCM Press, 1972.

Jewett, Paul K. *The Ordination of Women*. Grand Rapids, Mich.: Wm. Eerdmans, 1980.

Johansson, Shelia Ryan. " 'Herstory' as History: A New Field or Another Fad?" In *Liberating Women's History: Theoretical and Critical Essays*, ed. Berenice A. Carroll, pp. 400–30.

Johnson, Benton. "A Framework for the Analysis of Religious Action with Special Reference to Holiness and Non-Holiness Groups." Ph.D. dissertation, Harvard University, 1953.

———. "A Critical Appraisal of the Cult-Sect Typology." *American Sociological Review* 22 (1957):88–92.

———. "Do Holiness Sects Socialize in Dominant Values?" *Social Forces* 39 (1960):309–16.

———. "On Church and Sect." *American Sociological Review* 28 (1963):539–49.

———. "Church and Sect Revisited." *Journal for the Scientific Study of Religion* 10 (1971):124–37.

Johnson, Charles, ed. *God Struck Me Dead*. Nashville, Tenn.: Fisk Social Science Institute, 1945.

———. *The Frontier Camp Meeting*. Dallas, Tex.: Southern Methodist University Press, 1955.

Jones, Michael O. *Why Faith Healing?* Canadian Centre for Folk Cultural Studies (Ottawa, Canada), No. 3, 1972.

Jordan, David K. *Gods, Ghosts and Ancestors: Folk Religion in a Taiwanese Village*. Berkeley: University of California Press, 1972.

Jordan, Rosan A. and Susan J. Kalčik, eds. *Women's Folklore, Women's Culture*. Philadelphia: University of Pennsylvania Press and the American Folklore Society, 1981.

——— and F. A. de Caro. "Women and the Study of Folklore: Review Essay." *Signs* 11, 3 (1986):500–18.

Jorstad, Erling. *The Holy Spirit in Today's Church*. Nashville, Tenn.: Abington, 1973.

Joyce, Rosemary O. *A Woman's Place: The Life History of a Rural Ohio Grandmother*. Columbus: Ohio State University Press, 1983.

Kane, Steven. "Aspects of Holy Ghost Religion." Ph.D. dissertation, University of North Carolina, 1973.

———. "Holy Ghost People." *Appalachian Journal* 1 (1974):255–61.

———. "Ritual Possession in a Southern Appalachian Religious Sect." *Journal of American Folklore* 87 (1974):293–303.

Kelly, M. W. "Depression in the Psychoses of Members of a Religious Community of Women." *American Journal of Psychiatry* 118 (1962):423–25.

Kelsey, Morton. *Tongue Speaking*. New York: Doubleday, 1964.

258

Kendrick, K. "The Pentecostal Movement: Hopes and Hazards." *Christian Century* 80 (1963):608–10.

Kerr, Laura N. *Lady in the Pulpit*. New York: Woman's Press, 1951.

Kevelson, Roberta. "Language Games as Systematic Metaphors." *Semiotica* 19 (1977):29–37.

Key, Mary Ritchie. *Male/Female Language*. Metuchen, N.J.: Scarecrow Press, 1975.

Kildahl, John P. *The Psychology of Speaking in Tongues*. New York: Harper and Row, 1972.

Kingston, Maxine Hong. *The Woman Warrior*. New York: Vintage Books, 1975.

Kochman, Thomas. "Toward an Ethnography of Black American Speech Behavior." In *Rappin' and Stylin' Out*, ed. Thomas Kochman, pp. 241–65.

———, ed. *Rappin' and Stylin' Out*. Urbana: University of Illinois Press, 1977.

Knox, Ronald A. *Enthusiasm*. London: Oxford University Press, 1960.

Kroll-Smith, J. Stephen. "The Testimony as Performance." *Journal for the Scientific Study of Religion* 19 (1980):16–25.

Kuhlman, Katherine. *I Believe in Miracles*. Englewood Cliffs, N.J.: Prentice-Hall, 1968.

———. *God Can Do It Again*. Englewood Cliffs, N.J.: Prentice-Hall, 1969.

LaBarre, Weston. *They Shall Take Up Serpents*. Minneapolis: University of Minnesota Press, 1962.

———. "Snake-handling Cult of the American Southeast." In *Explorations in Cultural Anthropology*, ed. Ward Goodenough.

———. "Materials for a History of Studies of Crisis Cults: A Bibliographic Essay." *Current Anthropology* 12 (1971):3–45.

Labov, William "The Study of Language in Its Social Context." In *Sociolinguistic Patterns*, ed. Wm. Labov.

——— and Joshua Waletzky. "Narrative Analysis: Oral Versions of Personal Experience." In *Essays on the Verbal and Visual Arts*, ed. June Helm, pp. 12–75.

LaFontaine, J. S., ed. *The Interpretation of Ritual*. London: Tavistock, 1972.

Lakoff, Robin. "Language in Context." *Language* 48 (1972):907–27.

———. *Language and Woman's Place*. New York: Harper & Row, 1974.

Lamphere, Louise. "Strategies, Cooperation and Conflict Among Women in Domestic Groups." In *Woman, Culture and Society*, ed. Michelle Rosaldo and Louise Lamphere, pp. 97–112.

Langness, L. *The Life History in Anthropological Science*. New York: Holt, Rinehart, and Winston, 1965.

Laski, Margharita. *Ecstasy: A Study of Some Religious and Secular Experiences*. Bloomington: Indiana University Press, 1961.

Lawless, Elaine J. " 'What Did She Say?' An Application of Peirce's General Theory of Signs to Glossolalia in the Pentecostal Religion." *Folklore Forum* 13 (1980):23–38.

———. "Make a Joyful Noise: An Ethnography of Communication in the Pentecostal Service." *Southern Folklore Quarterly* 44 (1980):1–32.

259

———. "Women's Speech in the Pentecostal Service: An Ethnography." Ph.D. dissertation, Indiana University, 1982.

———. "Brothers and Sisters: Pentecostals as a Folk Group." *Western Folklore* 43 (1983):85–104.

———. "Shouting for the Lord: The Power of Women's Speech in the Pentecostal Service." *Journal of American Folklore* 96 (1983):433–57.

———. " 'I Know If I Don't Bear My Testimony I'll Lose It': Mormon Women's Testimonies." *Kentucky Folklore Quarterly* 30 (1984):32–49.

———. "Traditional Women Preachers in Mid-Missouri." *Missouri Folklore Journal* 6 (1984):47–60.

———. "Oral 'Character' and 'Literary' Art: A Call for a New Reciprocity Between Oral Literature and Folklore." *Western Folklore* 45 (1985):77–96.

———. " 'Your Hair is Your Glory': Public and Private Symbology for Pentecostal Women." *New York Folklore* 12 (1986):33–49.

———. "Tradition and Poetics: The Sermons of Women Preachers." In *A Memorial for Milman Parry*, ed. John Miles Foley.

———. "Piety and Motherhood: Reproductive Images and Maternal Strategies of the Woman Preacher." *Journal of American Folklore* 100 (1987):469–79.

———. *God's Peculiar People: Women's Voices and Folk Tradition in a Pentecostal Church*. Lexington: The University Press of Kentucky, 1988.

———. "Narrative in the Pulpit: Persistent Use of *Exempla* in Vernacular Religious Contexts." *Journal of the Midwest Modern Language Association* 20 (1988), forthcoming.

———. " 'The Night I Got the Holy Ghost . . .': Holy Ghost Narratives and the Pentecostal Conversion Process." *Western Folklore* 47 (1988):1–19.

Leach, E. "Social Geography and Linguistic Performance." *Semiotica* 15 (1975):77–97.

Lebra, Takie S. "Millenarian Movements and Resocialization." *American Behavioral Scientist* 16 (1973):195–217.

Lederer, Wolfgang. *The Fear of Women*. New York: Harcourt Brace Jovanovich, 1968.

Lee, Gary R. and Robert W. Clyde. "Religion, Socioeconomic Status, and Anomie." *Journal for the Scientific Study of Religion* 13 (1974):35–47.

Lefever, Harry G. "The Religion of the Poor: Escape or Creative Force?" *Journal for the Scientific Study of Religion* 16 (1977):225–36.

Lehman, Edward C., Jr. *Women Clergy: Breaking Through Gender Barriers*. New Brunswick, N.J.: Transaction Books, 1985.

Lenski, Gerhard. "Social Correlates of Religious Interest." *American Sociological Review* 18 (1953):533–44.

Lerch, Patricia. "The Role of Women in Possession-Trance Cults in Brazil." M.A. thesis, Ohio State University, 1972.

Leslie, Charles. *Anthropology of Folk Religion*. New York: Vintage, 1960.

Lessa, William A. and Evon Z. Vogt, eds. *Reader in Comparative Religion: An Anthropological Approach*. New York: Harper & Row, 1979.

Leuba, James H. *Psychology of Religious Mysticism*. New York: Harcourt, Brace, 1925.

Lewis, I. M. *Ecstatic Religion*. Middlesex, Eng: Penguin, 1971.

———. *Religion in Context: Cults and Charisma*. Cambridge: Cambridge University Press, 1986.

Lofland, John and Norman Skonovd. "Conversion Motifs." *Journal for the Scientific Study of Religion* 20 (1981):373–85.

Lord, Albert B. *The Singer of Tales*. New York: Atheneum, 1976 (First pub. Harvard University Press, 1960).

Lovekin, Adams and H. Newton Maloney. "Religious Glossolalia: A Longitudinal Study of Personality Change." *Journal for the Scientific Study of Religion* 16 (1977):383–93.

Lovell, John. "The Social Implications of the Negro Spiritual." In *Mother Wit From the Laughing Barrel*, ed. Alan Dundes, pp. 452–64.

Lowe, W. L. "Religious Beliefs and Religious Delusions: A Comparative Study of Religious Projections." *Psychoanalytic Quarterly* 13 (1944):1–15.

Luther, Gerlach P. "Pentecostalism: Revolution or Counter-Revolution?" In *Religious Movements in Contemporary America*, ed. Irving L. Zaretsky, pp. 669–700.

Mackie, A. *The Gift of Tongues*. New York: G. H. Doren, 1921.

MacCormack, Carol and Marilyn Strathern, eds. *Nature, Culture and Gender*. New York: Cambridge University Press, 1980.

Malpezzi, Frances M. and William Clements. "Tropological Allegory in Pentecostal Radio Sermons." *Midwestern Journal of Language and Folklore* 2 (1985): 31–39.

Maranda, Pierre and Elli Kongas Maranda, eds. *Structural Analysis of Oral Tradition*. Philadelphia: University of Pennsylvania Press, 1971.

Marsden, George M. *Fundamentalism and American Culture: The Shaping of Twentieth-Century Evangelicalism 1870–1925*. New York: Oxford University Press, 1980.

Marshall, Howard Wight. " 'Keep on the Sunny Side of Life': Pattern and Religious Expression in Blue-Grass Gospel Music." *New York Folklore* 30 (1974):3–43.

Martin, Ira Jay. *Glossolalia in an Apostolic Church*. Berea, Ky.: Berea College Press, 1960.

Marty, Martin E. *A Nation of Behavers*. Chicago: University of Chicago Press, 1976.

———. *Pilgrims in Their Own Land*. New York: Penguin, 1984.

Marx, Gary. "Religion: Opiate or Inspiration of Civil Rights Militancy Among Negroes?" In *Research in Religious Behavior*, ed. Benjamin Beit-Hallahmi.

Masson, Margaret. "The Typology of the Female as a Model for the Regenerate: Puritan Preaching." *Signs* 2 (1977):304–15.

May, I. Carlyle. "A Survey of Glossolalia and Related Phenomena in Non-Christian Religion." *American Anthropologist* 58 (1956):75–96.

McDermott, R. P. and David R. Roth. "The Social Organ of Behavior: Interactional Approaches." *Annual Review of Anthropology* 7 (1978):321–45.

McDowell, John Holmes. "The Corrido of Greater Mexico as Discourse, Music and Event." In *"And Other Neighborly Names"*, ed. Richard Bauman and Roger D. Abrahams, pp. 44–75.

McGuire, Meredith B. "Testimony as Commitment Mechanism in Catholic Pentecostal Prayer Groups." *Journal for the Scientific Study of Religion* 16 (1977):165–69.

McNamee, John J. "The Role of the Spirit in Pentecostalism." Ph.D. dissertation, Universität Tubingen, 1974.

McPherson, Aimee Semple. *The Holy Spirit*. Los Angeles: Challpin, 1931.

———. *Give Me My Own God*. New York: H. C. Kinsey, 1936.

———. *The Four-Square Gospel*. Echo Park, Ill: Evangelistic Association, 1946.

———. *The Story of My Life*. Hollywood: An International Correspondent's Publication, 1951.

Messenger, John C. "Folk Religion." In *Folklore and Folklife*, ed. Richard M. Dorson, pp. 217–37.

Miller, Terry E. "Voices From the Past: The Singing and Preaching at Otter Creek Church." *Journal of American Folklore* 88 (1975):266–82.

Minney, Robin. *Of Many Mouths and Eyes: A Study of the Forms of Religious Expression*. London: Hodder and Stoughton, 1975.

Mischel, Walter and Frances. "Psychological Aspects of Spirit Possession." *American Anthropologist* 60 (1958): 249–60.

Mitchell, Basil, ed. *The Philosophy of Religion*. London: Oxford University Press, 1971.

Mollenkott, Virginia R. *Women, Men and the Bible*. Nashville, Tenn.: Abingdon Press, 1977.

Morton, Robin. *Come Day, Go Day, God Send Sunday*. London: Routledge & Kegan Paul, 1973.

Morris, James. *The Preachers*. New York: St. Martin's Press, 1973.

Murphy, William P. "Oral Literature." *Annual Review of Anthropology* 7 (1978):113–36.

Neal, Sister Marie Augusta. "Women in Religion: A Sociological Perspective." *Sociological Inquiry* 45 (1975):33–39.

Neumann, Erich. *The Great Mother: An Analysis of the Archetype*. New York: Pantheon Books, 1955.

Newton, Judith Lowder. *Women, Power, and Subversion: Social Strategies in British Fiction, 1778–1860*. Athens: University of Georgia Press, 1981.

Nichol, John. *Pentecostalism*. New York: Harper & Row, 1966.

Noy, Dov. "Is There a Jewish Folk Religion?" in *Studies in Jewish Folklore*, ed. Frank Talmage, pp. 273–87.

Oats, Wayne E. "A Sociopsychological Study of Glossolalia." In *Glossolalia*, ed. Frank E. Stagg.

O'Brien, Mary. *The Politics of Reproduction*. London: Routledge & Kegan Paul, 1981.

Ochs, Carol. *Women and Spirituality*. Totowa, N.J.: Rowman and Allanheld, 1983.

Ochshorn, Judith. *The Female Experience and the Nature of the Divine*. Bloomington: Indiana University Press, 1981.

O'Connor, Edward D. *Perspectives on Charismatic Renewal.* Notre Dame, Ind.: University of Notre Dame Press, 1975.

Ong, Walter. *The Presence of the Word.* Minneapolis: University of Minnesota Press, 1981.

Ortner, Sherry. "Is Female to Male as Nature is to Culture?" In *Woman, Culture and Society,* ed. Michelle Rosaldo and Louise Lamphere.

———. "On Key Symbols." In *Reader in Comparative Religion,* ed. William A. Lessa and Evon Z. Vogt, pp. 92–99.

Otterland, Anders and Lennart Sunnergren. *Upwinds.* Nashville, Tenn.: Thomas Nelson, 1975.

Paredes, Americo and Ellen J. Stekert, eds. *The Urban Experience and Folk Traditions.* Austin: University of Texas Press, 1971.

——— and Richard Bauman, eds. *Toward New Perspectives in Folklore.* Austin: University of Texas Press, 1972.

Paris, Arthur E. *Black Pentecostalism: Southern Religion in an Urban World.* Amherst: University of Massachusetts Press, 1982.

Pascal, Roy. *Design and Truth in Autobiography.* Cambridge, Mass.: Harvard University Press, 1960.

Patterson, Daniel. *The Shaker Spiritual.* Princeton, N.J.: Princeton University Press, 1979.

———. "Ideological Support for the Marginal Middle Class: Faith Healing and Glossolalia." In *Religious Movements in Contemporary America,* ed. Irving L. Zaretsky, pp. 418–58.

Peck, Catherine. "Your Daughters Shall Prophesy: Women in the Afro-American Preaching Tradition." M.A. Thesis, University of North Carolina, 1983.

Pelto, Pertti J. and Gretel H. "Intracultural Diversity: Some Theoretical Issues." *American Ethnologist* 2 (1975):1–18.

Pentikainen, Juha. "Taxonomy and Source Criticism of Oral Tradition." In *Science of Religion,* ed. L. Honko.

———. "Religio-Anthropological Depth Research." In *Folklore Today,* ed. Linda Degh, Henry Glassie and Felix Oinas, pp. 403–14.

Phillips, Susan. "Sex Differences and Language." *Annual Review of Anthropology* 9 (1980):523–44.

Plaskow, Judith and Joan Arnold, eds. *Women and Religion.* Decatur, Ga.: Scholars Press for the American Academy of Religion, 1974.

Poblette, Renato and Thomas F. Odea. "Anomie and the 'Quest for the Community': The Formation of Sects Among the Puerto Ricans of New York." *American Catholic Sociological Review* 21 (1960):18–36.

Pohli, Carol Virginia. "Church Closets and Back Doors: A Feminist View of Moral Majority Women." *Feminist Studies* 9 (1983):529–58.

Pope, Liston. *Millhands and Preachers.* New Haven, Conn.: Yale University Press, 1942.

Porter, Judith and Alexa A. Albert. "Subculture or Assimilation? A Cross-cultural Analysis of Religion and Women's Roles." *Journal for the Scientific Study of Religion* 16 (1977):17–29.

Porterfield, Amanda. *Feminine Spirituality in America.* Philadelphia: University of Pennsylvania Press, 1980.

Pride, J. B. and Janet Holmes, eds. *Sociolinguistics.* New York: Penguin, 1972.

Quinn, Naomi. "Anthropological Studies on Women's Status." *Annual Review of Anthropology* 6 (1977):181–225.

Rabuzzi, Kathryn Allen. *The Sacred and the Feminine.* New York: Seabury Press, 1982.

Ramsey, Ian. *Religious Language.* London: SCM Press, 1957.

Rappaport, Roy. "Concluding Comments on Ritual and Reflexivity." *Semiotica* 30 (1980):181–93.

Redfield, Robert. "The Folk Society." *American Journal of Sociology* 52 (1947):293–308.

Reiter, Rayna. *Toward an Anthropology of Women.* New York: Monthly Review Press, 1975.

Rich, Adrienne. *Of Woman Born: Motherhood as Experience and Institution.* New York: Bantam Books, 1977.

Richardson, James. "Psychological Interpretation of Glossalia." *Journal for the Scientific Study of Religion* 12 (1973):199–207.

Richmond, W. Edson, ed. *Studies in Folklore.* Bloomington: Indiana University Press, 1957.

Rickel, Patricia. "Some Accounts of Witchriding." In *Readings in American Folklore,* ed. Jan. Brunvand, pp. 53–63.

Rogers, Susan Carol. "Female Form of Power and the Myth of Male Dominance." *American Ethnologist* 2 (1975):727–56.

Rooth, Anna-Birgitta. "Taxonomy and the Source Criticism of Oral Tradition." In *Science of Religion,* ed. L. Honko, pp. 53–70.

Rosaldo, Michelle Z. and Louise Lamphere, eds. *Woman, Culture, and Society.* Stanford, Ca.: Stanford University Press, 1974.

Rosaldo, Michelle Z. "The Use and Abuse of Anthropology: Reflections on Feminism and Cross-Culture Understanding." *Signs* 5 (1980):389–417.

Rosenberg, Bruce. "The Oral Quality of Rev. Shegog's Sermon in William Faulkner's *The Sound and the Fury.*" *Literatur in Wissenschaft und Unterricht* 2 (1969):73–88.

———. "The Formulaic Quality of Spontaneous Sermons." *Journal of American Folklore* 83 (1970):3–20.

———. *The Art of the American Folk Preacher.* New York: Oxford University Press, 1970.

———. "The Psychology of the Spiritual Sermon." In *Religious Movements in Contemporary America,* ed. Irving I. Zaretsky, pp. 135–50.

———. "Oral Sermons and Oral Narrative." In *Folklore, Performance, and Communication,* ed. Dan Ben-Amos and Kenneth Goldstein.

Rosengarten, Theodore. *All God's Dangers: The Life of Nate Shaw.* New York: Alfred A. Knopf, Inc., 1974.

Rothenberg, Jerome and Diane Rothenberg, eds. *Symposium of the Whole: A Range of Discourse toward An Ethnopoetics.* Berkeley: University of California Press, 1983.

Ruddick, Sara. "Maternal Thinking." In *Mothering: Essays in Feminist Theory*, ed. Joyce Trebilcot, pp. 213–30.

Ruether, Rosemary Radford. *Religion and Sexism: Images of Woman in the Jewish and Christian Tradition*. New York: Simon and Schuster, 1974.

———. *Sexism and God-Talk: Toward a Feminist Theology*. Boston: Beacon Press, 1983.

———. *Women and Religion in America II: The Colonial and Revolutionary Periods*. Cambridge, Mass.: Harper & Row, 1983.

——— and Eleanor McLaughlin, eds. *Women of Spirit: Female Leadership in the Jewish and Christian Traditions*. New York: Simon and Schuster, 1979.

——— and Rosemary Skinner Keller, eds. *Women and Religion in America I: The Nineteenth Century*. San Francisco: Harper & Row, 1981, (especially "Documents: The Struggle for the Right to Preach," pp. 207–61).

Ryan, Mary P. "A Women's Awakening." In *Women in American Religion*, ed. Janet Wilson James, pp. 89–110.

Samarin, William. *Tongues of Men and Angels*. New York: MacMillan, 1972.

———. "Sociolinguistic vs. Neurosysological Explanations for Glossolalia." *Journal for the Scientific Study of Religion* 11 (1972):293–6.

———. "The Linguisticality of Glossolalia." *Hartford Quarterly* 8 (1968):49–75.

Sanches, M. and B. G. Blount. *Sociocultural Dimensions of Language Use*. New York: Academic Press, 1975.

Sandeen, Ernest R. *The Roots of Fundamentalism*. Chicago: University of Chicago Press, 1970.

Sapir, J. D. and J. C. Crocker, eds. *The Social Use of Metaphor*. Philadelphia: University of Pennsylvania Press, 1977.

Sasson, Diane. *The Shaker Spiritual Narrative*. Knoxville: University of Tennessee Press, 1983.

Schermerhoren, R. A. "Ethnicity in the Perspective of the Sociology of Knowledge." *Ethnicity* 1 (1974):1–23.

Schwarz, Berthold. "Ordeal by Serpents, Fire and Strychnine." *Psychiatric Quarterly* 34 (1960):405–29.

Schwimmer, E. G. "Folkloristics and Anthropology." *Semiotica* 17 (1976):267–89.

Searle, J. "What is a Speech Act?" In *Language and Social Context*, ed. Pier Paolo Giglioli, pp. 136–154.

Sebeok, Thomas A., ed. *Style in Language*. Cambridge, Mass.: M.I.T. Press, 1960.

Sessions, Jim and Bill Troy, special eds. "On Jordan's Stormy Banks: Religion in the South." *Southern Exposure* 4 (1976).

Sherrill, John L. *They Speak With Other Tongues*. New York: McGraw-Hill, 1964.

Slobin, D. I., ed. *A Field Manual for Acquisition of Communication Competence*. Berkeley, Ca.: Language Behavior Research Lab, 1967.

Smart, N. "Interpretation and Mystical Experience." *Religious Studies* 1 (1965):75–89.

Smith, Page. *Daughters of the Promised Land: Women in American History*. Boston: Little, Brown and Co., 1970.

Smith, Robert J. *The Art of the Festival*. Lawrence: University of Kansas Press, 1975.

Sobel, Bernard. "The M'lochim: A Study of a Religious Community." M.A. thesis, New School of Social Research, 1956.

Spacks, Patricia Meyer. *The Female Imagination*. New York: Alfred A. Knopf, Inc., 1972.

Spender, Dale. *Male Made Language*. London: Routledge & Kegan Paul, 1980.

Spindler, George and Louise. *Dreamers Without Power: The Menomini Indians*. New York: Holt, Rinehart and Winston, 1971.

Spiro, Melford E. "Religion and the Irrational." In *Symposium on New Approaches to the Study of Religion*, ed. June Helm.

———. "Religion: Problems of Definition and Explanation." In *Anthropological Approaches to the Study of Religion*, ed. Michael Banton, pp. 85–124.

Spretnak, Charlene. *The Politics of Women's Spirituality*. New York: Doubleday, 1982.

Stagg, Frank E., ed. *Glossolalia*. Nashville, Tenn.: Abingdon, 1967.

Stahl, Sandra K. D. "The Personal Narrative as Folklore." *Journal of the Folklore Institute* 14 (1977):9–30.

Stanley, Gordon, et al. "Some Characteristics of Charismatic Experience." *Journal for the Scientific Study of Religion* 17 (1978):269–78.

Stanton, Elizabeth Cady. *The Woman's Bible*. New York: Arno Press, 1974 (first published 1895–98).

Stark, Rodney and William Sims Bainbridge. "American-born Sects: Initial Findings." *Journal for the Scientific Study of Religion* 20 (1981):130–49.

——— and Charles Glock. *American Piety: The Nature of Religious Commitment*. Berkeley: University of California Press, 1970.

Stekert, Ellen. "The Snake-handling Sect of Harlan County, Kentucky." *Southern Folklore Quarterly* 27 (1963):316–22.

———. "Focus for Conflict: Southern Mountain Medical Beliefs in Detroit." In *The Urban Experience and Folk Traditions*, ed. Americo Paredes and Ellen J. Stekert, pp. 95–127.

Stolz, Benjamin A. and Richard S. Shannon. *Oral Literature and the Formula*. Ann Arbor: University of Michigan Press, 1976.

Stone, Merlin. *When God Was a Woman*. New York: Dial Press, 1976.

Stone, O. M. "Cultural Uses of Religious Visions: A Case Study." *Ethnology* 1 (1962):329–48.

Sudnow, David, ed. *Studies in Social Interaction*. Englewood Cliffs, N.J.: Prentice-Hall, 1972.

Sunden, H. "Psychology of Religion, An Orientation." *Temenos* 6 (1970):142–99.

Suojanen, Paivikki. "The Contribution of Socio-Linguistics to the Study of Religion." *Temenos* 10 (1974):114–23.

Sutton, Joel Brett. "Spirit and Polity in a Black Primitive Baptist Church." Ph.D. dissertation, University of North Carolina, 1983.

Sweet, Wm. Warren. *Religion on the American Frontier*. New York: Henry Holt, 1931.

———. *Religion in the Development of American Culture*. New York: Charles Scribners, 1952.

Synan, Vinson. *The Holiness-Pentecostal Movement in the United States*. Grand Rapids, Mich.: Wm. Eerdmans, 1971.

Talmage, Frank, ed. *Studies in Jewish Folklore*. Cambridge, Mass.: Association for Jewish Studies, 1980.

Tavard, George H. *Woman in Christian Tradition*. Notre Dame, Ind.: University of Notre Dame Press, 1973.

Tedlock, Dennis. "Toward an Oral Poetics." *New Literary History* 8 (1977): 507–08.

———. *The Spoken Word and the Work of Interpretation*. Philadelphia: University of Pennsylvania Press, 1983.

Thomas, Keith. "An Anthropology of Religion and Magic." *Journal of Interdisciplinary History* 6 (1976):42–60.

Thorne, Barrie and Nancy Henley, eds. *Language and Sex: Difference and Dominance*. Rowley, Mass: Newbury House, 1975.

Titon, Jeff Todd. "The Life Story." *Journal of American Folklore* 93 (1980):276–92.

———. "Powerhouse for God." Liner Notes. Chapel Hill: University of North Carolina (American Folklore Recordings), 1982.

——— and Ken George. "Testimonies: Transcribed Testimonies of Rachel Franklin, Edith Cubbage, Rev. John Sherfey." *Alcheringa* 4 (1978):69–83.

———. "Dressed in the Armor of God." *Alcheringa/Ethnopoetics* 3 (1977):10–19.

———. "Some Recent Pentecostal Revivals: A Report in Words and photographs." *The Georgia Review* 32 (1978):579–605.

Trebilcot, Joyce, ed. *Mothering: Essays in Feminist Theory*. Totowa, N.J.: Rowman and Allanheid, 1984.

Turner, Roy, ed. *Ethnomethodology*. Middlesex, Eng: Penguin, 1974.

Turner, Victor W. *The Ritual Process*. Chicago: Aldine, 1969.

———. "Betwixt and Between: The Liminal Period in Rites of Passage." In *Symposium on New Approaches to the Study of Religion*, ed. June Helm, pp. 4–21.

———. *Dramas, Fields and Metaphors: Symbolic Action in Human Society*. Ithaca, N.Y.: Cornell University Press, 1974.

Uspensky, B. A. "The Influence of Language on Religious Consciousness." *Semiotica* 10 (1974):177–81.

van der Meer, Haye. *Women Priests in the Catholic Church? A Theological-Historical Investigation*. Philadelphia: Temple University Press, 1973.

van Vuuren, Nancy. *The Subversion of Women*. Philadelphia: Westminister Press, 1974.

Verdesi, Elizabeth H. *In But Still Out: Women in the Church*. Philadelphia: Westminster Press, 1976.

Waardenberg, Jacques. "The Language of Religion and the Study of Religions as Sign Systems." In *Science of Religion*, ed. L. Honko, pp. 441–57.

Warburton, T. Rennie. "Holiness Religion: An Anomaly of Sectarian Typologies." *Journal for the Scientific Study of Religion* 8 (1969):130–39.

Webster, Shelia K., ed. *Women and Folklore* (special issue *Women's Studies International Forum* 9, 3 [1986]). New York: Pergamon Press.

Wells, David F. and John D. Woodbridge, eds. *The Evangelicals: What They Believe, Who They Are, How They Are Changing*. Nashville, Tenn.: Abingdon Press, 1975.

Warner, Marina. *Alone of All Her Sex*. New York: Alfred A. Knopf, 1976.

Warner, Wayne E. *The Woman Evangelist: The Life and Times of Charismatic Evangelist Maria B. Woodworth-Etter*. Metuchen, N.J.: Scarecrow Press, 1986.

Weber, Max, *The Sociology of Religion*. Boston: Beacon Press, 1922.

Weidman, Judith L. *Women Ministers*. San Francisco: Harper and Row, 1981.

Weigle, Marta, ed. "Woman as Verbal Artists." Special Issue, *Frontiers* 3, Fall 1978.

Weisberger, Bernard. *They Gathered At the River*. Boston: Little, Brown, 1958.

Welter, Barbara, ed. *Dimity Convictions: The American Woman in the 19th Century*. Athens: Ohio University Press, 1976.

———. "The Cult of the 'True Womanhood.' " In *Dimity Convictions*, ed. Barbara Welter, pp.

———. "The Feminization of American Religion, 1800–1860." In *Dimity Convictions*, ed. Barbara Welter, pp.

———. "She Hath Done What She Could: Protestant Women's Missionary Careers in Nineteenth-Century America." In *Women in American Religion*, ed. Janet Wilson James, pp. 111–27.

Whitehead, Alfred N. *Religion in the Making*. New York: Macmillan, 1927.

Wilgus, D. G. "The Negro-White Spiritual." In *Mother Wit From the Laughing Barrel*, ed. Alan Dundes, pp. 67–81.

Willard, Frances E. *Woman in the Pulpit*. Boston: D. Lathrop, 1888.

Williams, Melvin D. *Community in a Black Pentecostal Church*. Pittsburgh: University of Pittsburgh Press, 1974.

Winner, Irene P. and Thomas G. Winner. "The Semiotics of Cultural Texts." *Semiotica* 18:101–56.

Wood, William. *Culture and Personality Aspects of the Pentecostal Holiness Religion*. The Hague: Mouton, 1965.

Yalom, Marilyn. *Maternity, Mortality and the Literature of Madness*. University Park: Pennsylvania State University Press, 1985.

Yoder, Don. "Official Religion vs. Folk Religion." *Pennsylvania Folklife* 15 (1964):36–52.

———. "Toward a Definition of Folk Religion." *Western Folklore* 33 (1974):2–13.

———. "Introductory Bibliography on Folk Religion." *Western Folklore* 33 (1974):12–34.

Zaretsky, Irving I., ed. *Religious Movements in Contemporary America*. Princeton, N.J.: Princeton University Press, 1974.

Zeman, J. Jay. "Modality and the Peircean Concept of Belief." *Semiotica* 10 (1974):205–25.

Zikmund, Barbara Brown. "The Struggle for the Right to Preach." In *Women and Religion in America*, ed. Rosemary Radford Ruether and Rosemary Skinner Keller, pp. 193–205.

Index

Index

Publications of the American Folklore Society
New Series

General Editor, Larry Danielson

DATE DUE

DEC 0 3 1999			
DEC 0 3 1999			
NOV 2 9 2004			
NOV 2 3 2004			
APR 1 8 2006			
GAYLORD			PRINTED IN U.S.A